P9-CFJ-896

High-Impact Hiring

High-Impact Hiring

A Comprehensive Guide to Performance-Based Hiring

Joseph Rosse

Robert Levin

Jossey-Bass Publishers • San Francisco

This publication is designed to provide accurate and authoritative information in regard to the subject matter covered. It is sold with the understanding that the publisher is not engaged in rendering legal, accounting, or other professional service. If legal advice or other expert assistance is required, the services of a competent professional person should be sought.

Substantial discounts on bulk quantities of Jossey-Bass books are available to corporations, professional associations, and other organizations. For details and discount information, contact the special sales department at Jossey-Bass Inc., Publishers (415) 433–1740; Fax (800) 605–2665.

For sales outside the United States, please contact your local Simon & Schuster International Office.

Jossey-Bass Web address: http://www.josseybass.com

Manufactured in the United States of America using Lyons Falls D'Anthology paper, which is a special blend of non-tree fibers and totally chlorine-free wood pulp.

Library of Congress Cataloging-in-Publication Data

Rosse, Joseph G.
    High-impact hiring : a comprehensive guide to performance-based hiring / Joseph Rosse, Robert Levin.
        p.   cm. — (Jossey-Bass business & management series)
    Includes bibliographical references and index.
    ISBN 0-7879-0995-5 (alk. paper)
    1. Employee selection.   I. Levin, Robert.   II. Title.   III. Series.
HF5549.5.S38R67   1997
658.3'112—dc21   97-24255

FIRST EDITION
HB Printing   10 9 8 7 6 5 4 3 2 1

The Jossey-Bass
Business & Management Series

Contents

To the Three Ps (Pam, Patrick, and Peter),
without whose patience and support this book
would never have been completed
                                        JGR

With love—for the love of learning
and of work given to me
by Mary Aberle Levin and George L. Levin
                                        RAL

Preface

People who hire are intrigued by hiring. Managers we know and work with get excited when they start discussing hiring with us, talking about their own experiences, asking questions, and debating different methods and ideas they've come up with or heard about. Those who have read and made comments on portions of this book as well as managers we have advised over the years have frequently engaged us in intense, almost philosophical, discussions. People we've met at social gatherings even stop talking about the weather, baseball, and politics to share their thoughts and ideas about hiring. We've been surprised by the amount of involvement in the topic that people have shown. Why is a potentially mundane topic like hiring interesting to people? We think there are several reasons.

- Hiring is challenging and intriguing. It's challenging to think about understanding another human being's skills, abilities, and motivation, for example, or trying to predict the future, or understanding more about your own goals, your organization's goals, and how the work of one individual worker can affect them.
- Hiring affects everyone who has a job. *You* probably have a job today because someone hired you. You may have been hired a few weeks ago or a few years ago, by an individual or a committee. You may have been hired for the job you have now or for the job you quit to do what you do today. On some glorious day, someone hired you.
- Hiring is a part of the job for everyone who supervises or works with other people. If you are a manager, supervisor, executive, professional, or business owner, hiring is something you do now and are going to need to do again. You may hire

well or poorly, by design or by luck, but you will be hiring
again, and you will have to live with the results of your hiring.

- Hiring affects how you work every day. Good hiring decisions
  make every working day more pleasant, while the effects of
  poor hiring decisions can linger for years.

- Hiring is essential to an organization's success. Most organizations are based on an idea—an idea for a product, a service,
  or a new way to meet a need. But ideas are realized only by
  people working at carrying them out. Hiring effectively is not
  sufficient to bring success, but it is absolutely necessary.

- Hiring affects your own success. If you are a manager, your
  own performance will be judged in part by your skills at hiring
  and assembling an effective team.

- Hiring requires a tremendous commitment of resources.
  When you hire someone, you will spend a lot of your own time.
  Your organization will spend money on the new employee's
  compensation and training. Large amounts of money may also
  be spent on headhunters' fees or assessment instruments.

Another reason that people are interested in hiring is that it
can be very frustrating. Hiring often is needed when someone
you've already invested time and effort in hiring and training
decides to leave. Or it may take place as a result of expansion, when
you're already stretched thin trying to meet demands from customers, suppliers, and current employees. Recruiting good applicants, trying to decide which to hire, making the actual job offer,
and then orienting and training the new hire—and waiting to see
if you've made a good choice—all take precious time that you can't
spare. We can't provide any magical shortcuts, because the truth is
that effective hiring requires an investment of time and energy. But
we can show you how to wisely invest your time and energy to get
the maximal return.

The interest that managers and professionals have in learning
to hire successfully shows up in a few of the questions we've been
asked and that we've asked ourselves over the years:

- Why does one employee do so well when the next person
  hired struggles to keep the job? In this book, you'll learn
  which hiring practices increase successful job performance.

You'll also learn what you need to do before and after you hire to increase your opportunities for success.

- What are the "secrets" to hiring successfully? There aren't any. But as with learning to play golf, ski, cook, play chess, or drive a car, certain techniques and tools can help you to hire more effectively. In this book, you'll learn about techniques and tools that really work. You'll learn the principles behind the techniques and how to apply these principles in order to hire effective employees.
- Is there a test that will predict who will be the best leaders among the job candidates? No, but you can spend a lot of money on tests that make claims like this. In this book, you'll learn how to use a variety of selection tools, such as structured interviews, reference checks, and different kinds of testing, to gather information that research has shown to help predict job performance.

This is a book, then, for the working manager or business owner who wants to do a better job of hiring employees. Not sure if you should read further? Maybe it will be easier to decide after we tell you what the book is and what it is not:

- The book is a practical guide to the latest in cutting-edge research and practice on hiring employees, not a dry summary of research data and theories. Although most of our recommendations are based on applied research, our goal is to translate the technobabble into the information you need to do hiring.
- It's based on the premise that employees should be hired strictly on the basis of their ability to contribute to the success of the organization, not on the basis of favoritism, irrelevant biases, or unsubstantiated hunches.
- Although it's based on the latest employment law, it isn't primarily concerned with legal mumbo jumbo, nor with ways to avoid legal hiring requirements.
- It provides a systematic approach to hiring for performance, a process that you can learn and then continue to adapt as your situation or needs change, rather than simply following the latest fads in hiring.

- It describes all the various selection procedures in current use, not just interviewing or testing.
- It's a comprehensive exploration of hiring for performance that provides you with tools and concepts you can use now and in the years to come.
- It gives you the information you need in order to learn about and develop a hiring system that works for you, rather than describing a generic hiring system that is "best" for everyone.

We obviously have some pretty strong feelings about what this book should be. How did we come to these feelings and why did we decide to write this book? The short answer is that the book grew out of two meetings, hundreds of hours of talking and working with managers and entrepreneurs on projects related to hiring and work performance, and thousands of hours of research.

The first of the two meetings took place when a personnel specialist from a state government agency walked into Joe Rosse's office at the University of Colorado and asked for help in using tests for hiring employees. She was referred to Joe by one of his past students, who had told her how Joe had covered that issue in a staffing class. Joe recalls the meeting:

In my course, I had thirty class meetings to explain everything involved in using tests for hiring employees. Now I was faced with answering in fifteen minutes this manager's question about how to choose particular tests and incorporate them into her organization's existing personnel system. She explained that her budget wouldn't accommodate my usual consulting role, I knew there weren't any books that I felt comfortable recommending to her, and she certainly didn't have time to try to wade through the textbook I use in my class!

I thought about suggesting that she attend a workshop, but too many of them pitch one form or another of snake oil, or are run by employment attorneys who emphasize only what you can't do rather than trying to meet employers' real need: hiring successful employees. She needed an answer that week, not the next month. What I did was block out the rest of my afternoon to give her a crash course. I tried my best, but as the afternoon came to an end I had the sinking feeling that I had raised more new questions than I had answered. That's when I resolved that I would come up with a practical guide to the state of the art in hiring to help managers like her.

The second meeting took place between the two authors of this book when Bob Levin moved his work performance research organization to Colorado to become part of the University of Colorado at Boulder Research Park. He'd started the organization a few years before out of frustration with what he saw as the poor quality of commercially available professional resources available to managers. One of his first meetings at the University of Colorado was with Joe Rosse. As Bob tells it:

> I knew that Dr. Rosse had his degree in industrial and organizational psychology. Before I met Joe, I was sure this meant he was someone who was likely to palm off the latest fads in personality testing, other kinds of selection testing, and motivational theory on unsuspecting businesses. Imagine my surprise when I found that instead, as part of his research, Joe made a practice of investigating the snake oil that permeates so much of hiring. But this also meant that before our meeting, Joe had me pegged as a snake-oil-peddling consultant. So our meeting almost never got off the ground. We spent the first half of it circling around each other like a couple of cougars. Then it slowly dawned on each of us that we saw things from largely the same point of view.

The two of us have been working together ever since, and this book is one result of our collaboration. Both of us feel strongly that workplaces should focus on work performance. This means, in particular, that hiring should be done in ways that improve the work performance of an organization. Both of us respect the results of both practice and research. Our questions and many of our answers come from hours of listening to and working with managers, workers, and business owners in private sector and public sector organizations, large and small, as they grapple with the daily challenges of performing work effectively and hiring others to do the same. Many of our answers also come from systematic, diligent research on these same problems. We do not recommend tools or procedures simply because they are popular. We describe what really works, based on rigorous field testing, and what doesn't work.

We also have a strong mutual respect for each other's capabilities. This means that every idea in this book is likely to have been written by one of us and then challenged by the other, before it ever got to you. We still go after an idea like a couple of cougars, all the more so if the idea is one of our own. A lot less hokum slips through this way. We hope that you'll find the result to be an interesting and informative way for you to learn what will really work for you in order to hire successfully for performance.

Overview of the Contents

In the first chapter, we develop a framework for successful hiring that emphasizes hiring in ways that have the highest impact on performance, a framework we call *high-impact hiring*. The next four chapters provide you with the foundation you'll need for effective hiring. Chapter Two explores the nature of work performance and explains the ways in which a thorough understanding of work performance is the key to high-impact hiring. Building on this foundation, the chapter then describes how to use work and job analysis, for both stable and dynamically changing jobs, to develop a Performance Attributes Matrix in order to identify the critical characteristics of successful applicants.

Chapter Three provides an approach to planning the hiring process so that you can break out of the cycle of crisis hiring. The concept of a PATH, or Planned Alternative to Hiring, is a unique feature of high-impact hiring that helps reduce time pressures to allow you to focus on higher-quality hiring. We also discuss continuous hiring and the use of temporary staffing and job design as alternative solutions to the problem of hiring well when you "don't have time to hire."

Chapter Four continues building the foundation of high-impact hiring by focusing on the critical importance of recruiting a good set of applicants. Since the quality of your final hires can be no better than the quality of the applicant pool from which they are selected, this chapter describes a number of techniques for high-impact recruiting.

Chapter Five completes the foundation of high-impact hiring by providing a nontechnical summary of the most important laws affecting hiring. Here you'll learn about the two most common forms of employment discrimination, as well as how to conduct your hiring in a way that is fair and legal and has the maximum impact on the bottom line of performance.

Having established a framework and laid the foundation for high-impact hiring, we then describe the tools of hiring in Chapters Six through Eleven. Chapter Six begins by presenting the "big picture," describing the range and variety of hiring tools available to you and using the Performance Attributes Matrix as a guide to focusing your hiring program. Chapter Six also describes the concepts of reliability, validity, fairness, and practicality and shows how they form the basis for determining which hiring tools should be included in your high-impact hiring system.

In Chapter Seven we describe hiring tools that can be used to assess background information about applicants at different stages of the hiring process. Since past performance is often one of the best predictors of future performance, this kind of information can be invaluable. It can also mislead you and leave you open to lawsuits if it is collected improperly. This chapter offers tips for evaluating résumés, designing effective application blanks, and obtaining useful information from reference checks.

Chapter Eight focuses on the employment interview, the most widely used—and misused—hiring tool. Used improperly, interviews can lead to hiring disasters and expensive lawsuits, but when they are designed around the simple concepts we describe in this chapter, interviews can be among the most powerful and flexible of hiring tools.

Chapters Nine through Eleven describe the use of different kinds of tests for screening applicants. Because tests are controversial and many managers have been given an unduly negative view of them, Chapter Nine begins with a brief review of the history of employment testing and of the controversies surrounding its use, with a particular emphasis on ability and personality testing. We describe the advantages of testing and explain why we recommend its use in many applications. We also describe the potential limitations of tests and provide detailed recommendations for selecting and using tests effectively.

Chapter Ten describes performance tests and other kinds of job samples. Unlike paper-and-pencil tests, performance tests have applicants actually perform a sample of the work they are being hired to do. By combining the rigor and standardization of traditional tests with the relevance of actual job tasks, performance tests represent a powerful and underused hiring tool. We provide a number of tips for adding this technique to your high-impact hiring toolkit.

Chapter Eleven shows you how to analyze potential "negative performance." Counterproductive behavior at work has become a critical concern of both employers and workers. Drug and alcohol use and theft at work create a financial and safety hazard for employers, and stories of worker retaliation are common. As a result, the use of integrity (honesty) and drug tests has mushroomed. In this chapter we describe the pros and cons of these tests, as well as other means of combating counterproductive behavior.

Chapter Twelve answers the important—and underemphasized—question, "How do I use all the information I've collected about my applicants to decide who to hire?" We provide an understandable and usable decision-making guide that applies recent research on decision making to the question, "Who should I hire?" We provide simple but powerful heuristic guides to help you to answer this question and make good hiring decisions. And, for readers who really like formulas, we also provide a simplified quantitative method of reaching the same answer. In effect, we provide a checklist for the hiring process.

The Afterword provides a guide both to what you've learned about hiring for performance and to where to go next. It includes a summary of the key high-impact hiring steps as well as guidelines for implementing your hiring decisions. There you will also find suggestions on how to continue with a high-impact approach after you make a hire, beginning with making sure that your new employees get a good start with you and your organization. You can use the information in the Afterword to guide you through the high-impact hiring process each time you make a hire, whether you hire once a week or once every six months.

As we've developed, tested, and learned about successful hiring techniques, we've been fascinated by how much we've learned about hiring, and about such areas as human behavior, job performance, information processing and decision making, and individual and organizational success. We hope you'll learn just as much, and be just as fascinated, as you learn with us how to build and use your own high-impact hiring system.

Boulder, Colorado
June 1997

JOSEPH ROSSE
ROBERT LEVIN

High-Impact Hiring

Chapter One

Developing a High-Impact Approach to Hiring

"Hiring employees is like a crapshoot most of the time, but if you've been playing as long as I have you start winning more." If this sounds familiar, it's no surprise. It was the reply we got when we asked a manager to describe why some of his hiring decisions were successful, while others were not. After asking this question of nearly one hundred working managers, we found that their most common responses referred to hiring by luck, chance, intuition, or gut feelings. It seems that many managers' experience has taught them that hiring is mostly a matter of rolling the dice. This book is dedicated to the proposition that hiring doesn't *have* to be a crapshoot.

It is certainly true that making hiring decisions is far from a certain thing; we do not doubt that experience and even intuition can play an important role in being more successful at hiring. But personal experience is a slow, painful, confusing, frequently erroneous, and often expensive teacher. Our position is that personal experience can be complemented by nearly a century's worth of scientific research showing ways to improve the hiring process for the maximum impact on work performance.

A problem is that most of this research is described in the arcane language of technical specialists and is not written to be accessible to managers who want to know how to do a better job of hiring their next employee. Our goal in this book is to develop instead a systematic approach to hiring for performance that builds on the experiences of both managers who are making hiring decisions and researchers who have studied hiring and

1

performance. We call this systematic, performance-oriented approach *high-impact hiring*.

Problems with Hiring

As the hiring manager, you are affected by many different factors during the hiring process: some good, others unhelpful. One of the most important factors is that hiring is unlikely to be one of your regular job duties, but when you do hire, it is likely to be one of your most critical responsibilities. The hiring decisions you make will have a big impact on your own performance, the performance of your work group, and the performance of your organization—perhaps for only six months to a year, but more likely for three to five years, ten years, or even longer.

When it comes time to make a crucial hire, therefore, you may be rusty and out of practice. You're in a situation similar to that of buying a car: you buy one only once every few years, whereas the salesperson sells them every day. You need both good information and effective tools to give you the edge in making a good buying decision—or a good hiring decision.

No matter how important hiring is to you, it's also likely to occur under significant time pressure, and this can affect how you hire. To save time, you are likely to eliminate one of the most crucial steps of the hiring process: thinking about how the job you are hiring for fits into the overall strategy of the organization and its work, and what performance is really required from the person in that job. This crucial step may only take fifteen to thirty minutes, but if you skip it, the remaining hours and days of time that you invest will largely be wasted and the hiring you do will really be a crapshoot.

We normally don't believe in viewing people in the same way as equipment, but an analogy between hiring a person and purchasing equipment can be useful in estimating the time and effort to devote to a given hiring decision. Consider the following approach:

1. Calculate the first-year salary and benefits that the person will be paid when he or she comes to work. For example, assume that the total salary and benefits will be $50,000.

2. Add the initial training and start-up costs, say, $20,000.
3. Estimate about how long the employee is likely to work with you, say, three to five years.
4. Ask yourself this question: "Suppose I had the responsibility of buying a piece of equipment for this organization, one that cost $50,000, not just to start with, but each year, plus $20,000 to get up and running. This is a piece of equipment that I need to work with every day for the next three to five years, and that I might not be able to change once I have it installed. How much time and how much attention would I put into this decision? What resources would I devote to it? Where would I place this decision on my priority list?"

All too often, there will still be a big gap between the time and resources the decision deserves and what you can devote to it. You need to be able to leverage your daily experience when you hire, particularly your experience with dealing with work performance. You'll want to use the time you spend on hiring effectively, by eliminating useless or harmful hiring practices. And you'll want to learn techniques that will help you to hire effectively, even when time is limited and you hire infrequently.

For a manager, then, learning to hire effectively is very similar to a police officer's learning to drive a patrol car. For the police officer, driving is just one part of a complex job. At the same time, driving effectively under extremely challenging conditions is essential to success, even if the need arises only once a year. So police officers need to gain some of the same knowledge and skills that race car drivers have.

If you were learning to drive a car down a winding gravel road at ninety miles per hour, you'd want to learn some effective cornering and braking techniques. You'd also want to know that the techniques you were learning had been shown to work. It would help if you gained some understanding of the fundamentals behind those techniques, such as how braking and downshifting affect weight transfer and skidding. Hiring is much the same for a manager. We want you to be able to perform effectively when it's time for you to hire. At the same time, we realize that hiring is only one part of your more complex job.

A Framework for High-Impact Hiring

Both of us have spent years looking at performance in a wide variety of contexts. Focusing on work performance has led us to conclude that hiring good people—that is, effective performers—is one of the most important factors in developing a successful organization. Of course, effective performance also depends on what happens with people *after* they are hired: job design, satisfaction, motivation, tools, training, and compensation all have important effects on employee performance and retention. Performance *begins,* though, with selecting effective performers for your organization, your work group, and the job. So how do you hire in a way that will have a high impact on performance?

The fundamental principles on which effective hiring is based are central to the effective management of any organization. You can utilize your managerial knowledge, skills, and experience to hire effectively, and you can use what you learn about effective hiring to develop other aspects of your managerial skills. Three fundamental principles that form a framework for effective hiring are:

1. Performance orientation
2. Systematic information-gathering
3. Rational, realistic decision making

Performance Orientation

The first and most fundamental principle of effective management underlying hiring is performance orientation. This principle recognizes that organizations exist to perform work toward a purpose. Every organizational decision should be based on contribution to performance, and hiring is no exception.

Consider, for example, how an effective manager bases a decision to purchase a forklift on performance toward organizational goals. Forklifts are purchased for their ability to move pallets. You purchase the forklift that can move pallets safely, reliably, and efficiently. The forklift's paint color isn't a performance-oriented basis for your decision. If your top-performing model comes in two colors, you can take advantage of this option, but that is different from making the nonperformance-oriented decision of purchasing a forklift because it came in green, or because the forklift sales-person gave you football tickets or a trip to Hawaii. Hiring is ex-actly the same.

Simply knowing that you need a forklift isn't enough; you need to know why you need a forklift and what you need it to do. Simi-larly, it isn't sufficient to simply know that you need a loading-dock worker or a computer programmer. You need to know why you need those people and what they will be responsible for.

In Chapter Two, you will analyze the work of your organization and use this information to understand the key performances re-quired from someone you hire. These techniques draw on your ex-perience as a manager and free you from relying, for instance, on standard job descriptions that may be inaccurate for the specific performances that are most critical to the work of your organiza-tion or work group.

Performance orientation is *necessary* to hiring (and, in general, to organizational effectiveness), but it is not *sufficient*. To be suc-cessful, performance orientation must be carried out systematically and implemented through effective decisions. Being systematic about hiring without orienting your hiring system to performance will not result in performance-oriented hires. It will just help you to make your nonperformance-oriented hires more efficiently. Decision-making techniques that are biased or that are focused on factors other than performance can't get you high-performance hires either. Performance always comes first in effective hiring.

Systematic Information Gathering

Organizational processes need to be systematic to be effective. Hir-ing, once again, is no exception. Think about the key processes that your organization uses to create, produce, or deliver its major products or services. Think about the systemization that goes into those processes and the quality of information that is required to make them effective. The master baker at an industrial bakery doesn't say, "Hey, let's bake thirty more loaves of whole wheat to-night. And let's try adding some honey and molasses to that vat of dough for the hamburger buns. Let 'em rise an extra hour or two tonight, too." Nor does the bakery's production manager decide that, tonight, the dough roller will be set an inch thicker and 20 percent faster. Universities don't run their classes by telling all the professors and students on campus to just get together in the main auditorium at 9:00 A.M. As a manager, you know that you achieve performance through sustained, systematic effort directed at your organization's key goals. You also know that good information is part of being effective and systematic: the baker needs product orders, the production manager needs quality feedback, and the university needs enrollment lists and course offerings.

Effective hiring also must be done systematically and based on high-quality information. Your hiring can have a dramatic impact on your organization if you make a systematic effort to analyze the work of your company, understand the performance requirements of a job, determine what capabilities are critical in job candidates, gather information about candidates, analyze that information, and make decisions based on that understanding. By *systematically* hiring for performance, you increase the performance capabilities of your organization's workforce each time that you hire. This impact becomes increasingly important as workforces get leaner and each hire counts for more.

In contrast, being unsystematic about hiring *reduces* the performance capabilities of your firm as poor hires and substandard performance accumulate. With an unsystematic approach that results in poor choices for one-sixth to one-third of the hires, about what you'd expect from a normal distribution of the labor pool, your organization and your work group will be functioning with 15 to 30 percent deadwood as those hiring mistakes accumulate. We feel strongly that performance-based firing should not be discouraged in organizations, but it is easier to avoid performance problems in the first place than to have to solve them later.

Two kinds of information are particularly relevant to the hiring process. One kind is foundation information like that provided in this book. You have a right to expect the foundation information for your hiring system to be as rigorous and of the same quality as the information or materials you get from other suppliers for your organization's key processes. A biotechnology firm expects to obtain well-formulated reagents, a computer firm expects well-developed code libraries, and a law firm expects accurate statute books. Information and tools you gather about the hiring process should be of the same quality. That goes for advice from in-house human resource managers and outside consultants, personality and ability tests, seminars and books. When you aren't getting that kind of quality, you need to do what you would do in other situations: switch suppliers.

The second kind of high-quality hiring information you need is the specific content that you develop for each hire, using your hiring system. A systematic approach to generating this information will help you to conduct an effective analysis of work. You can then use your analysis to identify the capabilities required for a candidate's success. Interviewing in a structured manner based on these capabilities will help you to gather high-quality information that you won't get by just asking questions as they come to mind. Working out what kind of testing is appropriate for a given position and what tests do the job of predicting performance for a specific job will help you to gather additional high-quality information. Such information is essential to making good hiring decisions.

An organization's key processes and the high-quality information they are based on are also more likely to be systematically effective when they are *research-based,* and your approach to hiring needs to be, too. By "research-based," we don't mean that your organization's processes were all developed by people in white coats, nor that hiring should be done by slide rule. Research means "systematic, diligent inquiry," and the first thing we mean by "research-based" is that you should be systematic, diligent, and inquisitive when you are hiring. Effective hiring processes are not thrown together haphazardly. You and your colleagues likely give your organization's key processes a great deal of attention. When you develop something new, you plan it (at least a bit), try it, see how it works, and change how you do things the next time based on how things went last time. This is a research-based approach. Our approach to effective hiring is also research-based, first, because our recommendations about hiring come from research on hiring and performance in many fields, and second, because we will provide you with methods for searching and re-searching in order to hire for high impact.

Rational, Realistic Decision Making

Making rational, realistic decisions about the future is the third fundamental principle of an effective hiring system. A rational decision is based on the best information possible, gathered systematically.

Realistic decisions take advantage of the fact that even with the most effective information gathering, decisions have to be made with limited and incomplete information.[1,2] Realistic decisions recognize that all organizational decisions, especially hiring decisions, are decisions about the future. This means that hiring decisions are not made about certainties, but about the probability of different options happening in the future. Realistic decisions are also made by recognizing that hiring decisions are made about people and their future behavior. This makes the outcomes of such decisions even more uncertain than if we were making decisions about complex physical systems, like the weather. Why? Because in addition to being complex, human behavior, especially behavior in the workplace, has two characteristics that are strongly related to future change:

1. *Cognition and learning.* People can know things in the future that are different from what they know today, and they can learn to do things in the future that they don't know how to do now. Two people with similar amounts of job knowledge today may have different amounts tomorrow. Someone who has done a job well in the past may be able to do much better at a similar new job than someone who will have to learn on the job. And even correct information will more accurately predict an applicant's initial job performance than it will performance over a long period of time.
2. *Choice and motivation.* People can choose to solve problems when they become dissatisfied at work, or they may choose to find a new job or slack off in their work. A person may have developed excellent math skills, for example, and may have a great deal of cognitive ability, but he or she may apply those skills with different amounts of effectiveness depending on whether the job involves ringing a cash register, designing a solar radiation model, or calculating an actuarial table. Also, more of the skills may be applied if the person is being paid $80,000 a year to develop an actuarial table than if the pay is $18,000 a year to complete someone else's calculations.

Human beings' ability to change means that, no matter how much you might want to, you cannot predict a candidate's future performance in the same way, and with the same precision and accuracy, that physicists can calculate the path a satellite will take to a distant planet. In fact, attempting to do so can lead to serious mistakes in decision making. We will present hiring decision methods that are effective precisely because they recognize the future-oriented, probabilistic nature of hiring decisions.

Performance orientation, systematic processes, effective decision making. These are the foundation of your high-impact hiring system, in the same way that they are the foundation of effective organizational management.

Low-Impact Approaches to Hiring

Hiring in ways that are systematically designed to increase the likelihood of high performance is an approach that we call high-impact hiring. But for all the reasons we've discussed, hiring is more frequently "high-problem" than high-impact. Time and resource constraints and managers' own concerns often shape the hiring process in ways that reduce the positive potential impact of hiring on performance. Before you can hire for high impact, then, it is important to understand why common hiring practices are high-problem and low-impact. In particular, we have observed two problematic kinds of hiring, which we call *warm-body hiring* and *ritual hiring*.

Warm-Body Hiring

Warm-body hiring is any approach to hiring that involves making selection decisions on some basis other than performance potential. One such warm-body approach is to hire available candidates without really evaluating their credentials. Managers most often hire on this basis when a large number of positions need to be filled out of a small applicant pool, when constraints of time or money do not allow credentials to be evaluated, or when differences in skill levels don't greatly affect performance. Managers who use this approach often say, "Look, all I need for this position is a warm body," or "All I need is someone who is breathing."

There are industries and jobs in which warm-body hiring predominates. Seasonal employers, such as ski resorts, often have to fill hundreds, even thousands, of positions in a short period of time. While resorts have become more sophisticated in the use of hiring tools, the tight labor markets often dictate that warm bodies fill a number of positions just before and during the ski season. High training and turnover costs—inevitable consequences of warm-body hiring—become part of the budget for these organizations. Over a period of time, managers can forget how these costs arose and may not realize that their organization need not be burdened in this way. One personnel director we know who worked for a ski resort that cultivated a highbrow reputation was chastised by his employer for telling the local newspaper, accurately, that the resort "would be hiring warm bodies" for the upcoming season. The corporation had long ago come to see warm-body hiring as inevitable, and the increased costs and reduced quality of service as unavoidable. Their personnel director's publicly stated reminder was unappreciated, but right on target.

More commonly, warm-body hiring occurs when managers choose not to put the time into meaningful evaluation of applicants. A human resource manager from a leading software company told us that her company had no need to evaluate the credentials of new software engineers in any detail. They simply hired graduates of the computer science departments of MIT and Stanford University. Many of these new hires were no doubt effective. Others, though, were likely to be ineffective for reasons unrelated to their educational background, or less effective than the aspiring engineers from other universities who never made it to the interview. The consequences of this approach only became clear when growth forced the company's recruiters to move beyond this warm-body approach based on old school ties.

Warm-body hiring is also a too-frequent response of some managers to equal opportunity or affirmative action mandates. Managers who follow a warm-body approach to such requirements take the first available applicant belonging to a given protected class. Not only is this approach at odds with the spirit of equal employment opportunity, but it is also one of the reasons such programs are often perceived as ineffective.

Other examples of warm-body hiring include: hiring friends or family members, hiring graduates of your own alma mater, over-relying on employee referrals, or hiring on the basis of prejudices, whether these are positive or negative (examples might include hiring or not hiring women, Californians, or MBAs). Warm-body hiring also occurs when hiring decisions are abridged by lack of choice, for example, when the first available candidate is hired.

What are the effects on performance of warm-body hiring? The best-case scenario is that you select new employees randomly from the available labor pool. By hiring randomly, you will hire good performers, average performers, and poor performers. You won't know which is which until turnover or mistakes on the job begin to appear. Even these consequences are hidden in rapidly growing companies, for whom they can appear to be the natural outcome of growth. Unfortunately, the negative impact of poor performers can far outweigh the positive impact of average and good performers. Consider how much time it can take you as a manager to deal with a poor performer. Where does that time come from? Most often, it is time you would rather be devoting to working with effective performers in your work group or to your own work.

Over a period of time, employers with a reputation for warm-body hiring are likely to attract less qualified applicants and to alienate high-potential applicants. Then they are no longer even sampling randomly from the whole applicant pool, but from a backwater of largely undesirable applicants. These firms become employers of last resort.

Ritual Hiring

After experiencing the consequences of warm-body hiring, many managers search for a more performance-oriented approach to hiring. But instead of analyzing the fundamental issue—how to hire in a way that maximizes performance in the organization—it's all too easy to turn to methods that *look* as though they might help and use them with blind faith.

Trying *something* seems like a reasonable thing, especially when tools are readily at hand. Managers in established organizations may have available to them such tools as standard lists of interview questions, expensive personality tests, or elaborate computerized systems that generate interview questions from job descriptions. Managers in start-ups or smaller organizations are likely to receive daily mailings from vendors who would be perfectly happy to provide the same tools to them. And managers also develop their own pet methods for avoiding the disasters they've encountered from previous bad hires.

Such an approach *feels* better than relying on blind luck, but it is really just a seat-of-the-pants approach to hiring dressed up. You are still hiring blindly when you are using tools without first having thought through the fundamentals of hiring with performance as the goal, and without working out a systematic approach to getting there. When you hire in this way, you have no way of knowing if the methods you are using actually predict performance, and you have no way to find out. This is literally a trial-and-error approach. Not first trying something, making errors, and using those errors to improve the approach the next time around, but instead just trial, then error, then trial, then error, repeated endlessly. Those of you who are reading this book because you are fed up with the results you get from using your organization's established system or a system of your own know exactly what we mean.

Why do managers hire this way? This approach doesn't actually predict performance, but it does make you feel better during the hiring process. You get a false sense of being in control over the hiring process, whether the process helps or harms. The hiring methods become a ritual—a ritual for your own reassurance or one you engage in because it is accepted. Thus, we call this approach *ritual hiring*.

Ritual hiring is any hiring method in which the hiring manager attempts to hire on the basis of performance, but does not do so systematically, because either the methods and tools are not directed toward performance, or there is no systematic approach, or a systematic approach is not focused on evaluating relevant performance potential. But it's a great ritual! Although the ritual makes you feel good about hiring, you aren't doing a better job than with warm-body hiring.

Take a minute to think about the rituals of hiring. Here are some examples we frequently encounter:

- Saying before you conduct an interview, "I'll ask my favorite interview question—that always works!"
- Knowing that your competitor (or the last organization you worked for) is using the Meyers-Briggs Type Indicator for hiring, so you will, too.

- Attending a professional conference that has a session on handwriting analysis and deciding to make that part of your hiring process because it is interesting (the vice president for human resources of a major corporation recently made just such a suggestion).

Rituals are attractive because they are comforting. Take a moment to think about the process you and your organization use to hire. Ask yourself, "Do we use this process because it is reassuring or because it actually does a better job of predicting future job performance?"

What are the consequences of ritual hiring? Ritual hiring may not be any better than warm-body hiring. In fact, it may be worse. With warm-body hiring, you will generally do about as well as hiring randomly: you'll get a lot of average employees and a few very good and very poor ones. Unfortunately, the consequences of ritual hiring are even harder to predict. If, by good luck, you happen to adopt hiring rituals that are related to your hiring situation, the outcomes should be better than with warm-body hiring. On the other hand, ritual hiring can provide even worse results if the tools you use lead you to systematically hire the wrong people. So once again, hiring is basically a crapshoot, one in which you may be shooting with dice you've loaded against yourself!

To compound the problems of ritual hiring, the faith invested in the hiring ritual may blind you to the problems the ritual creates. If you have just made a major investment in a new hiring system, it *must* be useful, right? If the system indicated that your new hire will be a stellar employee, that will come to pass any day now. You're sure of it. Admitting that the system may be ineffective destroys the whole basis for the ritual. At least with warm-body hiring, you know you are going to make some disastrous hires and are likely to be on the lookout for them. With ritual hiring, on the other hand, you have the disastrous illusion of having made reliably good hiring decisions.

Ritual hiring is also more expensive than warm-body hiring. The rituals of interviewing and testing, for example, all cost money. Ultimately, ritual hiring becomes frustrating. You have tried to do something better without getting better results. So what *are* you and your organization going to do? If what is known about ritual is any indication, you will most likely try to do the same old rituals more frequently and more intricately.[3] Or you may decide to give up and live with the results of warm-body hiring or the ritual selection system your organization is stuck with. A third choice is to ask: What's lacking here?

The High-Impact Hiring Solution

We wrote *High-Impact Hiring* to answer the question of what is lacking. First, high-impact hiring is based on a systematic analysis of the *performance requirements* of the job, the organization, and its work. You have to know what you are looking for before you can find it. This foundation is so important that the entire next chapter is devoted to understanding performance.

High-impact hiring also focuses on a second systematic analysis—an analysis of the *performance capabilities* that each applicant brings to the job. You can use high-impact techniques to assess the knowledge, skills, and abilities of applicants, using techniques and procedures that are job-related and effective.

Third, the high-impact hiring approach helps you to systematically relate and match the information you develop on the performance requirements for the job and organization to the performance capabilities you gather systematically from applicants. This systematic approach will help you to make effective hiring decisions and to recognize the strengths and limitations of these decisions. You will learn how to make the probabilities involved in hiring work for you instead of against you and how to make effective hiring decisions based on the unique kinds of information gathered in the hiring process. The remainder of this book will be devoted to teaching you these approaches to high-impact hiring.

In this chapter, we have laid the cornerstones of the foundation for high-impact hiring. You have learned three fundamental principles of effective hiring. You have learned the characteristics that differentiate low-impact approaches to hiring, such as warm-body hiring and ritual hiring, from high-impact hiring. And you have reviewed the high-impact hiring process, which uses the three fundamental principles in each of its phases. Now we will move on to build the rest of the foundation of your high-impact hiring system.

Chapter Two

Knowing Who You Want to Hire and Why

The first step in the high-impact hiring approach is to understand work performance. Being able to understand and analyze work performance will get you started down an effective path as you begin the hiring process. In this chapter, we'll show you how to understand work performance at the organizational and individual level and how to conduct an effective analysis of that work when you are hiring. We will also help you to recognize particularly difficult situations for analyzing work performance—for instance, when work is changing or jobs are less structured. We'll show you how, even in these situations, you can get a good understanding of performance outcomes so that you can still hire on the basis of performance, regardless of whether you are hiring for a job that has stayed the same for decades or one that is changing as rapidly as the industry it's in.

What do we mean by "understanding work performance" and why do we believe that your understanding of performance is so critical to high-impact hiring? These questions are far more controversial than you might guess. Recently, many experts have pointed out that both research and practice in hiring have focused too much on what *might* predict performance without first understanding what performance really *is*.[1-3] When hiring, it's easy for working managers to focus on the mechanics of finding "good people" without ever understanding what good performance is or how to recognize good performance when they see it.

Athletic competition, another area in which prediction of performance is critical, doesn't suffer the same problem. Sports science research, in fact, has produced some critical knowledge that we can apply to workplace performance. For example, sports scientists have noted that it's important to differentiate between a person's performance on a task and the *results* of performing that task. People perform better by getting information about how they performed on a task, such as keeping the forward arm straight in a golf swing, than about the *results* of their behavior, such as whether the swing resulted in a hole in one on a par-three hole.

Why is it more difficult to understand performance at work than in sports, and why is this critical step so often ignored in the workplace? In sports, the purpose and desired outcomes of the endeavor are well understood and define the sport. Thus, the act of swimming fast defines a swim meet, as does the desired outcome of swimming a given distance faster than the others in the pool. At a swim meet, one doesn't have to ask whether it's also important for a swimmer to be able to kick a field goal, solve differential equations, or design an effective multimedia presentation.

At work, though, things get more complex. In a large aerospace organization, skill with differential equations or multimedia might be critical. Yet in an early-stage start-up aerospace instrumentation company, the same person might need to *both* solve equations and prepare presentations; in addition, he or she would need to have a solid understanding of aerodynamics and the aerospace industry. To understand performance in a given job, then, you need to thoroughly understand the desired outcomes for the organization and the ways the organization wants to get to those outcomes. Understanding work, and learning how to analyze performance, is the critical first step in learning how to do high-impact hiring.

Work and Performance

To understand performance, you need to recognize and understand two kinds of work. The first is the work of your organization. This work produces the goods or services for which your organization receives an exchange of value. A computer hardware company produces machines, which it sells to customers for money. A law firm delivers legal services in exchange for fees. A nonprofit service organization delivers social services to clients and receives grants, donations, and fees. The exchange of value lies between the organization and its customers for the product or service produced; production of the good or service, together with other related goals, is *organizational performance.*

However, an organization cannot produce goods or services apart from the work of the individuals in that organization. This *individual work* may be aggregated and coordinated with the work of others; it may be amplified by the use of machines and technology. Nonetheless, the work of individuals is necessary to design and manufacture a computer, prepare a legal brief, or deliver assistance or an education. The organization receives value from its goods and services, which are created, produced, and delivered by the work of individuals.

Organizational and individual work performance are closely related but distinct. Organizational performance is directed at the creation, production, or delivery of goods or services, and other closely related goals, that bring inputs and surpluses into the organization. The organization depends on the work of individuals for its performance. Individual work performance is directed toward activities that result in sustenance, and related goals such as satisfaction. Where is there overlap? The overlap lies in the *work performances* that an individual directs to the creation, production, or delivery of the organization's goods or services. Work performances allow the organization to perform its work, receive value, and pay the individual for work performed. So although their interests may differ, both the organization and the individual have a strong interest in individual work performance.

Organizational performance is therefore built around individual work performances, centered on the match between the requirements for organizational performance (for the production of goods and services) and the capabilities for individual performances (for the work required to produce goods and services). A performance-oriented organization will make its hiring decisions based on this match.

As a manager, how can you conceive of work performance in a way that's useful? For many years, managers and researchers have conceived of performance as being one thing for one job.[4] The "overall" rating for job performance you often see as the last item on a performance appraisal form is a good example of viewing performance in a one-dimensional way.

It's easy to understand how this point of view arose. Much research on performance comes from areas such as sports, where performance is clear and specific. Performance in a single class in high school or college is reduced to a single performance measure, a letter grade; in the workplace, performance is often summarized in a single overall score on a performance appraisal. Studies of job performance try to connect a specific predictor with a single outcome, in the same way that medical studies try to show whether a specific drug was related to curing a specific disease. The pernicious effect is that such efforts to predict performance have narrowed our concepts of performance to a single measure, such as a supervisory rating of overall job performance, or production of a given number of units, or performance at a job trial done in an assessment center. Narrowing performance in this way may make it easy to study, but it no longer describes the full range of performance in a given job.

Our approach is to think of performance as multidimensional and to ask, "What are the performances that really count?" *Critical performances* are the behaviors that have the most effect on producing outcomes that contribute disproportionately to an organization's stated goals, particularly to the creation and delivery of the good or service that the organization produces. Performance is not a single thing—it has many components.[5] In the following sections, you will learn more about understanding and analyzing organizational and individual performances as the foundation for your high-impact hiring system.

Analyzing Organizational Performance

To analyze the performance of your organization, you will first need to understand the purpose of the organization's work, that is, the *desired outcomes* of its organizational performance. If you were looking at sports performance, the job would already be done for you. For instance, in basketball, the purpose or desired outcome would be to score more points by putting the ball through the hoop more times than the opponent. In analyzing organizational work, you first need to define what game your organization is playing. This step is fundamental to high-impact hiring. Without knowing your desired outcomes, there is no way to understand organizational performance, to know which individual performances will contribute most to organizational performance, or to predict or even define individual performance. If you skip this step, the rest of your hiring system is just a ritual. We suggest that you analyze your organization's work without relying on any existing mission statement. Think the work through for yourself. This should be a simple process in which you define the way that the organization receives value through creating, producing, or delivering a good or service.

Your analysis should have three parts: what your organization does, how it does it, and for whom it does it. It's also useful to describe how your organization receives money from people or organizations for its goods or services. For example, the regional manager of a national restaurant chain might say, "Our company is engaged in the commercial delivery of food service, and we do this by serving medium-priced Italian food to a sit-down clientele. Our clientele pays us for food and service."

Next, write a statement relating the purpose and activities of your work group to the organization as a whole. The kitchen manager in one restaurant in the Italian chain might say, "The kitchen prepares food from our menu in a timely manner based on orders from the wait staff. The food is then delivered to the wait staff for service to the customer."

Finally, write a statement that describes the work performed by your work group that contributes disproportionately to the organization's performance. The same kitchen manager might say, "Timeliness of preparation, quality of prepared product, healthiness of menu items developed for our target market, and sanitation are the four areas of my group's work that really make a difference to the restaurant's success."

Although this process requires some thinking, it is not time-consuming or burdensome. Once you have completed it, you are armed with three statements: the purpose and outcomes of the organization's work, the purpose and outcomes of your work group's work, and the key contributions of your work group to organizational performance. You have now completed the necessary strategic foundation for analyzing the performances that are required from individuals you will hire to be part of your work group.

You will refer back to these statements many times during the course of developing your own high-impact hiring system. We hope that you think about them often and revise them whenever necessary. With these statements as your cornerstone, you will be able to develop valid answers to questions that previously may have seemed mysterious or problematic, questions like these:

- "What am I really looking for in a person I hire?"
- "What questions should I ask in an interview?"
- "How do I use all the information we've gathered on job applicants?"

Let's turn to the first question on that list and explore ways to analyze the performance requirements for individual work.

Analyzing Individual Performance: Job Analysis

High-impact hiring is based on a thorough understanding of work performances and related requirements for successful performers. The practical question is how to develop this understanding so that it can be used to enhance your hiring. Traditionally, the answer to this question has revolved around a process of analyzing the individual performances required to perform a job successfully, a process called *job analysis,* which is performed to produce *job descriptions.* We often use the broader term *work analysis* to refer to the more comprehensive approach of analyzing both organizational and individual job performance. You have just learned how to develop a better understanding of the performances of your organization and work group. The remainder of this chapter focuses on the use of individual job analysis to extend this understanding to the level of individual job performances and hiring standards for making hiring decisions.

What Is Job Analysis?

Individual job analysis is a systematic process for collecting information about the work performed in a job. The most frequent "product" of job analysis is what is usually referred to as a job description. A job description is a summary statement of a job's *purpose,* essential *duties* (also known as tasks or responsibilities), and *context* (the physical and interpersonal context in which the duties are performed).

Just as with analysis of organizational performance, it is critical to understand the intended performances of the job for which you are hiring. Job analysis provides the basis for determining both desired job performances and employee characteristics necessary to attain those performances. By determining first what you will want an employee to do, you can focus your high-impact hiring system on assessing the critical capabilities for performance that applicants will need. Without this fundamental information, it is easy to lapse into warm-body or ritual hiring.

Traditional job analysis and the job descriptions it produces have recently come under fire from both managers and researchers as being archaic and useless. Our view is that job analysis is a critical component of high-impact hiring, although changing conditions in the workplace call for significant changes in how the process is undertaken for some kinds of jobs. To better understand the continued importance of job analysis, as well as how to conduct an effective analysis, let's look at four critical issues that are frequently raised about job analysis, along with our recommended solutions.

Issue 1: Are Job Descriptions a Help or Just a Bureaucratic Exercise?

As one personnel manager of a large company put it, "How many of the failures in recruitment are *because of* position descriptions written by the personnel department, who have no perception of the dimensions, demands, challenges, and opportunities of a vacancy?" Many managers have felt the same frustration with job descriptions that seemed to bear little resemblance to reality, were hopelessly out of date, or were so vague as to be useless (or worse) for hiring, evaluating, or compensating employees.

The problem here is not necessarily with the concept of job analysis, but with its implementation. Even one of the major proponents of job analysis has estimated that 90 to 95 percent of job descriptions are so vague or misleading as to be useless.[6] Why? He suggests that the problem is that most are written in a haphazard fashion, usually by a person who has little understanding of the job and little or no training in how to conduct job analyses. In some cases, the person writing the job description may even have a motive for providing inaccurate information, such as making a job look more difficult or valuable than it is. Expediency also leads managers to write a single job description so that it includes a variety of jobs. The description is then too broad to be useful. Even more importantly, the manager is not engaging in the job analysis process prior to hiring.

The High-Impact Hiring Solution

The solution is not to abandon job analysis but to do it better and differently. In some cases, the reluctance to carefully analyze a job's performance requirements is due simply to time constraints. In other cases, though, the reluctance may have more to do with an unwillingness to make performance expectations explicit. It's easy to skip the process of understanding the work at hand and hire based on your gut feelings, but it's a lot easier to live with the results produced by putting the work into high-impact hiring. Moreover, if 90 to 95 percent of your competition is ignoring this critical process, you are being handed a competitive advantage that you shouldn't pass up.

One clear message from the criticism that job descriptions are often useless is that the person doing the job analysis needs to understand the job. Ask yourself whether your knowledge of a subordinate's job is really up-to-date and comprehensive. Research shows that workers and their bosses usually have different views of the subordinates' work, so involving workers in the work analysis is generally a good idea.

Issue 2: Are Job Descriptions Too Static?

Too many managers assume that once they write a job description they don't have to worry about it anymore. For most jobs, either critical tasks or essential worker competencies change over time. Job descriptions should be reevaluated regularly, at least every three years for even the most stable and defined jobs. Highly dynamic jobs may require more frequent review, perhaps on an annual basis, or with each new hire. A practical rule of thumb is to do a quick reassessment every time you hire a new person or conduct a performance review; if conditions seem to have changed, a more thorough reanalysis is in order.

A more fundamental concern is that jobs may be changing so quickly that job descriptions are outdated almost as soon as they are written. Even if job descriptions are updated regularly, hiring decisions are based on requirements that will change by the time the new employee is on board and oriented. Our view is that such rapid change—while probably not characteristic of most firms even today—actually *increases* the importance of the work analysis process, although it makes it more difficult. Change makes it even more critical to have a clear direction for work performances; without this direction, dysfunctional stress and misdirected effort are almost inevitable.

The High-Impact Hiring Solution

The key is to adapt job analysis to better describe *future* needs. You can do this by thinking about how the work and related hiring standards are likely to change over the next few years, not just what the work is like today. Then follow the process we will describe shortly for both current and anticipated tasks and qualifications. The result should be that you hire employees who can perform the current work and can grow into future changes in performance requirements. As we will describe shortly, this may also involve hiring employees on the basis of their ability to adapt and grow.

With this approach, you can use different time periods for projecting changes in different jobs, depending on the volatility of your organization's situation and the typical tenure of new employees in the job in question. Assembling a team of experts within the organization or trade group can help you to make realistic projections about the future. Some firms find it useful to involve their customers and suppliers, gaining tremendous payoffs for rethinking business strategies as well as job descriptions.

Issue 3: Are Job Descriptions Too Narrow?

One of the reasons we prefer to think in terms of work analysis is that traditional job analysis has been too narrowly oriented to specific task requirements. Traditional job analysis consists of determining the essential duties of a job and then systematically linking these duties to the employee capabilities required to successfully accomplish them. Although this systematic, task-focused approach has many advantages (including compliance with legal standards, covered in Chapter Five), it can lead to a lack of attention to broader requirements, which often are not either tied directly to narrow, prescribed tasks or easily classified as a knowledge, skill, or ability.

Working safely is one example of a factor that all employers know is important but, in our experience, is rarely included in job descriptions. One reason is that working safely is an implicit factor in most tasks; only if it is made explicit, as when a rash of serious accidents occurs, is it likely to come to mind when writing a job description. Another reason for the absence is that it is unclear if "safety orientation" is a personal factor that can be used appropriately for hiring decisions. For example, if you learned from doing reference checks that an applicant had been involved in numerous accidents, it would be hard to determine if the applicant was accident-prone or was working in an unusually unsafe environment. Moreover, if working safely is a personal factor, it may have more to do with training than with personality or personal abilities. But even if working safely is hard to use as a hiring factor, it is likely to be useful as a performance evaluation factor for many jobs.

A similar argument applies to undesirable employee characteristics. The first step in hiring good employees is to avoid hiring bad employees. Looking strictly at task characteristics may not directly remind you that you do not want to hire an employee who will be chronically absent, who will steal or damage property, or who will create other problems for you, other employees, or customers.

The High-Impact Hiring Solution

Before focusing on specific task performances, it is important to first analyze how the job contributes to overall organizational performance. This more comprehensive analysis will help to illustrate the importance of such factors as safety or dependability. It may also be useful to incorporate what some researchers have referred to as "organizational analysis,"[7] which involves matching applicants both with the requirements of a specific job and with the requirements—and rewards—of the work group or organization. This type of match can be assessed by asking yourself such questions as:

- What is our company's way of doing things? What do we value?
- What is unique about this work group or organization?
- What do managers expect from workers?

- What do workers expect from each other and from the organization?
- What kind of person would enjoy working here? What kind of person would not fit here, and why?

Answers to these questions may provide you with a bigger picture of the requirements for work performance. For example, suppose that the organizational analysis describes a firm as an entrepreneurial start-up, with a participatory culture in which both coworkers and managers expect people to pitch in and work on whatever needs to be done and for however many hours are required to meet deadlines. Salaries are low but there is a generous stock option plan. If that is an accurate representation, it is unlikely that an applicant who is risk-averse and likes working in a highly structured work environment will be either effective or satisfied.

Issue 4: Aren't Jobs, and Therefore Job Analyses, Obsolete?

Rapid change in our global competitive environment has led many managers and researchers to become discontent with the very notion of a "job." A fundamental assumption of most job analysis techniques is that a job exists apart from the employees who hold it, and that the job can be objectively described in terms of observable behaviors or tasks.[8] Many critics of traditional job analysis feel that these assumptions were once valid and useful, but are now anachronisms.[9, 10] They point out that many organizations are being "de-jobbed," and that most employees in these organizations now work on a fluid set of activities that change rapidly. No longer do such workers have an obvious set of tasks that can be defined in advance and for which clear performance expectations can be set. Traditional jobs in such organizations are being replaced with project or consulting work in which employees are given only general objectives. Some researchers conclude that in such circumstances, task-specific skills are less critical than more general abilities to adapt, problem-solve, and define one's own direction.

These issues may be particularly important in team-based work, where the sharing of roles and responsibilities is based on the particular skills and abilities of the current job incumbents. Adding or losing a team member requires reevaluating how work gets done.

Under these conditions, many managers and researchers feel that traditional task-based job analysis simply doesn't work, and the very notion of job-specific hiring standards is irrelevant. This "new view" advocates establishing broad employee "competencies" that are more likely to be useful over a wide range of work activities and to be more stable over time.[11] Examples of such competencies include leadership, initiative, problem solving, interpersonal relations, and decision making.

The High-Impact Hiring Solution

These criticisms of traditional job analysis raise a number of important challenges about the most effective ways to analyze work and hire successfully in a wide variety of situations, including rapidly changing ones. These important challenges don't necessarily mean that effective job analysis is no longer appropriate. Organizations that uncritically embrace the "new view" risk discarding useful tools without having effective replacements. One of our goals in high-impact hiring is to provide you with a set of tools that can work under a wide variety of circumstances. Some work and jobs are much like what critics of traditional job analysis describe, and they may require new approaches to work analysis and hiring. However, these new approaches should still meet the test of performance orientation that's at the core of high-impact hiring. Many other organizations continue to have relatively distinct, defined jobs with reasonably specific, stable roles and performance expectations, for which well-implemented traditional job analysis can have a significant performance impact.

Even for dynamic, de-jobbed organizations, we believe that it is irresponsible to assign employees to project work, or to hire new employees into the organization, without providing them with a clear set of performance expectations. Work should not be defined in terms of the person doing it, nor even in terms of tasks. Rather, it should be defined in terms of its intended *outcome* and how that outcome relates to the intended outcome of the firm.

You can think about these issues using the analogy of a road map. In the traditional view, job descriptions provide employees with a road map that describes how to get from point A (starting the job) to point B (performance that contributes to the organization's objectives). Managers bear the responsibility for determining what point B is and the best route to get there. The "new view" points out that what has changed is that there are many equally good routes to get to point B and that employees are often in the best position to determine which route is optimal. With market and technology changes constantly creating detours and new routes, job descriptions may not be able to specify in advance what the best routes will be.

Our own view is that the contribution of work analysis to high-impact hiring rests with having the manager take responsibility for defining point B (including involving employees in this process). You can't use a road map effectively until you decide where you are going. As work changes, point B may become region B (or even multiple region Bs) and where point B or region B is may change as time goes on. You may decide that there are many routes to get there. You can decide what kinds of maps are needed and how detailed they need to be. You can also involve team members in helping to scout out the region and possible routes.

But none of these changes affects our fundamental point: the most important part of the process is defining the *outcomes of work* and determining suitable means of attaining them through your hiring and your work assignments. That's why work analysis is so important and why you as the hiring manager need to be directly involved in the process. If this means reevaluating performance objectives and job descriptions every six months, with every new hire, or with every product or market change, so be it. This is a necessary cost of doing business in a changing working environment. The alternative is to have employees shooting randomly at a moving target or shooting with no target at all, the result of which is sure to be many performance misses.

An additional concern with the "new view" is that it too easily leads to vague or irrelevant competencies in the name of being broad or general. For example, a CEO of a publishing company criticized a division manager for not specifying leadership as a desired performance for the manager's administrative assistant. The division head responded that leadership was not really a part of that job, and defining the job in that way unfairly subjected the assistant to lower performance appraisals. Even when such broad competencies are used benignly, it is often difficult to determine how to accurately measure them in job applicants. The combination of vague and irrelevant traits not only seem to us a lot like ritual hiring, but it also smacks of the subjectivity and potential bias that lead to poor hires and invite lawsuits.

Instead of thinking exclusively in terms of either the traditional or the new view of job analysis, we propose a continuum of hiring that ranges from hiring for stable work under conditions that are certain to hiring for dynamically changing work under conditions that are uncertain. As we'll explain, these different conditions have different implications for the role of traditional job analysis and for the way work should be analyzed, critical worker traits should be determined, and hiring practices should be validated. This integrated approach to work analysis allows you to develop the approaches that are best suited to your situation.

The High-Impact Approach to Analysis of Work

We want to take the different points of view about job analysis and use them to develop an approach that you can use under a wide variety of conditions. Debating traditional job analysis as an all-or-nothing proposition ignores two facts of managerial life. The first fact is that managers need to have some basis for deciding how to hire and how to staff a team. The high-impact hiring perspective is that focusing on intended outcomes is fundamental, even when performance, work, and outcomes are dynamic and changing, and therefore more difficult to describe.

The second fact is that while some jobs are changing and dynamic, others are stable for long periods of time. In still other jobs, some or even most elements of the job will be quite stable, while certain critical elements may be dynamic. In fact, how dynamic a job is will itself usually change over time. After all, one of the main purposes of an organization is to take work that may be unique when it is done the first time and provide the stable setting that allows that same work to be done more predictably and cost-effectively over a long period of time.

You need an approach to work analysis that can deal effectively with this wide range of situations and that can generate solutions that will be effective in differing situations. The first critical step will be to have a way for you to determine what kind of situation you are looking at, what kind of solutions you are looking for, and what kind of work analysis is required.

Our solution draws on recent research that looks at the effectiveness of different kinds of solutions under different amounts of uncertainty.[12] When conditions are certain, or stable, the most effective strategy is to find the single best solution—an optimal solution. But when conditions are uncertain, or are changing most of the time, the most effective strategy is to use multiple approaches to find workable, robust solutions. A robust solution is one that works under a wide variety of conditions and fails under none, though it may not necessarily be the "best" solution for any one situation. (When conditions are uncertain, you can determine if a solution works or not, but not necessarily whether it is "best.") Under conditions that are certain, you try to answer the question, "What is best?" and under uncertain conditions, you try to answer the question, "What works?"

This means that the first question you must ask when preparing to hire for a job is, "How certain (predictable or stable) is the work for this job?" Your reference point for your estimate of the amount of change should be the range of time that you expect the people you are hiring to stay in the job—for example, two to five years or three to six months. If you're not sure, you can start by using one year. If a work situation is more stable and defined than it is changing and dynamic, you can proceed to conducting a traditional job-based task analysis of the kind we will shortly describe in more detail.

If you determine that a job is more uncertain than certain or more changing than unchanging over the reference time, you will want to conduct a more robust work analysis. Your aim will be to describe the job in a way that will guide you to hire people with the capability of doing the work both as it is presently done and as it will be done as conditions continue to change. This means that you will need to take multiple approaches to developing a robust analysis of the job: your task analysis will need to be future-oriented, you will want to look for applicants who have relevant experience working effectively in changing and uncertain conditions, and you will want to account for characteristics that may help people to work effectively under uncertainty.

Even when a job's conditions are uncertain, you still want to understand what the outcomes of the work are (although they will be changing) and everything you can about the critical components of work performance. The fact that some of the work cannot be described does not mean that nothing can be described. Nor does the fact that descriptions must account for change in order to be accurate mean that you cannot develop accurate and helpful descriptions of the desired outcomes of the work and the kinds of performance required to attain these outcomes. When jobs involve a combination of certain and uncertain elements, you will want to conduct traditional job analysis on the certain elements and more robust analysis of the uncertain ones.

Let's look in more detail at which practices are more likely to be helpful under stable (certain) conditions, and which may be helpful under dynamic (uncertain) conditions. (See Figure 2.1.)

An example of effective hiring for a more stable situation would be that of a general contractor who is selecting electricians, plumbers, and other tradespeople for a large-scale housing development. Because the homes will be standard, required tasks can be specified in advance and are unlikely to change during the duration of the contract. In this situation, traditional task-based job analysis leading to specific performance expectations and job-specific hiring standards is wholly appropriate and effective. Hiring practices for more stable jobs will focus on hiring applicants based on their job-specific skills (that is, their demonstrated proficiency at a particular task) and their knowledge, rather than on more general abilities or competencies. In this case, the focus is on selecting experienced, skilled workers, since contractors have neither the time nor the resources to hire inexperienced people, even if they have the potential to develop into good electricians.

In more dynamic, uncertain situations, hiring focuses on evaluating a broader set of abilities and competencies, rather than task-specific skills and knowledge. This broader set, while more general, still must be job-related. Specifying broader job competencies is not an excuse for eliminating the task of work analysis from high-impact hiring, nor for using fancy-sounding competencies that may glorify a job but that are vague or irrelevant. Hiring in the less certain situations is more likely to consider basic abilities or competency sets,

Figure 2.1. Two Models of Hiring.

Hiring in Stable Situations

Primary job analysis approach:
- Task analysis

Hiring qualifications:
- Primarily task-specific skill and experience
- More general abilities are secondary

Approaches to validating selection system:
- Any, including content validation

Appropriate for:
- Traditional jobs for which performance requirements can be readily anticipated and described
- Work that is changing either slowly or in ways that can be readily anticipated
- Task-specific skills that are both *identifiable* and *immediately necessary*, though these skills may continue to develop and change as the hired employee gains more experience, and as need and technology change
- Situations in which employers need to hire employees who are immediately ready to work, rather than going through an extensive training period

Hiring in Dynamic Situations

Job analysis approach:
- Multiple strategies for robust solutions

Hiring qualifications:
- General abilities and broader "competencies"
- Ability to adapt to changing situations

Approaches to validating selection system:
- Criterion-related or construct (but not content) validation

Appropriate for:
- Broadened, flexible jobs in which requirements are likely to change over time or assignment
- Team-focused work in which requirements change as team composition changes
- More generally, situations in which employers prefer to hire based on "raw talent" and then develop employees in-house

with the expectation that employees will need to rapidly or repeatedly adapt these competencies to evolving job requirements.

You need to think carefully about the specifics of work in your organization before determining where your analysis should fall on the certainty-uncertainty continuum. Consider the example of hiring aircraft pilots. Commercial airlines have traditionally used certainty-based hiring, with an emphasis on hiring people with demonstrated skill in flying a jet aircraft, primarily by hiring pilots trained by the military. Based on this approach to hiring, larger airlines invest a considerable amount in aircraft-specific training—for example, by adapting the skills of flying a high-performance F-16 fighter to transporting passengers in comfort on a 767—rather than devoting resources to basic flight training. In contrast, the military traditionally selects candidates for flight school based on a comprehensive evaluation of the basic abilities necessary to *learn* to fly. This approach allows the military to recruit from a much broader applicant pool and also allows them to socialize pilots in the "Air Force" or "Navy" way of flying.

The appropriateness of hiring solutions for situations with more or less certainty may change depending on differences in the cost of training for different jobs within your organization. For example, while airlines have traditionally hired pilots on the basis of demonstrated skill and experience, flight attendants, for whom training costs are far lower, are often chosen on the basis of general abilities and then trained in-house. Hiring approaches for the same job also vary across companies within an industry. For example, smaller airlines are more likely to hire both pilots and flight attendants with some prior experience, largely because they cannot afford the substantial investment in training.

The distinction between hiring for stable and dynamic jobs also affects how hiring tools are developed and validated. Because hiring for stable jobs focuses on job-specific tasks and employee capabilities, selection tools can be chosen or developed based on their similarity to actual tasks involved in the job, a process called content validation that is discussed in Chapter Six. For example, if the analysis of an electrician's job shows that knowledge of the Uniform Electrical Code is essential, it is a fairly straightforward task to develop and justify a test that measures electricians' knowledge of the code. It is much more difficult to develop and validate mea-

sures of more abstract competencies that are relevant to high uncertainty, such as adaptability to change or initiative. Thus, the
more straightforward certainty-based hiring may be more practical in many situations as a first approach.

Summary of Job Analysis Recommendations

Before describing how to use job analysis information to establish
hiring standards, we want to summarize the high-impact hiring
approach to the job-analysis process:

- Job analysis—thought of as a systematic approach to defining
  job performance and hiring standards—is the foundation of
  high-impact hiring.
- To be useful, job analysis must be done thoughtfully, by people
  who understand *why* they're doing it, *how* to do it well, and
  what the job really involves.
- Job analysis for stable jobs consists of identifying critical tasks
  and the worker capabilities necessary to perform them. This
  approach is most appropriate for jobs that are well defined
  and unlikely to change dramatically over a new employee's
  tenure.
- Traditional, task-based approaches to job analysis are less
  appropriate for jobs that change rapidly, that are based on
  team or project work, or that require extensive training and
  socialization. In these cases, hiring standards that take into
  account the dynamic nature of the job are recommended.
- Whichever approach is used, job descriptions need to be
  periodically reevaluated to ensure that they remain relevant
  and accurate. When conditions are more uncertain, reevalua-
  tion must occur more frequently and have more of a future
  orientation.
- Managers need to be involved with work analysis each time
  they hire. In some situations, a detailed, formal job analysis
  will be a good use of your time. In other cases, something
  broader may work better. Even when a current, updated
  description is available, though, you need to take the time to
  review the description and ask yourself, "Does this description
  describe the work I want to be hiring for?"

Using Your Work Analysis to Define Critical Success Attributes

Although the information from work analysis can be used for many purposes, our immediate concern is using it to determine the attributes of job applicants that are related to successful job performance. Making the link between a description of work and the necessary worker characteristics to perform the work is both crucial and difficult. In this section we will describe the process in terms of the basic steps involved for both stable and dynamic jobs.

One frequently used strategy, useful to both hiring models, is to differentiate attributes into four categories: knowledge, skills, abilities, and other characteristics of employees (generally referred to as KSAOs). *Knowledge* refers to a body of information that an employee must know to be an effective performer. In our previous example, we described knowledge of the electrical code to be a prerequisite for electricians; for programmers, the requisite knowledge might include various programming languages. Additionally, when describing knowledge requirements, it is important to specify what the person must know at the time of hire, as compared with knowledge that she or he is required to attain on the job. Of course, this will differ if you are taking a certainty-based approach and expect the person to work almost immediately after being hired, rather than an uncertainty-based approach in which much of the necessary knowledge may be learned on the job.

Skill refers to proficiency at a specific task and is a function of both underlying knowledge or ability and practice. Electricians may require skill in wiring an electrical panel, which in turn involves knowledge of the code requirements, experience in pulling wires and knowing what inspectors are looking for, and a certain level of physical ability, such as manual dexterity. Similarly, programmers' skill in writing code involves both knowledge of the programming language and practice in applying it to the task of developing programs that meet the organization's objectives in an efficient manner. Specifying skills as hiring standards implies that you want to limit your job search to applicants who have already gained proficiency in the required skills.

Abilities are attributes that indicate the *potential* to do a job, given subsequent training or experience. Although some abilities are reasonably observable, such as the ability to lift a fifty-pound load of tools and carry them up a ladder, most are more amorphous than knowledge or skills, and they often require a good deal of experience to estimate.[13] Abilities are particularly important for uncertainty-based hiring, in which you are looking for potential that can be developed, rather than immediate expertise. Relevant abilities may include cognitive abilities (such as comprehension of oral or written communication, mathematical fluency, selective attention, or memory), psychomotor abilities (for instance, manual dexterity or reaction time), physical abilities (such as static or dynamic strength or stamina), and sensory and perceptual abilities (for example, visual acuity, depth perception, or hearing sensitivity). Realistically, you are wise to consult with hiring experts, such as industrial psychologists, if you intend to place a significant emphasis on abilities.

Other characteristics is a catchall that includes any critical attributes that are not readily categorized as knowledge, skills, or abilities. Examples might include required licenses or certificates, possession of required tools, or the ability to be bonded and insured. This is also a good category in which to include integrity, attendance, and other more general job requirements, as well as relevant personality characteristics. Although it is useful as a reminder to include otherwise overlooked requirements, you need to avoid the temptation to include factors that are not essential to job performance.

Developing Performance Attributes for More Stable Hiring Situations

We will describe the traditional process first, not only because it is still useful for most jobs, but also because it forms one foundation of hiring for more dynamic jobs as well. Weighty volumes have been written on how to do job analysis, and we won't duplicate their contributions. Rather, we will provide a streamlined approach that is designed to meet the practical needs of managers who are primarily interested in improving the effectiveness of their hiring. Our approach may not meet all the technical standards specified by the job analysis experts, but it will provide a far better alternative to setting hiring standards by the seat of the pants or not setting them at all.

Our streamlined approach to job analysis consists of two simple steps: (1) determining the critical tasks or duties involved in a job and (2) determining the attributes required of applicants to accomplish these tasks. Once you have developed this information, you can move on to the next step in the hiring process—determining how to measure these attributes in job applicants (described in Chapter Six).

Determining Critical Tasks or Duties

Hiring effective employees first involves determining what you expect them to do. Although you probably already have a good idea of this in your head, an essential aspect of job analysis is putting these notions on paper. Writing down your ideas about desired performance forces you to make your assumptions explicit. In particular, writing makes clear your assumptions regarding the *relative* importance of the various tasks. This is also a good opportunity to obtain input from others who understand the job, particularly job incumbents, but often also internal and external customers and suppliers of the work produced by the job. This inclusiveness both ensures the accuracy of information and allows for a better understanding of different parties' performance expectations. Finally, written work analyses will meet any legal requirements that may apply to your organization (see Chapter Five).

The first outcome for this step should be a list of tasks, weighted in terms of relative importance. We prefer to assess importance by rating *how often* the task is done, *how difficult* the task is to do or to learn, and *how critical* are the consequences of doing the task wrong. We recommend rating task frequency, task difficulty, and task criticality individually and then combining them into an overall rating of importance. An example of such a listing is shown in Table 2.1 for the job of hotel clerk. To keep things simple and to avoid overemphasizing relatively unimportant factors, only tasks that are rated highly enough to be considered essential should be included in the subsequent steps of job analysis. Limiting hiring decisions to essential duties is also a legal requirement under the Americans with Disabilities Act and other equal employment opportunity legislation.

Determining Necessary Applicant Attributes

Once you know what you expect employees to do, the next step is to determine which KSAOs make it more likely that an applicant will be successful in performing the critical duties. This can be done

Table 2.1. Task Importance Ratings.

Position: Hotel Clerk

Task	Task Description	Rating
Task 1	*Answers phone and greets guests*	
1a	Develops positive guest relations by promptly and courteously answering phone	4.5
1b	Refers guests to other representatives, such as the concierge, as needed	2.5
Task 2	*Books lodgings*	
2a	Asks guests when they are planning to visit, what type of room (size, cost, nonsmoking, and so on) is preferred, and whether any special services are desired	4.0
2b	Answers questions about hotel amenities or local activities	3.5
2c	Determines room availability	4.0
2d	Books lodgings in reservation system	4.3
2e	Provides guests with price of complete accommodations package	3.5
Task 3	*Concludes reservation*	
3a	Provides deposit and refund policy	4.5
3b	Takes deposit information and guest's credit card information	4.0
3c	Summarizes reservation for guest	3.3
3d	Concludes call in friendly and courteous manner	3.0
3e	Asks guests if any additional information or assistance is needed	2.0
3f	Checks record for overall accuracy	4.5

by evaluating each critical task in terms of the KSAOs needed to accomplish it successfully. This is the essence of the task-based job analysis used in certainty-based hiring. Seeking input from other people who are familiar with the job is likely to provide more accurate information; this may be critical if a legal challenge later arises.[14]

To return to the example of hiring an electrician, a critical task might be wiring electrical switches. This may require knowledge of electrical code requirements that specify the size of wire to be used, the distance from the floor to the switch opening, and the proper means of grounding the switch. Required skills might include proficiency in stripping the wire insulation to the correct length and attaching it safely to the switch. Relevant abilities include normal eyesight to correctly identify wire colors and the ability to work while standing, sitting, or lying in awkward positions, which is common in many of the electrician's tasks.

After listing attributes, two optional but desirable steps are (1) explicitly rating the importance of the KSAOs and (2) linking the KSAOs back to specific tasks. Rating the importance of the KSAOs involves asking how strongly the KSAOs are related to work performance, or how serious the consequences would be if an applicant did not possess the KSAOs. This can be scored on a scale of 1 to 5. Only the KSAOs that are rated as essential (for example, a score of 4 or more) should be used for hiring. To link the KSAOs to specific tasks, you need to describe the essential tasks for which each KSAO is needed. For example, normal (corrected) vision might be linked to such electrician's tasks as identifying wire colors, reading work orders, and observing unsafe working conditions. This can be documented either narratively, as was done in the preceding sentence, or with a simple spreadsheet that lists the essential duties from step 1 in the rows and the essential KSAOs from step 2 in the columns. Check marks (or, even better, the numerical ratings of importance) will readily show how the KSAOs are related to the key aspects of the work. An example is shown in Table 2.2.

The idea underlying these steps is central to effective hiring: hiring should be based only on attributes that are critical to essential job duties. Hiring based on other factors is inefficient, unfair, and quite possibly illegal. (Courts and regulatory agencies generally require documentation of KSAO relevance, but for our streamlined approach this documentation is not absolutely essential.)

Developing Performance Attributes for More Dynamic Hiring Situations

The process of setting hiring standards when conditions are less certain has several options. One important consideration is that hiring attributes should not be focused around narrowly defined

Table 2.2. Determining Critical Performance Attributes.

Position: Hotel Clerk

Attribute	Rating	Rationale
Ability to work accurately	4.9	It is important to correctly book reservations to ensure customer satisfaction and to avoid costly adjustments or upgrades.
Ability to work well with customers	4.7	Guests often form their first impressions of the hotel based on their interactions with the clerks.
Stress tolerance	4.5	Many customers are rude and demanding.
Willingness to do repetitive work	4.4	Answering many phone calls and making reservations involves the same basic steps.
Verbal fluency	4.1	The agent must clearly and concisely converse with guests in order to obtain reservation information and answer questions.

Note: Importance ratings are based on a five-point scale ranging from "minor importance" to "absolutely critical."

tasks, since these jobs are dynamic. This leaves us with two approaches to recommend. The first is to describe the tasks or factors of the jobs more broadly; the second is not to describe them at all.

Using Broad Descriptions

Jobs that are more dynamic or more complex don't lend themselves to narrow task descriptions, but this doesn't mean that you should avoid work analysis. Instead, you need to change the description to fit the task. Describe the work using active verbs, thinking first about the desired outcomes of the work today and over a five-year period or other long time frame. Then describe the smallest number of most critical actions that someone will need to do to achieve those outcomes. Limiting the number of actions will force you to write in broad terms; relating these actions to critical outcomes will keep you from being vague or irrelevant. Do this in terms that will apply even as the work changes.

For example, suppose that you were responsible for hiring a research and development (R&D) director for a company in a competitive market that is increasingly reliant on new technologies. Telecommunications companies have faced just such a challenge. Perhaps the smallest number of most critical outcomes for the R&D director would be these:

- Developing an R&D department with the capability of both developing new technologies and evaluating promising and threatening technologies developed elsewhere
- Guiding R&D to a market focus, while maintaining the high quality of basic research critical for long-term success
- Changing the R&D operation so that it functions effectively with the reduced resources brought on by increasing market competitiveness

You can see that the above descriptions are broad. They are also job-related, accurate, and descriptive of some of the contradictory outcomes required in the position. You could look at such a description in a few years and rationally evaluate whether the R&D director had done his or her job. Notice, too, that many factors you might traditionally associate with the job aren't even listed, such as administering the R&D function or reporting to the board of directors on technology issues. In a stable environment these would be important, but they are less so in the environment this organization is confronting.

The knowledge, skills, and abilities required for such outcomes are also broader, and your KSAO statement needs to reflect this breadth. For example, one of the KSAOs that you might develop would be:

Knowledge

Broad knowledge of technology development related to communications. Includes knowledge of traditional telecommunication technologies, as well as knowledge of technology development, computing, communications, and materials science technologies, and knowledge of basic science required to effectively guide the development of new technologies and the evaluation of technologies emerging from competitors and from other industries.

Note that this KSAO statement, like the work description, is broad, but it accurately characterizes a key requirement for the work at hand. You can also see that relevant work experience is still important. Under changing conditions, it's important for people to be able to apply relevant knowledge to new conditions.

Eliminating Task Descriptions

A second approach to less certain hiring situations, one that must be used with caution, is to delete the steps involving identification and rating of tasks and move directly to determining the knowledge, skills, abilities, and other attributes necessary to perform well on the job, a process technically called worker-oriented job analysis. As you might guess, trying to estimate worker standards without having a set of tasks to base them on is difficult, and most organizations using this approach have relied on the use of standardized questionnaires such as the Position Analysis Questionnaire (PAQ).[15] The PAQ contains 187 questions on which you or a well-educated incumbent rate a job in terms of five "generic" dimensions of work (Information Input, Mental Processes, Work Output, Relationships with Others, and Job Context). These ratings are then used to create a computer-generated list of critical employee attributes that is based on expert judgments. Although quite useful, the PAQ is fairly expensive and time-consuming and can be challenging to interpret without training.

A more practical alternative is to ask people who are familiar with the job to describe the worker characteristics necessary for successful job performance. To do this, job experts are asked such questions as "What personal characteristics make for an excellent worker on this job?" or "What factors distinguish employees who have been successful from those who have not?" Coaching the experts to think in terms of KSAOs may help to provide a more comprehensive list of hiring standards. The experts' answers are then summarized in a list. The experts rate the importance of the KSAOs that have been compiled, and the KSAOs that are rated most important are used as hiring standards.

To ensure that the resulting hiring standards really are essential, it is important to think about why the differences seem to be relevant, to reach consensus among as many knowledgeable people as possible, and to evaluate how well hiring decisions based on these standards turn out. One person's unsubstantiated opinion is not likely to be effective—or to pass legal muster.[16] It's also essential for differences in job performance to be great enough so that you know you are evaluating the differences between successful and unsuccessful performance, not just between different shades of mediocrity.

Some experts suggest that extending this process to the specification of "universal" competencies would dramatically increase the efficiency of job analysis, while also accommodating changes in how work is done.[17] For example, many researchers believe that general mental ability, or "intelligence," is a prerequisite for all jobs, because of the importance of general mental ability for learning and problem solving (see Chapter Nine for further discussion of this position). Similarly, a growing body of research suggests that the personality trait of Conscientiousness may be relevant to all jobs (this is described in more detail in Chapter Nine).

While still controversial, there is at least substantial evidence behind the claims of universality for general mental ability and Conscientiousness. This cannot be said for other popular claims of generic competencies, such as flexibility or leadership, which makes their use risky. At some point in the future, we may be able to identify both universal and occupation-specific competencies, making the task of determining job standards no more difficult than clicking a website's browser button. (Some vendors are marketing computerized programs today that make such claims, which are well beyond the findings of even the most enthusiastic researchers.) For now, this is a highly controversial approach, and little in the way of professional or legal consensus has yet emerged regarding how these competencies should be defined or identified. Until this process is better understood, we recommend that you carefully determine the relevance of hiring standards for your specific situation.

Summary: Incorporating Performance Attributes into Your Hiring System

At this point, you have developed a set of critical hiring attributes for the job in question. You did this by:

1. Describing the essential duties the job holder will perform, if you used the traditional high-certainty hiring approach.
2. Determining what knowledge, skills, abilities, or other worker characteristics (KSAOs) are essential to perform these duties.
3. Documenting that these KSAOs are associated with the essential duties of the job or, in the case of uncertainty-based hiring, documenting agreement among experts that they are essential to successful performance.

One additional step remains before your work is done:

4. Determining if the hiring standard is necessary *at the time of hiring*. In many cases, knowledge, specific skills, or other requirements are learned on the job; an example might be the use of a particular software package. Skill in using this software may be essential to job performance, but it is not likely to be something you expect job applicants to have already acquired.

Congratulations! You have completed a performance foundation for your high-impact hiring system. You've gained a solid understanding of what you expect the new employee to contribute and what characteristics are most likely to produce excellent performance. You're now ready to go on to plan the hiring and recruiting process around this understanding.

Chapter Three

Breaking the Cycle of Crisis Hiring

When we stress the importance of taking a systematic approach to hiring, we are not trying to idealize the conditions most managers face when it's suddenly time to hire. Hiring often takes place in a crisis atmosphere, triggered by such events as employee turnover, promotions, and business expansion. In a crisis, grabbing an available warm body, with or without any accompanying ritual, looks like a pretty good option. Breaking out of the habit of crisis hiring is essential to conducting high-impact hiring. That doesn't mean that you only can hire well under ideal conditions. This chapter presents you with practical ways to anticipate the events that trigger hiring and to develop plans and alternatives that will get you out of the vicious cycle of crisis hiring.

Change is part of all hiring, and part of the normal operation of any organization. You can't eliminate change from your organization, but you can anticipate and plan for changes so that when they occur you can respond effectively. Changes that trigger hiring (what we call *hiring events*) may be broad or narrow in their effects on your organization. Any hiring event affecting your work group, though, has a big impact on *you:* you are compelled to respond and you will live with the consequences of the effectiveness of your response. Even when the attention of your organization may be focused on the major expansion of another division or the elimination of a key product, learning that your key assistant or expert is leaving your work group in two weeks has a much greater impact on your work life.

Rather than resisting or ignoring change—which would be counterproductive—or trying to anticipate extremely specific future changes—which would be impossible—it will be more effective to implement some simple strategies that can help you to prepare for and respond to a variety of future changes and hiring events. In the absence of such strategies, it's too easy to fall into a pattern of repeated hiring crises. Such crisis hiring occurs when we respond in a panic mode to a hiring event we could have anticipated and planned for. Then not only do we have an unnecessary crisis, but it's easy to respond with a solution that doesn't match our needs. It's also easy to get in the habit of responding to all hiring events in this way, and then to develop the belief that this process, and the hiring disasters that go with it, is just how hiring is done.

The CEO of an organization with which we have worked for many years asked us a question to which this chapter is an answer. We had developed a selection system that the company was using to hire for performance, a forerunner of the high-impact hiring approach. The CEO said, "I'm always fighting fires around here, and then I have to hire in the middle of it. So how do you hire well when you don't have time to hire?" Our answer was, and is, "In those situations, when you have no time, fire fighting is actually a fine way to hire. Only you want to fight fires the way a fire department does: you anticipate that you're going to need to fight a fire in the near future, you outline what will trigger that need, you plan how you will respond to that need, you make sure you have the tools you need to respond effectively, and you assemble them in advance so that you can respond rapidly when it's time to fight the fire."

What will cause you to need to "fight a hiring fire" in the near future? To anticipate hiring events, it can be helpful to think about the kinds of events that can trigger hiring: employee turnover, business expansion, operational changes, seasonal fluctuations, changes in needs, and retrenchment. Because having an employee leave your work group is a common and frequent event that triggers hiring in both established and start-up organizations, we'll develop a method for anticipating, planning for, and responding to hiring events caused by employee turnover, and then use this foundation to generalize to other hiring events.

It's not possible to predict exactly when and how individuals will leave your work group, but it is possible to anticipate that workers will leave at some point. We can also say this with more certainty than we can say that your organization or your work group will, for instance, expand or contract. Since this fact is absolutely certain, you can have the greatest impact on hiring by planning for the departure of each employee from the position he or she now holds in your work group.

Strategies for Responding to Hiring Events

Strategies that you can use to prepare effectively for hiring events include replacement planning, PATH development, succession planning, continuous hiring, job design, and temporary staffing.

Developing a Replacement Plan

A replacement plan for a work group is designed to answer the question that is at the heart of crisis hiring: "What would I do tomorrow if so-and-so departed today?" Developing a replacement plan before anyone actually departs will help you to understand both the operational and hiring consequences of a departure. An additional benefit of such a plan is that you have a preplanned work flow for dealing with *any* absence from the work site.

To develop your plan, draw up a piece of paper or create a spreadsheet with four columns, as in the example in Table 3.1. In the first column, list each job position in your work group. In the second column, write the names of the people who are in your work group next to their primary job assignment. To complete the third column, ask yourself, "If this person was unable to be at work for a day, a week, or a month, who would I want to have perform his or her essential tasks?" Put your answer to that question, the name of the primary replacement person, in the corresponding slot in the third column. To complete the fourth column, ask the same question again: "If this person was unable to be at work *and* his or her primary replacement wasn't available, who would I want to perform the essential duties of the first person's job?" A replacement chart that's two-deep gives you depth for the changes that occur when you move one person as a replacement, or for situations in which two people leave. Such an operating replacement plan is common for mission-critical situations (for example, an organization's disaster plan, or the plan for handling a computer system failure). You can use the replacement plan as the foundation of planning for hiring as well as to help solve operating problems.

Table 3.1. Sample Replacement Plan.

Position	Primary Assignment	Primary Replacement	Secondary Replacement
Director	Alan	Janice	Yem
Managing Director	Janice	Alan	Yem
Operations Manager	Yem	Janice	Alan
Marketing Specialist	Charles	Alan	Jerry
Technical Specialist	Jerry	Janice	Janice
Receptionist	Andrea	Charles	Temporary staff

By preparing such a plan for your work group, you begin to turn the most common cause of unanticipated hiring events into anticipated events. Having more control over the timing of hiring, which replacement planning helps you do, will make it easier to increase the quality of hires.

Developing a PATH

You can make the replacement plan you developed even more useful by asking, "What are the most critical consequences of a person's not being available for his or her job?" It may be helpful to break that question down into these four questions:

1. What *can't* get done if this person is not in his or her job?
2. Of these things, which are critical to the work of the organization?
3. What is the impact?
4. Over what period of time is that impact felt?

Armed with your answers to these questions, you can ask, "In the event that the person currently in this position leaves, what is the best way to perform the most critical duties that otherwise won't get performed, *until an effective hire can be made?*" Your answer to this question is what we will call your Planned Alternative To Hiring, or PATH. Your PATH for a given position doesn't relieve you of the need to hire when a departure occurs, but it does provide you with better alternatives at that time. Understanding and planning a PATH for each position in your work group also pays benefits during the hiring decision-making process: your decision-making effectiveness is improved by having attractive alternatives.[1]

The critical impact of a departure will vary by job and organizational level. In less skilled positions, the impact will occur when departures create inadequate staffing for the organization to deliver a needed service or product to standards of quality or safety. Skilled employees, those with mission-critical roles, and specialized and experienced midlevel managers often have the kinds of responsibilities for which the immediate short-term substitution provided in your operating replacement plan is likely to be most essential.

Using PATHs to Improve Hiring

The time you have available for hiring can profoundly affect your ability to hire for high performance. Developing a PATH for every position makes it possible for your hiring process to operate independently of immediate time constraints, allowing you to focus on hiring for performance, rather than simply putting a body in a position.

Having a PATH gives you a wider time window that allows you to be hiring at the same time that a highly qualified applicant is in the labor market. You *need* to hire candidates who you predict will deliver at least minimally acceptable levels of performance. You *prefer* to hire those who you predict will deliver desirable levels of performance, and who are highly qualified with the critical attributes you identified in your work analysis in Chapter Two. Hiring great people from the available candidates on any given day (or any other short period of time) is difficult to do. So it's important to increase the time available to conduct your hiring, which gives you more time and opportunities to hire great candidates when they are in the labor market.

Highly qualified candidates may be present in the labor market in fewer numbers and for shorter periods of time than less skilled individuals. This means that if you are overly constrained by urgency, you may be trying to hire when no one you want is available. This can be particularly true for specialized positions and for expanding organizations: the greater your demand and the greater your urgency, the more likely it is that your demand will completely exceed available supply at desirable levels of performance. It is possible, for example, that at any given time a labor pool will contain few or no great candidates or even acceptable ones. Or all candidates may just be acceptable when you really need a great one. The difference between minimally acceptable and desirable performance levels may be large or small; this affects how important it is to have a PATH that allows you some flexibility. When a hotel hires laundry workers, there may be little distinction in performance between workers who are minimally qualified and those who are desirably qualified, and the minimal standard for a board-qualified neurosurgeon may be so rigorous that there also is little difference between minimal and desirable levels. For most jobs, though, there is an important performance difference between those with minimally acceptable and desirable performance.

The essence of high-impact hiring is to hire as many well-qualified people as possible. How well-qualified depends on the performance requirements for the job and on the costs of hiring. However, the distribution of performance in the labor pool that's available to you for hiring fluctuates from day to day as people enter and leave the pool, and that fluctuation is completely independent of your need to hire. Crisis hiring leaves you at the mercy of the existing labor pool at the time you go to hire. Hiring with the backup of a PATH, on the other hand, gives you more opportunity to select an employee who is highly qualified for the position.

Hiring at the mercy of the labor pool is an almost certain ticket to low-impact hiring. For example, if a high-quality director of quality control (QC) is crucial to the performance of your own job, and your QC director quits, there may be no one in the available labor pool at that time who comes close to having outstanding qualifications. It doesn't help you at all that six outstanding performers were available last month and four will be available next month if you have to fill a position this week.

Similarly, if your hospital needs three experienced burn unit nurses, the chances are much better that you can find them in the labor pool over the next sixty days than over the next forty-eight hours. This will be even more true if you want to hire nurses with the necessary specialized experience who are also high performers. The same would be true of hiring experienced C++ programmers, or research technicians for a biotech company. Overloading a labor pool with demand at any one time results in your being at the mercy of the labor pool, which in turns results in lower quality and higher costs. Companies that are particularly vulnerable to such effects include those with large numbers of technical specialists, those with technical specialists in crucial positions, rapidly expanding companies of any size, and organizations that are hiring large numbers of seasonal employees.

Succession Planning

You can also use your replacement plan and PATH as a starting point for a longer-term succession plan. Succession planning takes a longer-range, more developmental approach than the replacement plan, focusing on how to develop people to become ready to move into a position instead of simply asking who is ready now to act as a replacement. Succession planning can be an effective strategy for anticipating hiring events when a position is staffed by one person or a small number of people, such as managerial or key technical or operational positions.

In a succession plan, you begin with a given position in your work group and ask yourself who the possible successors would be. You can create a succession plan in which the intended successor or successors begin to receive the training or experience necessary for the position and sometimes fill the position on a temporary or acting basis. An advantage of succession planning is that it tends to encourage internal promotion at the time of hiring events. At the same time, succession planning will help you to see the holes in your work group's depth, showing you when you need to be prepared to go outside for a successor.

Your succession plan also helps to make your decision to promote internally or recruit externally understandable and fair to others in your work group. If a possible successor lacks specific training that would make succession successful, then you and the potential successor can agree to focus development efforts in that direction. If no internal successors can reasonably attain desirable performance or develop enough to do so, then you will want to create a PATH that includes both having an internal operational replacement who can perform critical tasks at a minimal level and attracting a permanent replacement with desirable qualifications. Remember that it's always important to be clear to a temporary replacement about whether he or she can expect to be promoted as a successor, considered with other internal and external candidates, or not considered as a successor at all.

Continuous Hiring

Continuous hiring is a term that we use for hiring outstanding candidates when they become available, whether or not there is an immediate need for them. This strategy is one way of making your hiring time-independent. Continuous hiring is most appropriate as a hiring strategy in situations in which the same position is held by a large number of employees and in which you anticipate regular turnover. If your work group, for instance, has a large number of customer service positions, these positions would be a good candidate for continuous hiring.

Continuous hiring can be particularly effective when the difference between the minimal and desirable qualifications for a job is significant. Using continuous hiring to bring in workers with desirable qualifications when they are available to you reduces the number of workers with minimal qualifications you will end up hiring when you must respond immediately to a hiring event. For example, if the minimal qualifications for the customer service positions in your software company require basic telephone-answering and computer skills, but desirable qualifications include technical knowledge that can be related to your organization's products, then you would want to be able to hire people who have both technical knowledge and telephone and computer skills whenever they become available. The key to continuous hiring is to hire workers with desirable or outstanding qualifications when they are available, not when you have an immediate need for them. (In Chapter Four, we'll talk about how to find these folks.)

Suppose that you are engaging in continuous hiring for the customer service position in your software company and you find that Tanya, who has in-depth knowledge of technical products and the required telephone and computer skills, is looking for employment.

You decide to hire her as part of your continuous hiring strategy. The fact that you are hiring on a continuous basis instead of a crisis basis means that you can hire with some additional advantages. You would *like* to hire Tanya, but it's not essential that you hire her in order for your operation to run today. Your PATH, therefore, if you and Tanya are unable to reach agreement on her hiring, is simply not to hire right now. If instead you had to hire Tanya today because your key product was completely unsupported, you would not have a viable alternative to hiring her, and if she was unavailable, you might end up hiring someone less qualified.

If you are going to hire Tanya even though you don't immediately need her, what will she do when she's hired? You have four basic options. The first, possible in many service organizations, is for her to start with part-time or short-term work, which can serve in part as a job trial. Your candidate is more likely to be receptive to this option if she or he is currently without employment, or perhaps still in school. Second, and more likely to be mutually acceptable, is for the candidate to come to work for necessary training, which should then be combined with a job trial. In a position with a large number of employees and high rates of turnover, you can predict whether a position is likely to open up during the training and job trial period.

A third option is to utilize the new hire in a "utility" position until a specific position becomes available. An example would be to hire an experienced nurse into a float position as part of his or her initial work at your hospital. To make this more attractive, you could offer the new hire the options of taking the first staff position that comes open or using the float position to identify desirable units, continuing to float until a desired position becomes open.

The fourth option is to use continuous hiring to actively manage the quality of performance in your work group, rather than to wait for a hiring event to occur. Specifically, once you have hired a candidate with desirable levels of qualifications, trained the new hire, and are comfortable with the results of any job trial, you can review your current work group. Ask yourself if workers who have substandard performance need to reduce their hours, upgrade their performance, transfer to a better job match, or leave your organization. You should look for two types of candidates. The first type is workers whose performance is not acceptable. They may currently have a job as a result of your own inertia or lack of an acceptable PATH. They can now leave your organization. The second type is workers who have minimal, but not desirable, levels of performance. For example, if you hired Tanya for your customer support department based on her specific product knowledge, you could then turn your attention to Mike, who was hired six months ago with only basic telephone skills. You could change Mike's responsibilities to include only basic call screening and routing, making better use of your technically qualified support staff. You could then also provide Mike with a time frame to upgrade his technical skills in order to move into a customer support position.

Job Design

Another approach to unanticipated hiring events is to redesign how the work performed by the person gets done. In fact, the loss of an employee is always an opportunity to rethink work design and flow. You may find that changing your operations will allow you to get by without replacing the person for a while, perhaps even permanently. You can also use proactive job design to avoid having a crisis when a person leaves.

Designing jobs to ensure cross-functional capabilities increases your PATH options for any given job. Options are increased not only for jobs that are lateral to each other, but also for those that are at different organizational levels. When you both provide opportunities for line workers to be promoted to managerial positions or positions with greater technical responsibilities and encourage or require line-work experience in the training and development of managers, you develop breadth of experience (and multiple PATHs) throughout the work group. The practice of moving responsibility to the lowest possible level of the organization encourages development, skill, and responsibility and lessens the dependency of an organization on any key manager. Such effects can be profound. During the Cold War, the United States emphasized the decision-making and combat roles of noncommissioned officers, while the Soviets reserved decision making for superior officers. This provided the United States with a strategic advantage: a U.S. attack could immobilize large Soviet forces by targeting their control and staff capabilities.

Temporary Staffing

Temporary staffing is another way to increase options for your PATH. Particularly if your options for in-house alternatives are limited, your PATH may consist of staffing a position with a temporary worker while a permanent replacement is being found. Temporary workers, dealt with effectively, may be just as committed as permanent employees.[2] Specialized agencies now provide not only temporary office and manufacturing workers, but health care workers, finance specialists, and executives. In other cases, "temporary-to-permanent" arrangements may provide an effective way to conduct continuous hiring and job trials, either with positions traditionally associated with temp-to-perm, or by utilizing a specialized agency that will arrange temp-to-perm placements for less traditional positions.

Responding to Different Types of Hiring Events

The strategies for anticipating hiring can be applied, individually or in combination, to help you respond effectively to prevalent causes of hiring events in your organization. There are three broad categories of causes: growth, recurring hiring trends, and employee turnover.

Growth

Change is inevitable in an organization's work. When you are planning for or confronting an organizational change, particularly one related to growth, the high-impact hiring perspective is to always ask, rigorously and at the earliest opportunity, "What are the consequences of this change for hiring events?" Decisions to produce a new product, expand the production of an existing product, eliminate a service, or grow a new company all have effects on hiring. Repeatedly, even incessantly, ask yourself and others about the consequences of proposed changes for hiring events, and note the hiring-event consequences of any strategic or operational change. You want to know what these effects are and how to anticipate them and respond most effectively.

In some cases, effective response means understanding the consequences of the change in terms of hiring events and responding to the events using the strategies outlined above. For example, your hiring analysis of a proposed new software product may indicate that the new product will require five new programmers next quarter and ten new customer service agents a year from now, so you anticipate this demand and plan for making these hires. In other cases, you must instead rethink your strategic or operating goals *because* of the hiring-event consequences, for example, when developing a new product would require you to create and staff an entire materials science R&D operation over the next six months. If you don't have sufficient expertise to staff this operation in-house and can't get desirable performance through hiring, you must change either your time frame (make it longer), your approach (pay a contract R&D lab), or your goal (find options for the new product that don't require innovations in materials science).

We have repeatedly found that analyzing an entrepreneurial venture's business plan in terms of hiring events is an effective tool for understanding the quality of the assumptions underneath the plan and the plan's strengths and weaknesses. In a similar way, entrepreneurial managers, whether in start-up or established organizations, will do well to subject their own plans to the same "reality therapy" of hiring-event analysis. Ask the high-impact hiring question: "What are the consequences of this plan for hiring events?" Ask it for every item on a plan. When you get done, you'll have an effective hiring plan for the entrepreneurial activity. But future issues about assumptions, quality, cash flow, and expansion will come to light, too. And this approach need not be limited to entrepreneurial business plans. You can ask this question of any proposal. There has never been a plan developed that didn't require people to carry it out, but there have been planners who forgot that fact. Hiring-event analysis helps you to remember that fundamental and use it to guide your planning and decision making.

Recurring Trends

You can use a similar approach to analyze hiring events that may have become commonplace at your organization and may be affecting your organization's performance in unanticipated and unnoticed ways. Your business may regularly experience increased hiring events with each new product release or development effort, or during tax season, Christmas retail season, tourist season, or vacation periods. Too often, we respond to these events with a look of shock and horror: "Can you imagine, we had to go through this *last* year (or last product release), too?" Anticipate hiring events by reviewing the operation of your business with high-impact hiring analysis of the hiring event. Ask, "How does this aspect of the operation affect hiring events?" Then translate your answers into hiring events you need to anticipate. When you can attach specific numbers to your answers, so much the better: "Each summer, we need to staff thirty more machines for our greeting card company to print Christmas cards." If you have historical data that can help you predict both your staffing needs and the rate at which people leave the same positions, so much the better.

If you haven't been tracking historical trends, you can make an estimate. To get an estimate of the number of hiring events for a given position, start with the number of people you will need after the anticipated change, or at the time of the peak, or at any other time in the near future. Subtract the number of people who currently staff the position. Now *add* the number of people you anticipate leaving their current positions by that time. Remember that people can leave because of getting a new job, transferring or being promoted, quitting, being fired, retiring, or becoming disabled. Account for all these sources. The result will be an estimate of the number of hiring events for a given position over that period of time.

Now you are faced with the issue of how to find and attract the number of workers you will need in order to complete an effective response to this hiring event. In the next chapter, we will look at how to do this through high-impact recruiting strategies.

Employee Turnover

One additional approach should be part of your repertoire for anticipating hiring events and reducing unanticipated ones. The formula you used in the last section shows that the number of hiring events you will need to respond to over any time period is directly related to the amount of turnover in a position. If you lower the amount of undesirable turnover occurring in your work group, you will have fewer hiring events to which you need to respond.

Turnover can be classified as desirable or undesirable. Once you have a poorly performing employee who does not improve performance, it is considered desirable turnover for the person to leave. In the short term, the high-impact hiring approach to desirable turnover is to anticipate the event, plan for it, and develop a PATH, so that it is not a crisis when it happens. In the longer run, though, the high-impact hiring approach is to *make desirable turnover unnecessary.* Conducting high-impact hiring in the first place, followed by effective training and development and organizational practices that encourage retention of employees with desirable performance, all help to reduce the incidence of turnover and of related hiring events.

High-impact hiring can also be one part of a comprehensive approach to undesirable turnover. Effective hiring practices help to reduce the number of poor matches between qualifications and needs that occur in the first place. But reducing turnover ultimately requires a comprehensive, performance-based approach to identify and retain employees with desirable levels of performance. An effective effort to reduce turnover will reduce hiring events, particularly unanticipated ones.

One difficult question is how to respond to turnover caused by internal promotion. One likes to see one's colleagues succeed, but frequent promotions from a work group can cause as many problems as frequent quits. We have two approaches to recommend. If the promotions are part of development (such as management training programs), then the promotions and hiring events must be anticipated and planned together in a coordinated fashion. Another possibility, though, is that your work group is just a convenient place for other departments to go when they hire. In this case, your first response should be to ask, "Is there something that makes other positions more desirable than the positions here?" and make the changes that are indicated by the answers to that question. Your second response should be to conduct a careful job analysis before the next hiring event (see Chapter Two). Specifically, make sure that the attributes you are profiling are really essential for success in the positions in your work group and that you aren't recruiting employees who will soon be motivated to seek different or more challenging work elsewhere in the organization.

Identify the attributes that are uniquely related to the positions in your work group, compared with other positions in the organization, and target those attributes in recruiting a high-performing candidate pool. Recruiting that high-performing pool will be the next portion of the foundation of your high-impact hiring system.

Summary

Changes—such as employees leaving your work group, expansion and contraction of your workforce, and recurring trends in your business operations—are inevitable, and so are the hiring needs they create. But crisis hiring need not be the inevitable response to these changes. You can respond more effectively if you develop strategies in advance that will help you to reduce hiring crises and the unanticipated hiring events that trigger them. Preparing a replacement plan helps remove the operational crises that can be brought on when an employee quits. Developing some Planned Alternatives To Hiring (PATHs) allows you to make the best hires possible even under difficult conditions. Succession planning, continuous hiring, job design, and temporary staffing can be used to improve the quality of your workforce through hiring and development, rather than resulting in the reduced quality of staff that is brought on by repeated cycles of crises hiring. Changes brought on by growth, recurring business trends, and turnover are always part of the operating environment for any organization. Using the strategies presented in this chapter can ensure that high-impact hiring, and not crisis hiring, can always be part of your operating environment as well.

Chapter Four

Attracting the Right Employees

Finding and attracting qualified applicants is one of the greatest challenges in the high-impact hiring process. You can't make a good hiring decision unless you begin with a pool of qualified applicants. Too often recruiting begins only *after* a hiring event occurs and an immediate need is identified. Then it suddenly seems like the time to write a want ad or call a search firm—in other words, crisis hiring. In contrast, high-impact recruiting presents a performance-oriented, systematic approach for attracting workers who meet your performance needs.

In this chapter, we present proactive strategies that, together with the ideas on planning hiring presented in Chapter Three, will help you to build an effective foundation for making good hiring decisions and avoiding crisis hiring. Our approach to recruiting is based on three key themes:

1. *High-impact hiring cannot occur without high-impact recruiting.* The quality of your applicants sets the upper limit for the quality of your new hires. You can only select from the pool of people who actually apply for work, and you can't hire better workers than those who apply, or those who already work there: recognizing talent within your organization is as crucial as attracting talent from outside.

2. *Hiring is a mutual decision between you and potential workers.* This is why we used the word "attracting" rather than the more typical term "recruiting" in the title of this chapter. High-impact hiring recognizes that the employment decision is a two-way

street in which both candidate and company make a choice. It's important that the entire hiring process be conducted in a way that presents your organization as the employer of choice for qualified applicants. Unfair, arbitrary, or invasive hiring procedures that turn off desirable applicants are not going to get you to that goal.

3. *Desired performance, not time constraints, should guide your efforts to attract qualified workers.* One implication is that you want to attract such workers without regard to whether you are looking for candidates right now or whether they are looking for work right now. Building a *recruiting foundation* with this principle in mind will expand your options in attracting workers. An effective recruiting foundation will also make it easier to respond to a specific hiring event.

Building Your Recruiting Foundation

The basic question to ask as you plan your recruiting efforts is: "Why would qualified applicants want to work here rather than at another organization?" To answer this question, you need to ask two others: "What do desirable workers want?" and "What does our organization have to offer?" One of the important aspects of high-impact recruiting practices is representing the strengths and weaknesses of a job accurately and targeting your recruiting toward candidates who will be a good match with the job as it really is. With that in mind, here are some more specific questions you can ask yourself, job incumbents, and even potential applicants to get the point of view of someone applying to your organization for work. Honest answers will help you to get a good understanding of what your organization and the job may look like to a desirable applicant:

"What aspects of a job, in general, would make it highly desirable to you?"

"What aspects of a workplace or work environment would make it desirable to you?"

"What aspects of this particular job, or this kind of job, are particularly crucial in making it desirable to you?"

"Generally, what makes a job undesirable to you?"

"Specifically, what makes this job, or this kind of job, undesirable?"

"What aspects of working for this organization make a job particularly desirable? Undesirable?"

"Thinking back over all of your responses, which are the key factors that would make the *most* difference to you in choosing whether or not to work for an organization in a particular job, or for choosing one organization over another?"

By reflecting on the answers to these questions, you can list three sets of information that form the foundation for your recruiting efforts. First, list the factors that make the job, the organization, or the work in general desirable. Second, list the factors that make the job, the organization, or the work undesirable. Be sure to note factors that come up frequently, and the frequency of such responses. Third, make a smaller list of the factors that are most important to potential employees in deciding about a job. These most critical factors will help you to determine which factors to emphasize in your recruiting efforts. They can also help you to analyze your organizational practices for possible changes that would make the job or the organization more desirable to qualified candidates.

Making Your Organization an Employer of Choice

You can use your recruiting foundation to determine which factors your organization should emphasize in order to have a competitive advantage in attracting qualified employees. We call an organization that has such an advantage an *employer of choice*. The positive factors that are present in an employer of choice's jobs and workplace and the negative factors that are absent will be most effective in attracting workers to a position. Positive factors that are absent and negative factors that are present, on the other hand, need to be dealt with in one of two ways. The first option is to change them. Changes that are simple to make should probably be made. Others may take more time and be more difficult, or even impossible, to make. The second option is to objectively describe both the desirable and undesirable factors in a job and work environment in a *realistic job preview*.

Realistic Job Previews

Realistic job previews are an approach to recruiting that recognizes that hiring is a two-way process, involving decisions by both the candidates and the hiring organization. It's tempting to make a job sound attractive to potential applicants, perhaps more attractive than it really is, either so that you can be more selective or so that you can put a body in place when you're crisis hiring.

An effective realistic job preview, in contrast, gives candidates an accurate representation of the job to help them make a valid decision about their interest in the job.[1] By providing an *accurate* and *representative* overview of both the strengths and limitations of the job, realistic job previews result in more satisfied employees who are less likely to quit. This occurs for three reasons:

1. Applicants can opt out of the application process if they decide they aren't interested in the job. In addition to avoiding bad hires, having a realistic job preview early in the selection process can save you time and energy by keeping you from recruiting the wrong people.
2. Applicants who decide to accept the job can psychologically prepare themselves for the negatives, as well as the positives, of the job. This "inoculates" the applicants from unnecessary dissatisfaction based on unrealistic expectations.
3. Applicants appreciate the honesty and are more likely to see you as a trustworthy employer.

To prepare a realistic job preview, return to the aspects of the job that your survey showed you were important to potential workers, either positively or negatively. When jobs have qualities that workers found desirable, by all means stress these aspects in describing the job. When your survey showed less desirable aspects of a job, especially if they are inherent in the nature of the work, you should describe those aspects, too, making sure to do so in objective language. Some aspects that you view to be less desirable won't be so to an applicant, and things that you view as strong points may not be appealing to others.

One of the best sources for the content of a realistic job preview is the work analysis you completed in Chapter Two. Tying the job preview to the work analysis ensures that both you and the candidates will be focusing on the key performances at hand. The last part of the realistic job preview would be a selected list of key employee attributes, also taken from the work analysis. You want to list the most critical desired attributes on which candidates can self-select and that don't make it easy for them to claim they have qualifications that they in fact lack. For example, "self-motivated" is a factor one should *not* list in a realistic job preview. Most people view themselves as self-motivated, so it is unlikely to meaningfully guide candidates, and it provides candidates with a clue about how to describe themselves in order to look attractive. On the other hand, "extensive experience developing vertical market software programs for inventory control using C++" helps make it very clear to candidates what the work involves, yet it is not a qualification that can easily be faked.

At its best, a realistic job preview is more than words on paper. You should utilize any opportunity you have to give candidates a realistic view or experience of the job, and one that is as specific as possible to the work to be done. It's one thing to tell the retail clerks you hire in October that work will be intense between Thanksgiving and Christmas. It would be far more accurate and representative to give the candidates the opportunity to observe or experience the work that will be done during the high-volume retail season. If that's not practical, another alternative would be to videotape work during the holiday rush to create a job preview videotape. One organization we've worked with makes a well-known consumer product with a fun image. The organization takes pains to give candidates tours of the factory floor and the offices (which look much like other factories and offices) so that candidates know they won't be "coming to work in Santa's workshop."

The practice of providing representative job previews ties closely to the rest of high-impact hiring. Throughout this book, we emphasize the need for obtaining valid information about candidates and using valid tools to gather this information. When you are recruiting, representative job previews allow you to help applicants make their own valid decisions, by providing them with valid information about the job at hand and the performances and attributes required for the job.

Developing a Recruiting Repertoire

A high-impact approach to recruiting is systematically aimed at your desired performance outcomes. Using your work analysis will allow you to develop a profile of the candidates you would like to attract. Your recruiting analysis, described above, will help you to plan how you can best attract desirable candidates to the job in question. The practice of anticipating hiring events will help to provide the opportunity for you to attract such candidates. Now you need to develop an effective repertoire of recruiting methods.

Frequently used methods of recruiting include:

- Classified advertising
- Employee referrals
- Employment agencies and executive search firms
- College and high school recruiting
- Community training organizations
- Job fairs
- Electronic and on-line recruiting

Each of these has advantages and disadvantages and can be employed in a low-impact or high-impact way. Before we look at how to make each of them a part of your recruiting repertoire, we want to give you our primary recommendation for moving beyond ritual recruiting to a high-impact approach: get out and meet potential employees before they even apply for a job.

People who are looking for employment frequently receive advice to forget about responding to want ads, usually accompanied by a statistic showing that only a small proportion of jobs are actually advertised. Job seekers are then advised to find jobs through networks or by finding other opportunities to interact with companies. We suggest that you use an analogous approach to locate desirable employees—especially those who may not be currently reading the want ads. Here are a few examples of how you can take a high-impact approach to networking as a recruiting tool:

- Holding professional meetings or events at your organization
- Hosting an open house in your organization or, even better, in your work group, either for workers in your specialty or for the broad community

- Attending professional or technical-society meetings
- Scheduling interviews or lunches with targeted individuals
- Attending or supporting civic organizations that appeal to a wide range of participants or to targeted groups
- Most importantly, always pushing for new avenues and approaches to reach qualified applicants you're not aware of

Developing a long-term approach to attracting candidates—without regard to whether they are looking for work—should form the foundation of your recruiting repertoire. If you are currently hiring, the contacts you make will provide you with some candidates. If not, you have a group of candidates and contacts to turn to when a hiring event occurs. You will also need to use other recruiting approaches to fill out your repertoire, and to use when you are recruiting in response to a specific hiring event.

It's also important to understand how some approaches to networking result in a long-term *low*-impact approach. The biggest shortcoming to recruiting by "traditional" networking is that you potentially limit your contacts to people you know or are likely to meet, rather than those who might be the best performers for a job. There's no particular reason to assume that qualified applicants for a position are likely to know you or are likely to meet you. Overrelying on networking can also make it difficult to develop diversity in your workforce.

Classified Advertising

Classified advertising is a frequently used method for recruiting applicants, a fact that would seem to contradict information provided in many books on how to get hired.[2] Classified ads provide you with several advantages when hiring, particularly as a supplement to the method we've described. First, they allow you to broaden your applicant pool, reaching applicants you don't know. You can also target applicants at the same time that you broaden your pool, for instance, by advertising in trade publications or professional journals. You can be specific about desired or required qualifications. And your broad potential pool of applicants from classified advertising serves as an effective comparison group for your other efforts. An additional advantage is that, as we've noted, traditional networking tends to produce applicants much like your existing workforce, which can create legal problems if your workforce is mostly white and male; it can also result in less than outstanding performance if your network is too narrow to include potential stellar performers in your field. Classified ads can broaden your applicant pool and increase the range of performance, as well as providing one part of a defense against adverse impact (adverse impact and discriminatory hiring are discussed in more detail in Chapter Five).

Classified advertising also has several disadvantages. The first can be cost. Local classified ads for an occasional job can be quite cost-effective, but repeated advertising, or advertising in a national publication, a trade magazine, or a professional journal, can be expensive. Tracking costs and effectiveness, as we'll describe later, is critical when using classified advertising.

The second disadvantage is the sheer volume of responses that can be generated. In general, increasing the number of responses of qualified applicants allows you to be more selective when you hire. But along with this selectivity comes the logistic burden of responding to all of the applicants. Particularly in smaller organizations or work teams, you should consider the added, hidden costs of responding to applications. These costs occur because it is essential to respond to all applicants, successful or unsuccessful, who apply to you for work. Doing so is courteous, helps maintain a good relationship with applicants who may be potential future candidates or who may talk with future candidates, and maintains good relationships with your local community or larger, professional community.

A third concern about classified advertising is that it broadly communicates information about your organization that you may not want disclosed. Classified ads placed by your organization may indicate that your organization is either expanding or experiencing high turnover. An advertisement for a key position indicates a critical change in your organization. Advertising for technicians to help develop or deliver a new product or service can telegraph your innovation.

One alternative approach that alleviates problems with both the volume of responses and disclosure is to use a blind-box ad.

You can either arrange for a box through the publications in which you advertise or rent a post office box for this purpose. The former gives applicants more assurance that your ad is legitimate; the latter will be less expensive if you advertise a lot and in many publications. Blind boxes relieve you of the necessity of responding to every application and of having readers glean information about your company, because the applicants don't know what organization they are applying to. Therein, unfortunately, lies the significant drawback of blind boxes: applicants are more reluctant to apply to them, which has the potential of reducing your qualified applicant pool. For specialized positions in which blind boxes are used frequently, knowledgeable applicants who understand the blind-box process will prefer to respond to a box run by the publication, rather than to a post office box. This reassures them that they are responding to a serious job opportunity and usually affords them the opportunity to specify an organization, such as a current employer, that the application should not be sent to.

Advertising Your Position Effectively

Your advertisement should communicate what you are looking for in performance-oriented language, focused on key duties that produce critical outcomes, key attributes needed to perform the key duties effectively, and key factors that realistically describe the job. The most important principle is to write the ad emphasizing the critical information that will help potential applicants to realistically differentiate the desirability of the job you are advertising from that of other jobs, and to make a realistic decision about whether to apply. Think about the advertisement from the applicant's point of view, not from yours, and decide if the information you are listing helps the applicant to differentiate your job from others and decide about the job.

You may find it enlightening to take some time to read through help-wanted ads from the applicant's perspective. A quick review will show that most ads fail to make this differentiation. Here are examples modified from two advertisements for a marketing assistant. Wouldn't almost all candidates see themselves as fitting the descriptions in the first ad?

Marketing Assistant: Progressive, rapidly growing company is looking for a smart, proactive person with strong organizational skills to
support a marketing department. Responsibilities include general
administrative support, responding to inquiries, setting up client
meetings, and handling travel arrangements. Requirements: excellent communication skills, attention to detail, familiarity with data
bases and word processing, and the ability to juggle many tasks at
once. For the right person, we offer a very competitive compensation and benefits package.

Now contrast the specific expectations communicated with the
following example of an ad for a marketing assistant. You get a
clear picture of what you would be doing in the job and what qualifications you must have to get the job, which gives you a basis for
deciding if you want to apply for the job.

Marketing Assistant: Assists Vice President of Marketing in scheduling trade shows, communications with sales reps, regional managers, and customers, prepares price quotations and coordinates
demonstrations. Must be able to work independently and follow
instructions. Excellent secretarial and organizational skills, ability
to deal with specific deadlines, accurate typing of 75 wpm, and a
pleasant phone manner are essential. Experience with data entry
using word processing and spreadsheet software and data entry exp
are also required. Must have both 3 years of office management
experience and experience marketing/sales customer relations.

Employee Referrals

Employee referrals are another common method of recruiting
applicants, in which employees are encouraged to refer people
they feel would be good candidates for employment.[3] The employees often receive an incentive payment for applicants who are hired
and stay with the company. The advantages of employee referrals
are that employees are likely to understand the job requirements;
they may also have an interest in having fellow employees who pull
their own weight. Employees recruited through referrals are less
likely to quit than those recruited through other methods. The disadvantages are that problems can arise with both employees if the
referred employee develops performance problems and that incen-

tives paid to referring employees are often too small and deferred too long to be a real incentive.

The success of employee referral programs depends on implementing them with a high-impact focus. You can do this by making sure that you communicate clearly to employees the desired performance and attributes for the position for which you are hiring. Even better is to have employees involved directly in developing these critical elements. Here are additional specific steps you can take to make employee referrals a high-impact practice:

- Make sure that you already have a high-performing work group. It does you little good to have a group of poor performers refer people they would like to work with.
- Provide your referring employees with information about the critical performance attributes for the job. Make sure they know that you will be hiring on the basis of those attributes.
- Encourage your referring employees to think broadly and refer people they think have these key attributes, not just people they know and like. And be sure to do the same yourself!
- Encourage high-performing employees to make referrals.
- Supplement employee referrals with classified advertising: overreliance on nonperformance-oriented employee referrals carries the performance risk of creating a homogenous, mediocre work group and the legal risk of adverse impact.
- Consider carefully whether you will offer a bonus to employees who refer someone for employment. You want employees to refer candidates because the candidates are qualified, not simply to obtain a bonus. One approach is to begin your referral program without a bonus and monitor quality carefully if you implement a bonus later. If you do offer a bonus, make sure that it's paid soon enough to be meaningful to the referring employee.

Employment Agencies and Executive Search Firms

Employment agencies and executive search firms are vendors who provide candidates to you in exchange for a fee. Fee arrangements vary, but one-third of a candidate's anticipated first-year salary is common. In some specialized searches, fees are paid regardless of whether the search firm provides a candidate you hire. In most other instances, the search fee or agency fee is paid after you hire a candidate provided by the firm. Frequently mentioned advantages of search firms and employment agencies are the applicant pools they will already have in place or can obtain quickly, the pre-screening they can provide, and the ability of the firms to replace your time and effort with theirs. The most commonly cited disadvantage is the cost.

These touted advantages and the stated disadvantage all miss your most crucial concern. As long as this concern is addressed properly, employment agencies and search firms can be of great help to your organization. Central to evaluating the advantages and disadvantages of using search firms and employment agencies is understanding that a *vendor* relationship exists between your organization and the firm, and that there may be a conflict between your organization's best interests and your vendor's. You can evaluate whether or not you want to use such a firm, and whether a given firm will do a good job for you, as long as you remember how a search firm gets paid: it is almost always in a firm's best interest that you hire a candidate they provide, but it is not always in your organization's interests. A few firms take these differing interests even further. They will work to convince you that you need to initiate a key hire or develop a new position, when you really have no need for a new position or a new person in a given position. Some firms also use the opportunity of doing a search for your organization to target employees in your organization for later raiding.

Thus, two primary factors in deciding whether to use a search firm at all and which firm, if any, to use are the quality of a search that the organization can conduct and the organization's business practices. Just as you want to be clear about a firm's business practices, it's wise to get beyond a sales presentation to understand the firm's quality; like any pool you would recruit, the firm's "stable" or pool of applicants could be good or poor depending on the quality of their recruiting techniques. Similarly, their ability to select good candidates for you depends on the quality of their selection techniques. These may be warm-body, ritual, or high-impact techniques, depending on each firm's practice. High-impact hiring provides you with effective guidelines for evaluating the quality of the techniques a firm utilizes.

Also remember that when you recruit a poor pool of applicants yourself, or are unsure about your selection tools, you have no incentive to hire an unqualified applicant into your organization (especially if you took the time to develop a PATH for the position before the hiring event) and plenty of disincentives. A search firm or employment agency, on the other hand, has a considerable incentive to get you to hire any applicant they put in front of you: that's how they get paid.

The key, then, to using a search firm or employment agency effectively is to understand that you will need to put time and work into evaluating the search firm. If you will put more work into selecting an agency than you will into selecting an employee, do the employee search yourself. If you decide that you will use an outside vendor, use the same care in choosing the vendor that you would in choosing an employee. Ask for specifics on how applicants are recruited and selected. Armed with information about high-impact hiring, you can make some determination about the quality of these processes, and therefore the quality of a hire you are likely to make using the search firm. As you would with any other vendor, look for a quality process, a quality product, fair and understandable pricing, and ethical business practices.

If you are using a search firm or employment agency, it is also critical that you not abdicate ultimate responsibility to the firm for the hiring decision. Use such firms to *help* you obtain applicants, but not to make critical decisions about the future of your organization.

Public Employment Agencies

Public employment agencies can be good sources of applicants when utilized effectively. This means matching their strengths to your needs and engaging in high-impact hiring of applicants referred from an agency, just as you would with any other applicants. As with private employment agencies, it is important for you to understand what you are looking for in applicants and communicate that clearly to the agency. Although state employment agencies may offer less rigorous screening than the best private agencies, you may be surprised at the quality of applicants sent to you when you take the time to carefully document your needs.

There are three situations in which public employment agencies can be quite useful. First, they are useful when economic or industry conditions have resulted in higher unemployment among your target hires. For instance, if you are looking for an in-house programmer when a major software company in your area files for bankruptcy or is downsizing, you might find a supply of qualified applicants through the unemployment agency. Second, they can be helpful when you are looking for a large number of workers to fill an immediate need, and you have the capability to train workers whose experience does not exactly meet your needs. This might be the case for seasonal employers. Third, you might use them when it is critical to make sure that you are making the job available to a broad applicant pool, and even more so when you want to be able to substantiate that you did so.

School Recruiting

We'd suggest two ways to make your school recruiting efforts effective and consistent with the high-impact hiring approach to recruiting. The first is to make use of cooperative education and internship programs at both the college and high school levels. You need to structure co-ops or internships to focus on job-related activities. In this way, you make your college recruiting a high-impact, performance-oriented effort. You will be recruiting and selecting from a job trial, which has high validity compared with other hiring methods (see Chapters Six and Ten). You are also creating a system analogous to continuous hiring: when a recruit produces an exceptional job trial through a co-op or internship, you have a strong reason to hire the recruit when he or she becomes available.

The second way to increase the quality of this type of recruiting is to host or become involved with events that have intrinsic interest to the students you most want to recruit. As an example, biotech companies from around the United States sponsor an annual symposium organized by the graduate students of one of the leading molecular biology departments in the country. Exposure for these companies is targeted to a pool of qualified future applicants. Two companies make a point of not only sponsoring the conference, but making sure that their researchers are directly involved with it and attend, providing exposure to cutting-edge research and content-oriented interactions with promising scientists.

Community Training Organizations

Community organizations of different kinds offer tremendous opportunities to reach a wider range of qualified applicants than you may be reaching today. Job referral and placement programs are often maintained by seniors' organizations, women's organizations, youth service organizations, and organizations serving different geographic areas and communities. Even when organized job referral programs don't exist, such organizations can often help to link you with qualified applicants whom the organization serves.

Some community organizations also have developed extensive job training operations, which often can provide you with trained applicants who are motivated to succeed and who may also bring additional support or supervision from the training operation. Community training organizations exist, for example, for single parents leaving welfare, people with physical and mental disabilities, disadvantaged youth, and people returning to work from a variety of situations, from parenting to prison terms. Many large corporations have learned to make use of these organizations so that they can recruit from a predictable source of trained workers, many of whom bring a strong motivation to excel. You can get your best results by finding community training organizations that have excellent reputations for the quality of the workers they train and developing a close and ongoing working relationship with these organizations.

Job Fairs

Job fairs are events at which multiple employers, often from the same community or the same industry, gather to recruit employees. As with any other recruiting method, you should take a high-impact approach to deciding whether and how to be involved with a fair. The most critical consideration is whether the fair is likely to bring you in contact with employees who have the desirable qualifications that you identified in Chapter Two. A well-organized and thoroughly publicized fair can bring you in contact with a wide range of applicants with an interest in working for your organization. Your recruitment efforts at job fairs, and your decision to participate in them, should also take into account the fact that some of the other organizations at the fair will be directly competing with you for applicants.

You will often find it advantageous to focus on job fairs that are planned by organizations that have an ongoing interest in your business, such as professional organizations and chambers of commerce. You can also organize your own job fair for your organization or work group. Use it as an opportunity to present positive, realistic pictures of your organization, its work, the work of your work group, and any jobs you are hiring for. Provide an attraction that is interesting and job-related in addition to the possible draw of getting a job, such as a speaker or a demonstration. And recruit for the near future, not just for your immediate needs. In addition to featuring jobs you are hiring for now, make sure your job fair appeals to those who are not in the immediate job market.

Electronic and On-Line Recruiting

Certainly the latest innovation, as well as the latest craze, to hit recruiting is using the Internet and the World Wide Web as a recruiting tool. Consider whether and how electronic recruiting can help your own high-impact recruiting efforts. Will recruiting on the World Wide Web help you to target applicants with the desired performance attributes for the job at hand? If so, you will want to move forward; if not, you'll want to avoid being drawn into high-tech ritual hiring.

How can you use Web-based recruiting in a high-impact way? As with all other recruiting, start by establishing whether a match exists between candidates you can recruit with this method and the attributes you've identified in your work analysis. If so, there are several routes you can take to effectively utilize the Web for recruiting:

- Local chambers of commerce, community networks, and government-industry partnerships are developing websites that often have as one purpose creating matches between employ-

ers and job seekers. These can be particularly helpful for
small- to medium-sized employers.

- If you currently have a website and have ongoing expenses
  already allocated to maintaining the site, you may well want to
  add the capability of posting jobs and receiving résumés, inquiries, and applications. At the very least, you will want to be
  aware that savvy job applicants will be searching your site for
  information about your organization before applying for a job.
- Commercial Internet job services facilitate postings by employers and candidates and can be particularly helpful for
  extensive recruiting efforts. CareerPath is an example of a
  commercial service that can be found at www.careerpath.com.

Websites that offer employers the service of posting job open-
ings and recruiting information are analogous to job fairs, with
similar advantages and disadvantages. Determine which course of
action will provide you with the greatest competitive advantages in
attracting the most desirable employees to your workplace. If your
competitors are all using electronic services, for instance, you may
want to also do so in order to maintain visibility with applicants. Be
sure to monitor the effectiveness of your efforts, and try to learn
about other organizations' experiences. If none of your competitors use this approach, you can decide if this means that you can
get a leg up on top prospects or if, instead, it means that it's not a
method suited to the jobs for which you recruit.

Here are some additional recommendations:

- If your organization has a website, encourage applicants to
  learn about your organization by visiting the site. (Internet-
  savvy applicants will be searching for your site anyway.)
  Consider specifically devoting a part of your existing site to
  recruiting. On the other hand, if you are thinking about developing a website simply for recruiting, carefully analyze the
  effectiveness of the time and resources spent on a site in comparison with other methods in your recruiting repertoire.
  Use guidelines similar to those listed for classified advertising:
  emphasize the information that will most help applicants to
  differentiate you from competitors for their labor. At the same

time, be sure that your recruiting information does not provide business competitors with useful information they don't already have.

- It's appropriate to offer an E-mail address as one way for applicants to route résumés or applications, particularly for positions that utilize electronic communication or computing. Commercial job-posting sites will offer applicants options for sending résumés to you electronically. If you do offer an E-mail route, you also need to be prepared to reply to applications and queries you receive.
- Material received, and material you transmit in response, should be considered to be public information; it is not currently subject to the same legal protection as documents transmitted through the mail.
- Work closely with the system administrators in your organization or with your Internet service provider to make sure that any interactive parts of your recruiting effort, such as electronic résumé submission, are developed with the security of your organization's computing resources in mind.
- Be sure to evaluate the effectiveness of electronic recruiting just as you would the effectiveness of other sources.

Evaluating Recruiting

For any of your efforts at attracting and recruiting employees to be high-impact hiring techniques, you have to know that they will have a positive effect on later work performance. The best way to make sure that your recruiting efforts are having this impact is to measure the results. Each time you recruit, track the following information for each recruiting method and source:

- Type of recruiting
- Specifics of the information presented: samples of copy or advertising tear sheets, lists of vendors (periodicals or search firms), and so on
- Costs of using each source
- Number of applicants produced by each source

You will want to have a way to determine which recruiting source produced each applicant. The simplest way is to ask applicants, on the application form or on a supplemental form, how they learned of the position. If you are advertising in several publications, for example, be sure to provide a blank or a check-off box for the applicant to indicate which source was used.

After your search process is completed, you can do an informal or formal evaluation of the information. You'll get the most helpful results by analyzing which sources produced:

- Applicants
- Applicants with minimally acceptable qualifications
- Applicants with desirable qualifications

The way you hire will determine how you would like your sources to be effective at producing the three categories of applicants. If you hire *deeply,* accepting a large number of people in any given applicant pool, then the most important target will be recruiting sources that provide applicants with *minimally* acceptable qualifications. If you hire *narrowly,* limiting yourself to a small number of select hires, your target will be sources that provide applicants with *desirable* qualifications. In the latter case, you could then move away from using sources that provide you with large numbers of applicants but smaller numbers of qualified applicants. This applies not only for general categories, such as advertising and job fairs, but also to specific efforts within a category. You can use this kind of analysis to determine, for instance, whether one ad copy or job fair was more effective than another.

If you hire large enough numbers of people, you can also track which sources produced the most candidates hired and their success after hiring. It's then possible to select recruiting sources that are more likely to provide successful employees. We caution, though, that unless you are hiring many people for similar positions, you will draw better conclusions by evaluating recruiting effectiveness in terms of qualified applicants than in terms of successful hires.

Summary

Attracting qualified applicants is critical to high-impact hiring, because your pool of applicants sets the upper limit for how effective you can be in hiring. If you've recruited only mediocre applicants, no amount of interviewing, testing, or background checking will allow you to hire excellent employees. The first step toward developing a quality pool of applicants is to actively seek desirable employees *before* they begin looking at you as a potential employer.

A second critical step is to analyze your job and organization from the perspective of potential applicants. Determine what factors are likely to appeal to and what factors are likely to create concerns in the most qualified applicants, and present applicants with a balanced picture that will allow them to make an informed decision to work for you.

The third step is to use high-impact approaches to recruiting that broaden the range of qualified individuals interested in working with your organization. Making sure that your recruiting is fair and reaches out to qualified applicants not only helps you increase the qualifications and performance of the candidates you can hire, but it also helps you ensure that your recruiting efforts—along with your entire hiring system—operate legally. Understanding the legal considerations in recruiting and hiring is the subject of the next chapter.

Chapter Five

Doing the Right Thing

High-Impact Hiring and the Law

One of the reasons many managers dread hiring is that hiring has become the target of challenges and expensive litigation. Rather than asking themselves "What characteristics are most critical for making a good hire?" too many managers instead fixate on legal constraints on what they can or cannot say, ask, or do while interacting with job applicants. The theme of this chapter is that employment law is a reality that employers cannot and should not avoid, but that legal requirements need not interfere with a high-impact hiring approach to selection. Instead, we see high-impact hiring as complementary with legal and ethical standards for hiring.

Our primary objectives in this chapter are to provide a brief description of employment law related to hiring and to help you to use this information to make hiring decisions that are both effective *and* legal. As a hiring manager, you need to understand the basics of employment law so that you can manage the legal risks involved in making a hiring decision. At the same time, you need to avoid the temptation to overemphasize legal principles to the detriment of business principles when you are developing a hiring system.

Employment laws are mostly useful for telling you what you *cannot* do; they're not very useful for advising you how to attract and hire the best talent for your organization. By way of analogy, can you imagine trying to learn how to drive a car by reading the traffic code? Just as the traffic code was not written to teach people how to drive, employment law was not written to teach employers the best way to hire employees. In general, employment laws only outlaw employment practices that are unfair; they do not constrain you from using practices that are effective and fair.

A key principle in this chapter is that high-impact hiring practices are also legal hiring practices. That is, as you learn how to hire effectively, you receive the additional benefit of being more likely to hire legally. Note that the converse is not necessarily the case: plenty of hiring practices are completely legal and also ineffective. Our approach is to focus first on what makes the best sense for hiring effectively, and then to make sure that hiring is done legally. Putting the legal cart before the effectiveness horse means that you may hire using methods that meet legal scrutiny but won't help you to find a better employee.

The Social and Legal Context of Hiring

It's important to remember that the laws that affect the hiring process were written to solve societal problems by correcting the poor management practices that helped to cause some of these problems. Early employment legislation, such as legislation concerning wages, hours, and health and safety, focused on improving working conditions for all workers. During the 1950s and 1960s, the civil rights movement highlighted the disparities in the way the benefits of employment were spread across society. Resulting equal employment opportunity (EEO) legislation was designed to open access to desirable employment to a much larger proportion of the workforce.

To a large extent, employment laws have been productive for groups that have historically been discriminated against, for society, and for most employers. Many of the employment practices that have been legally mandated make good business sense and were already being implemented by many firms before they became law. EEO laws provide for a larger pool of skilled employees than when social pressures kept qualified applicants from being considered because of reasons unrelated to performance, such as not attending the "right" college or not originating from the "right" social group. They also remind employers of the need to use hiring procedures that select applicants on the basis of legitimate, job-related factors. These are sound business practices that also underlie high-impact hiring.

One unfortunate consequence of increased regulation of employment has been a significant increase in paperwork for employers. The only consolation we can offer is that following the high-impact hiring principles of performance orientation, systemization, and effective decision making will produce information that fulfills many of the existing legal documentation requirements.

Let's consider some examples of the kinds of issues that hiring managers wrestle with, and we will see how they can be addressed from legal, ethical, and performance perspectives:

"I own a small business, and I can't afford to hire enough employees to cover for our current receptionist when her children are sick. She's going to be leaving, and I'm wondering if I can ask applicants for this position if they have children and, if so, what their plans are if the children get sick."

"We have a person applying for a clerical position. He tells us that his vision is so bad that he cannot take our usual written employment test, so he wants to either skip the test or have someone read it to him. If we hire him, he says he'll need an extra-large computer screen to do his work. Do we really need to make these special accommodations just for him?"

"We do a lot of business in South America, where managers are often uncomfortable working with women. Stephanie is one of our best salespeople, and she keeps asking to be assigned to our South American region to get some international experience, which is critical for advancement in our company. But our customers there flat-out told me that they don't want to work with a woman. I want to be fair to Stephanie, but I can't afford to lose business."

"I've been thinking about using some employment tests as part of our hiring process. They seem more objective and they're pretty quick and inexpensive. But a friend tells me not to touch them, because I'll end up being sued for discrimination. Testing still sounds like a useful tool, but is it too much of a gamble?"

"We realized that we have too few women in our management group, so we made a special effort to recruit Sally for the position of vice president of operations. But now James, the previous heir apparent, is threatening to charge us with reverse discrimination. We're damned if we do and damned if we don't."

Deciding What Is "Right" to Do When Hiring

When you are faced with difficult situations like these, the hardest challenge is deciding what is right to do and how you will know that your chosen response is the right one. There are at least three perspectives that can help you to decide on an appropriate course of action: (1) determining what response is most appropriate from a *performance* orientation, (2) determining what relevant *legal requirements* dictate, and (3) determining what approach is most compatible with relevant *ethical* standards. Much of the time these perspectives will lead to about the same decision, but differences exist often enough to make it productive to understand each perspective.

The Performance Perspective

As we described in Chapter Two, we believe that hiring decisions should be based on contribution to the performance of the organization. The fundamental question is whether the capabilities you are basing your hiring decisions on—and the indicators (tests, interview questions, and so forth) you are using to measure these capabilities—are really *essential* to job performance. If they are not, they are not high-impact hiring methods, and they also may put you at greater risk for violating the law. Consider, for example, the first case, the manager who wants to cut down on absenteeism by asking applicants about their child care plans. It would be illegal to ask only women about their child care plans, since this involves treating female applicants differently because of their gender (not to mention the dubious assumption that men with children are not affected by family illness). If regular attendance is essential to the receptionist's position, it's appropriate to describe the attendance requirements and ask if the applicant would have any problem meeting those requirements. It would also be appropriate to ask about attendance when seeking references from prior employers. In either case, you should ask these questions of both male and female applicants.

The performance perspective we are describing throughout this book should not be confused with a cynical, expedient approach to difficult ethical questions. Let's use the case of the job applicant with poor vision as an example. The Americans with Disabilities Act prohibits discriminating against an applicant with a disability who is otherwise able to perform the *essential* tasks in a job. It further requires that you go to reasonable lengths to accommodate otherwise qualified applicants so that their disability does not interfere with work performance, with the definition of "reasonable" being a function of your resources, among other things. A cynic might be tempted to distort the performance perspective by arguing that the best business decision would be to avoid the cost of accommodating applicants with disabilities. Such a perspective is shortsighted for a number of reasons:

1. It ignores the question of whether the applicant has the essential capabilities to do the job. The applicant in question might be a very good employee once a larger computer monitor is made available. The key is to focus on job-related capabilities, not irrelevant disabilities.
2. The cost of accommodating this applicant by reading the test questions to him (or just providing him with a magnifying glass) and later providing him with a larger computer monitor is trivial for most employers when you consider the investment that is made in any new employee. In fact, the Job Accommodation Network, a nonprofit consulting service of the President's Commission on Employment of People with Disabilities, reports that 66 percent of accommodations cost less than $500; Sears, Roebuck & Co. found the cost to be less than $100 in 89 percent of their accommodations.[1]
3. The investment you have made in accommodating an employee is likely to pay dividends in increased loyalty. Many employees who have been accommodated realize that finding other equally willing employers is likely to be difficult.

Our approach is to rely primarily on the performance perspective. This perspective's emphasis on job-relatedness also forms the core of the legal and ethical perspectives we describe next, and it capitalizes on what you know as a manager, rather than forcing you to rely too much on an attorney or other specialist. Nevertheless, there are times when the other perspectives are important complements to the performance perspective.

The Legal Perspective

The legal perspective is often important in determining the best means of reaching your performance objectives. In other words, once you know *what* you are looking for in applicants, legal considerations may affect *how* you assess these factors. Let's consider the case of the employer who was worried that employment tests might discriminate against racial minorities. The performance perspective indicates that the employer should first determine if the capabilities measured by the test are really essential to work performance; if they are, the test may be a useful tool. The legal perspective can then be helpful in determining how to administer the test and document its job-relatedness in a way that will reduce the likelihood of an expensive lawsuit. Knowing what is required to show that a test or other hiring tool is valid and non-discriminatory is vital to determining whether using it is a gamble or a reasonable business risk.

The problem with the legal perspective—aside from all the paperwork it tends to generate—is that it can too easily distract you from performance issues. Deciding not to use tests because you might get sued, even if the tests are the best way to measure essential employee capabilities, abdicates your fundamental responsibility to accomplish the work of the organization. Yes, the risk of lawsuits or other adverse consequences is part of any business decision, but risks need to be weighed against potential benefits. This kind of rational cost-benefit analysis, or risk analysis, is a routine part of most business decisions but is too often lacking in decisions about how to hire.

We have worked with many organizations that conduct inherently risky business and have an active program of reducing risk and effectively managing the unavoidable risks that remain. Your risk involved in daily business is generally greater than your legal risk during hiring, as long as you follow basic practices for reducing and managing risks. We encourage businesses to reduce their risks during hiring by following a performance orientation such as high-impact hiring and by being attentive to legal requirements. Doing so makes litigation less likely to occur and easier to defend against. If you conduct your hiring in a way that doesn't focus on performance, isn't systematic, and isn't explicit about effective decisions, you won't be likely to make high-impact hires, and you will have a greater likelihood of being involved in a legal action.

Another problem with the legalistic perspective is that the mere fact that a practice is legal does not mean that it is the right thing to do. There is an important distinction between illegal and unfair hiring decisions. As a practical matter, most employers need to conform to legal requirements whether or not they agree that the requirements are fair or practical. But you often have an option when it comes to practices that may be unfair but on which the law is silent. This is where the moral-ethical perspective becomes salient.

The Moral-Ethical Perspective

An example of an ethical issue that has recently become controversial concerns hiring decisions based on sexual preference. Federal EEO law does not address the issue, so employers are on their own to determine whether or not to use sexual preference as a factor in hiring (unless relevant state or local regulations apply). Although our own perspective is that sexual preference is not likely to be job-related, some employers feel that a different standard applies in cases such as this.

Affirmative action provides another example of an ethically charged hiring issue. In our case describing Sally, the woman who was appointed to the position of vice president of operations instead of an equally qualified male, the employer made a decision to actively target female applicants. Such affirmative action programs may be defended from the performance perspective; for example, as a woman, Sally will bring a more diverse perspective to management decisions, which may be more effective as a result. In many cases, however, the rationale is an ethical argument that society is better served by aggressive actions to overcome the effects of past discrimination. Even though courts have become increasingly critical of this type of argument, some employers have chosen to accept this legal risk because of their philosophical beliefs.

The High-Impact Hiring Approach

As we have already noted, our approach in this book is to focus primarily on the performance perspective. We are management researchers and consultants, not lawyers or ethicists, so we can speak most directly to performance issues. In most cases, the performance perspective—with its focus on job-relatedness as a central principle—will present recommendations that are compatible with legal and ethical perspectives.

We recognize the practical importance of legal considerations in making hiring decisions. The question is not whether they are important, but how much priority to place on them. Our strategy, even in this chapter, might be thought of as a commonsense approach to legal issues. We want to draw your attention to legal issues that are likely to be important, but we will not attempt to deal with all legal factors that could possibly apply. The legal environment is changing and is likely to continue to move toward a performance-based analysis of employment discrimination. That is, hiring procedures that can be shown to improve performance and are not blatantly discriminatory are likely to be acceptable to the courts. Although we certainly don't advocate a cavalier approach to legal responsibilities, we also want to avoid an overly defensive legal strategy that imperils good decision making about performance and business issues.

Our approach may not be suitable for managers who are risk-averse or who work in particularly litigious environments, as many public sector organizations do. In such instances, it is a good decision to work closely with a legal counsel who is well versed in employment law. In fact, most readers will find that it is necessary and a wise idea to work with such a specialist at least occasionally. In these situations, it is important to pick an attorney who specializes in employment law; this usually will not be the same person who provides general legal counsel to your firm.

Where Do All These Rules Come From?

Various sources of legal guidelines affect hiring, and each affects different kinds of employers in different ways.

Constitutional Law

Despite all the arguments about the constitutionality of hiring requirements such as drug testing, the U.S. Constitution is not directly relevant for most employers. That's because the Constitution was written to protect citizens from the excesses of government, not to regulate the behavior of private sector employers. Thus, the Fifth Amendment (pertaining to the federal government) and the Fourteenth Amendment (pertaining to state and local governments) guarantee equal protection under the law, but only to public sector employees.

In some cases state constitutions provide additional requirements that employers need to be aware of. For instance, California's constitution includes a right to privacy that is not incorporated in the U.S. Constitution and that has been used to litigate employment procedures that may be perceived as invading applicants' privacy rights.

Statutory Law

Statutory law is legislative law, that is, laws that are written by elected representatives to federal or state congressional bodies. Most important pieces of EEO law are statutory law, generally written by the U.S. Congress under the Commerce Clause of the U.S. Constitution and thus applying to most firms doing business in the United States. State and local laws may be more inclusive than federal law, so you need to be aware of them as well.

The most important statutory law regarding hiring is Title VII of the Civil Rights Act of 1964 (most recently amended in 1991), generally referred to simply as Title VII. It is the most comprehensive statement of EEO law and provides the model on which most other antidiscrimination laws are based. Table 5.1 provides a listing of the key federal EEO laws and briefly summarizes their requirements. The next section of this chapter will help you to determine which laws may regulate your own organization.

Common Law

Common law refers to laws made by the courts, rather than laws written into the Constitution or enacted by legislative bodies. As

Table 5.1. Primary Equal Employment Opportunity Laws.

Law	What Is Covered
Equal Pay Act (1963)	Prohibits gender-based discrimination in pay.
Civil Rights Act (Title VII) (1964, amended 1991)	Prohibits discrimination in all aspects of employment on the basis of race, color, religion, national origin, or gender.
Age Discrimination in Employment Act (1967, amended 1987)	Prohibits discrimination on the basis of age for employees aged forty or over. Also prohibits age-based mandatory retirement.
Pregnancy Discrimination Act (1978)	Prohibits discrimination on the basis of pregnancy or pregnancy-related conditions. Covered employees must be treated in accordance with an organization's short-term–disability provisions.
Immigration Reform and Control Act (1986)	Prohibits discrimination on the basis of national origin. Requires employers to verify employment eligibility of all job applicants.
Americans with Disabilities Act (1990)	Prohibits discrimination on the basis of disabilities that are not critically related to job performance. Requires "reasonable accommodation" of qualified applicants with disabilities.

employers often lament, laws are frequently written in rather vague terms. Therefore, it falls to the courts to interpret how they actually apply to specific workplace situations. Within the federal court system, where many precedent-setting decisions are made, cases are first heard in district courts. Decisions may be appealed by either party to the corresponding circuit court of appeals for each of the twelve judicial circuits. Decisions by a court of appeals create a precedent for all the district courts within that circuit, but not for courts in other circuits. This explains why the "law of the land" may differ depending on where you do business. Circuit court decisions may be appealed to the U.S. Supreme Court, whose decisions set precedents for the whole country.

Three aspects of common law are particularly relevant to hiring and other personnel decisions. *Tort law* concerns situations in which a person can be held liable for intentional harm inflicted on another. An example, discussed in Chapter Seven, is the possibility that a previous employer may be held responsible for defamation of an applicant's character when providing unfavorable information during a reference check. *Contract law* determines the conditions under which an agreement, such as an agreement to be hired, is legally binding. Contract law is an important consideration when describing the terms and conditions of employment to a new hire, to be sure that you are not unintentionally implying contractual obligations that you do not intend. Finally, the common *law of agency* describes situations in which you as an employer are responsible for actions taken by your agents, such as supervisors who may be asking illegal questions in interviews.

The significant differences in common law in different states and localities—as well as the complexity of the jurisdictional and precedent-setting processes—are among the reasons that it is important to choose an attorney who specializes in employment law when you have a tough question.

Regulatory Agency Guidelines

Because statutory law is generally written in general language, government regulatory agencies are often given the responsibility of developing more detailed enacting regulations. Although these regulations are not always "laws," courts generally use the guidelines as a basis for determining if you are acting within the bounds of the law.

Title VII created the Equal Employment Opportunity Commission (EEOC) as the primary EEO regulatory agency. In addition to its enforcement and record-keeping responsibilities, the EEOC has written a variety of regulations concerning everything from sexual harassment to disabilities in the workplace. Its key document is the *Uniform Guidelines on Employee Selection Procedures,* which forms the legal basis for most of what is discussed in this book. Comparable agencies, generically referred to as Fair Employment Practices Commissions, exist in most states, and sometimes at local levels as well. The other primary regulatory agency is the Office of Federal Contract Compliance Programs, which sets hiring standards for companies wishing to do business with the federal government.

Executive Orders

Executive orders are policy decisions made by the president of the United States. Much like decisions made by the CEO of an organization, executive orders prescribe how business with the federal government will be conducted. Executive orders are not "laws" in the same sense as constitutional or statutory laws, but they are necessary requirements if you wish to be a federal contractor or otherwise receive federal funds. For example, Executive Order 11246 requires federal contractors to make hiring decisions in a nondiscriminatory fashion and to utilize affirmative action in hiring targeted groups in order to receive a contract.

Are You Affected by All of These Laws?

Not all employers are affected by all laws. As we already mentioned, only public sector employers are substantially affected by U.S. constitutional law, and only federal contractors, subcontractors, or those otherwise receiving federal funds are covered by executive orders. Most private employers are affected by Title VII as long as they employ fifteen or more employees. The threshold level for coverage by the Age Discrimination in Employment Act is twenty or more employees; for the Family and Medical Leave Act it is fifty or more employees. Title VII also covers labor unions, hiring halls, and employment agencies. Private clubs are excluded from EEO legislation, and religious organizations may be allowed to consider religion when hiring. Firms doing business in the United States—regardless of their country of incorporation—must comply with federal EEO laws. U.S. companies with offices or plants in foreign locations must comply with both U.S. and host-country requirements in their overseas locations.

State or local regulations may have a broader scope than federal laws. For example, in some states all employers are covered by state regulations regardless of size. Some states or localities have also extended EEO legislation to include a wider range of characteristics, such as sexual orientation, or to provide added protections against invasion of privacy, such as bans on the use of drug tests, honesty and personality tests, or restrictions on employee behavior off the job.

What Is Prohibited?

Generally speaking, the intent of EEO laws is to prohibit discrimination based on certain "protected characteristics." These characteristics include race or color; gender, including pregnancy; religion; national origin; age (being older than forty); and disabilities. There are two important but subtle points in this statement. One is that we prefer the term *protected characteristics* to the more widely used *protected groups*. The latter term leads to the misconception that EEO laws protect only certain groups, such as racial minorities or women. In fact, EEO laws prohibit making hiring decisions that are based on characteristics, such as race and gender, that are irrelevant to job performance. These laws protect characteristics, not groups. Thus, it is equally illegal to discriminate against a white, male applicant based on his race or gender as it is to discriminate against a Hispanic, female applicant. The second point is that EEO laws only prohibit employment decisions that are based on these targeted characteristics. Decisions based on other equally irrelevant characteristics, such as hair color or being right-handed, are perfectly acceptable from a legal point of view, although they are wholly contrary to a high-impact approach to hiring. Thus, while the legal perspective probably weeds out some of the worst bases for hiring, *EEO laws do not require that employers use sound, job-related hiring procedures,* unless the procedures create adverse impact, which we will describe shortly. That is why the legal perspective needs to be complemented by the performance perspective that is fundamental to high-impact hiring.

It is also important to understand what is meant by "discrimination." Fundamentally, to discriminate means to make distinctions among people. Discrimination on the basis of performance is the whole point of effective hiring, which makes distinctions among applicants in order to hire those who will be most effective. From a legal perspective, however, the term *discrimination* implies distinctions made on the basis of protected characteristics that have no rational relationship to job performance. Hiring decisions that are based on such distinctions are a primary target of EEO law.

There are two forms of illegal discrimination, referred to as *disparate* (unequal) *treatment* and *adverse impact*. You should review your hiring procedures to make sure that neither form of discrimination occurs.

Disparate Treatment

The most obvious form of discrimination, disparate treatment involves treating people differently because of their age, sex, skin color, and so forth. Examples of disparate treatment include:

- Asking only women about their ability to meet attendance requirements. As we described in the example at the beginning of this chapter, if regular attendance is essential, it may be appropriate to ask applicants about their ability to regularly be at work on time. But asking this only of female applicants is illegal because it treats them differently from male applicants, who may also have problems with regular attendance.
- Not hiring older job applicants because you're concerned that they won't learn as quickly as younger applicants. If the ability to learn quickly is really essential, you should assess this in all applicants rather than assuming that younger applicants are better in that regard. (An older fast learner will learn faster than a younger slow learner.) Excluding older workers may also reduce overall performance by lessening job-related experience in your workforce.
- Requiring applicants with disabilities to have a medical examination, or asking them how their disability would affect their job performance. If physical ability is important, all applicants should have a job-related medical evaluation, which must occur *after* a job offer has been extended.
- Asking only "foreign-looking" or "foreign-sounding" applicants to prove that they are eligible to work in the United States. This represents discrimination on the basis of national origin. The Immigration Reform and Control Act requires employers to verify *all* applicants' eligibility to work; it also prohibits discrimination against noncitizens who are eligible to work in the United States.

Although disparate treatment is relatively obvious and is usually considered to be intentional, the underlying motive may not necessarily be malicious. In fact, disparate treatment can occur with the best of misguided intentions. For example, one employer took pains to explain to a female applicant that she would be working in a male-dominated group and asked her if she felt that she could be productive in such an environment. The woman sued, arguing that she was being treated differently from male applicants and that the interviewer's motive was to discourage her from applying for the job. While that may not have been the interviewer's true motive, he exposed his company to a lawsuit by treating the applicant differently because of her gender.

Adverse Impact

Not all instances of discrimination involve the "smoking gun" that usually characterizes disparate treatment. Adverse impact, also known as disparate impact, includes discrimination that is usually a consequence, either intentional or unintentional, of what appears to be a reasonable (or "facially neutral") hiring procedure. Examples of adverse impact might include:

- Specifying minimum height requirements that are not really necessary but that have the effect of excluding women and some ethnic groups, such as Asian Americans, who have more members who are shorter than the general population.
- Using employment tests that are not job-related and on which minorities score lower than majority-group members.
- Using employee referrals as the sole recruiting procedure, when the employees refer primarily people who are like themselves. A common example at executive and professional levels is the "good old boy" network, in which white, male executives hire other white males they know from their fraternity, country club, or church.

Adverse impact is considerably more controversial than disparate treatment because there is no requirement to show that the discriminatory effect was intentional. The focus is entirely on the consequences of a particular hiring practice and whether the practice is job-related.

What Happens if Someone Sues You for Discrimination?

If you follow the high-impact hiring approach, treat applicants fairly, and make hiring decisions based on job-relevant performance factors, you reduce the likelihood of being sued. Overall, the odds of being sued for discrimination in hiring are not large, particularly if you're a smaller employer. Adverse-impact cases in particular appear to be on the decline, and the vast majority of lawsuits today pertain more to unfair treatment of *employees* (for example, cases of age discrimination or sexual harassment) rather than of job applicants.[2] Nevertheless, lawsuits and complaints to the EEOC do occur, and even unsubstantiated complaints can be unnerving. As attorneys say, you can be sued by almost anyone for almost anything. The real issue is whether the person suing you can convince a jury that the complaint is valid.

In this section we provide a brief, informal description of how a *plaintiff* (the person making the complaint) files a charge of discrimination, and what you (the *defendant*) can do to defend yourself. This will help you to understand the process so that you can design a hiring system that can both reduce the likelihood of such a challenge and stand up to a challenge if one is raised. (If you are currently facing or anticipating a discrimination claim, our treatment of the topic will not suffice. You need to consult an employment attorney immediately.)

The Plaintiff's Burden of Proof

Normally, applicants who feel that they have been treated unfairly will first contact a state Fair Employment Practices Commission (or the federal EEOC). The agency, or in some cases the plaintiff's attorney, investigates the case and, as a first step, looks to see whether the plaintiff has what is called a prima facie case. Prima facie evidence is tentative evidence of discrimination, what might be called reasonable suspicion. The purpose of prima facie evidence is to show that a strong enough case exists to require you to defend your actions, much as a prosecutor in a criminal case needs to develop an adequate case before a defendant is indicted. Obligating plaintiffs to provide prima facie evidence as a required first step serves to minimize unsubstantiated, nuisance lawsuits that waste your time and the court's.

For *disparate treatment* cases, the U.S. Supreme Court outlined the basic elements of prima facie evidence in *McDonnell Douglas Corporation* v. *Green* (1973)[3]. Plaintiffs must show that they:

- Are protected by a relevant EEO statute
- Applied for a job for which they were qualified
- Were not hired, with the job remaining open to applicants with qualifications similar to their own

More generally, plaintiffs making a disparate treatment case must show that they were treated differently in the hiring process because of their race, national origin, gender, or other protected characteristic.

For *adverse impact* cases, plaintiffs usually establish a prima facie case through the use of statistics. One type of statistic involves showing that the number of *employees* in a company who belong to one group, such as African Americans, is not proportional to the number of qualified workers of that group in the relevant labor pool. For example, one employer's workforce included less than 1 percent black workers, while the local labor market was 30 percent black (*United States* v. *Hayes International Corporation*, 1972)[4]. This raised sufficiently serious questions about possible discrimination to require the firm to defend its hiring practices.

Another type of statistic used to establish a prima facie adverse impact case compares the hiring rate for *applicants* of different groups. If the "pass rate" for one group is less than 80 percent of the pass rate for the majority group, there is reasonable suspicion that the hiring practice may be discriminatory. (See Exhibit 5.1 for an example.)

It is important to remember that prima facie evidence is not definitive proof that you are guilty of discrimination; it simply provides a sufficient basis to compel you to respond to the charges. If you have been practicing performance-oriented, nondiscriminatory hiring, you can show that the hiring practices are in fact legitimate and that discrimination did not take place.

Defending Your Hiring Practices

The type of evidence you need to provide to defend your hiring practices depends on whether the plaintiff has filed a disparate treatment or adverse impact claim. For *disparate treatment* cases, you need to provide a sound nondiscriminatory reason for not hiring the

Exhibit 5.1. Calculating Adverse Impact.

In a typical year, Mall Fashions hires over 100 retail sales clerks for its five stores in Metroville. In reviewing the last year, Mall Fashions finds the following hiring trends for different racial groups:

Racial Group	Number of Applicants	Number Hired	Pass Rate (Percent)
White	150	60	40
Black	60	15	25
Hispanic	50	5	10
Asian	40	20	50

Mall Fashions obviously hires far fewer Hispanics than applicants of other races, in both absolute and percentage terms. They hire nearly as many blacks as applicants of Asian descent, though the pass *rates* for the two groups are quite different. Notice also that the pass rate for white applicants is lower than that of Asians, though far more white applicants are hired than applicants of any other group. Is there evidence of adverse impact, and if so, against whom?

A rule of thumb known as the "Four-Fifths Rule" can be used to estimate whether disparate impact exists. The Four-Fifths Rule indicates that disparate impact exists if the pass rate for any racial, ethnic, or sex subgroup is less than four-fifths (or 80 percent) of the pass rate of the group with *highest* pass rate. In this example, the group with the highest pass rate is Asians (with a pass rate of 50 percent). Any group with a pass rate of less than 40 percent (four-fifths of 50 percent) would be experiencing adverse impact; this includes black and Hispanic, but not white, applicants. Mall Fashions would be wise to explore why this level of disparate impact is occurring, to make sure that it is not based on discriminatory factors.

plaintiff. This might involve showing that the person was not actually qualified for the job, or that the person you hired instead was more qualified than the plaintiff. The more compelling case you can build, the better off you are. Remember that the plaintiff is likely to respond by saying that your explanation is nothing but a pretext and that your actual motive was discriminatory. Your best defense is a good set of records, developed at the time of the hire, that document the reasoning behind your hiring decisions and show that your hiring decision in this case was consistent with your overall orientation to performance-based, nondiscriminatory hiring.

In certain, quite limited, circumstances you may be able to show that excluding applicants with a particular characteristic is a "bona fide occupational qualification" (BFOQ). Title VII provides an exemption allowing a firm to hire on the basis of religion, national origin, gender, or age if such hiring is justified by business necessity and if no applicants in the excluded group are able to perform the job. For example, public safety officials have pressed for an exemption for police and firefighters to the Age Discrimination in Employment Act's ban on mandatory retirement ages, arguing that police officers and firefighters over fifty-five years of age are physically unfit to do the work and thus pose a greater risk to the public. BFOQs are only rarely upheld, for the very good reason that it is rare for all members of any particular group to be unable to perform the work successfully. Moreover, race can never be used as a BFOQ.[5]

Evidence to defend against an *adverse impact* charge can be particularly difficult to amass and present, because the prima facie case will have already established that a pattern of hiring exists in which people with protected characteristics are hired significantly less frequently. When this is the case, you will need to prove that your hiring procedures are justifiable, despite the disparate impact they create against a particular group. By "justifiable," we mean that you must show that the procedures are job-related and consistent with business necessity. Unlike disparate treatment, you need to show proof—evidence—to support your argument that the hiring procedures are job-related. This can be done in two ways.

The first way is to validate the selection procedures. This requires empirical evidence that differences among applicants on the challenged hiring procedures are actually related to corresponding differences in job performance. Validation is the most common means of defending hiring procedures against adverse impact claims. It also is a technique that can indicate whether a selection procedure is performance-based, and it is complex enough to merit a more extended discussion in the next chapter.

The second way to support your argument is to argue that the practice is a business necessity, or "that which is reasonably necessary to the safe and efficient operation of the business."[6] While this may sound easier than validating selection tools, courts have frequently rejected business-necessity claims that are not well substantiated with hard evidence. Subjective opinions about what is necessary or blindly following industry practices are usually not sufficient. Nor are customer preferences. To return to the case of Stephanie, the sales representative who was the victim of discrimination by international customers, the courts have ruled that a threatened loss of business is not an adequate basis for assigning a man to work in countries that have traditionally not worked with women (*Fernandes* v. *Wynn Oil Company,* 1982)[7]. In fact, many companies have found that cultural biases such as these can be overcome and that women can be very effective working in other cultures.

About the only area in which business necessity has consistently been upheld is situations in which employee or public safety is affected, as with mandatory retirement of airline pilots. The problem with a business-necessity defense is that it is hard to predict what evidence the agency or judge will accept as compelling. These decisions are made on a case-by-case basis, so you won't know in advance if your defense will be successful.

Defending yourself against an employment discrimination charge is unpleasant and time-consuming. But before getting fixated on the legalities of hiring, it's important to remember a few key points:

- Doing business, as with all aspects of life, involves taking risks. The risks involved with making hiring decisions are probably lower than most of your other business decisions, and they can be effectively managed.
- A challenge to your hiring procedures—even one that is supported by the EEOC—does not necessarily indicate that you are guilty of wrongdoing.
- Developing a performance-based hiring system that has been shown to be job-related and applying it consistently to all applicants minimizes the likelihood of a challenge and maximizes your likelihood of successfully defending hiring decisions that are challenged.
- Your primary concern when hiring should be selecting effective employees, not worrying about being sued.

Affirmative Action

Affirmative action is a controversial topic that in many ways lends itself better to the ethical perspective than to the legal or performance perspectives. It is particularly difficult to describe the legal limitations affecting affirmative action, since whatever we say today is likely to have changed by the time you read this. Nevertheless, we feel that affirmative action is an important topic to discuss if for no other reason than the many misconceptions about it, which can confuse the hiring manager about its actual impact on hiring decisions.

What Is Affirmative Action?

Affirmative action means different things to different people. The term originated in 1965 when President Lyndon Johnson issued Executive Order 11246, prohibiting discrimination and ordering federal contractors to take affirmative steps to hire more women and minorities. Its original intent was to encourage more targeted *recruiting* of traditionally underemployed groups. It was not intended to create quotas or to require employers to hire unqualified individuals, but simply to encourage employers to develop more diverse applicant pools. Once the enhanced recruitment pool has been developed, the "pure" affirmative action approach requires that final hiring decisions be conducted in a color- and gender-blind fashion on the basis of the applicants' job-relevant qualifications. Over time, however, affirmative action has come to represent more than this "pure" targeted recruiting approach.

Affirmative Action and Reverse Discrimination

Much of the distress about affirmative action comes from notions that it requires employers to give preferential treatment to targeted groups and places white males at a disadvantage (so-called reverse discrimination). Yet as we just noted, preferential treatment and quotas were not included in the language of Executive Order 11246. In fact, preferential treatment of *any* group is explicitly prohibited by Title VII. So where did the notions of quotas and preferential treatment come from? To better understand this, it is important to know the various ways in which affirmative action plans come about.

Affirmative Action Among Federal Contractors

Like all executive orders, Executive Order 11246 applies only to federal contractors and subcontractors. It provides that, as a prerequisite to doing business with the federal government, contractors must determine whether their workforce mirrors the racial and gender composition of the relevant labor pool. If not, the contractor must establish goals and timetables for rectifying any underutilization of employees with protected characteristics. These goals and timetables are supposed to be flexible, not hard-and-fast quotas, though some regulators and employers have undoubtedly treated them that way. The Office of Federal Contract Compliance Programs has in recent years placed less emphasis on specific goals and timetables, and courts have struck down certain "set-aside" provisions of public works contracts.

Court-Mandated Affirmative Action

Title VII specifies that courts may impose mandatory affirmative action plans as part of the settlement of discrimination charges. These plans, which often include hard quotas, are only to be imposed if the firm has been found guilty of past discrimination; in practice, they are rare, since courts limit their use to particularly egregious cases of discrimination.[8] Requirements for affirmative action that involve hard quotas *do not* affect you as a hiring manager unless you are working for an organization that has been found guilty or has settled on past charges of discrimination.

Voluntary Affirmative Action

Employers may also choose to voluntarily incorporate affirmative action into their hiring plans. "Pure" affirmative action—involving only targeted recruiting—is perfectly legal, and it can be an excellent tool for adding diversity to your workforce. The most controversial and risky plans are voluntary ones that involve preferential treatment of targeted groups at the point of selecting employees from the applicant pool. While this may involve explicit quotas, such as having every other new hire at middle-management levels be a woman, it is more likely to involve more subtle factors, such as requiring fewer years of prior managerial experience for female applicants than are expected of male applicants.

The legal standing of preferential treatment in voluntary programs is currently in flux. In 1979, the U.S. Supreme Court ruled in *Kaiser Aluminum and Chemical Corporation* v. *Weber* (1979)[9] that such preferential treatment is acceptable only if it is:

- Part of a formal affirmative action plan intended to overcome historical imbalances
- Temporary—that is, ending when the imbalances are corrected
- Not unduly harmful to other applicants, for example, by completely excluding other applicants or by requiring that existing workers be fired to make room for affirmative action hires

Although the *Weber* rules are still the law of the land, recent lower-court decisions have been more restrictive about using race as a factor in hiring decisions. It is likely that the Supreme Court will revisit this issue in the near future; based on the Court's precedents in other cases, affirmative action programs will likely be restricted even more than in the past. Until then, the safest approach to enhancing the scope and diversity of your workforce is to broaden your recruiting efforts in order to attract the most capable candidates of both genders and all ethnicities, ages, and levels of disability. Hiring should then be based on selecting the applicants who best match the profile of capabilities identified in your work analysis (see Chapters Three and Twelve).

Employment at Will: Don't Promise More Than You Plan to Deliver

Most of the legal issues we have discussed have concerned unfair discrimination against applicants with protected characteristics. There are other legal considerations that we have not addressed; a complete treatment of all of them would be a book in itself, and it would also likely distract from the performance focus of high-impact hiring. But one additional legal issue has become so important in the hiring process that it needs to be discussed here: the possibility that you might unintentionally promise the applicant more than you intend. You realize that it would be a breach of contract to exaggerate a job's earning potential just to get an applicant to accept a job, but did you realize that you can also, probably unintentionally, promise an applicant unplanned job security by making inflated claims during the hiring process?

According to long-standing common law, and statutory law in some states, most employees are hired on an "at-will" basis.

Essentially this means that either the employee or the employer may terminate the employment relationship at any time and without any requirement that the decision be justified. "Standard" exceptions to this rule are explicit employment contracts or collective bargaining agreements, both of which generally require that terminations be based on just cause, and terminations that violate EEO or labor law, such as firing employees because of their race or sex or because they filed a grievance. Various states and local governments have additional restrictions that you need to be aware of.

In addition to these exceptions, court decisions have increasingly eroded the employment-at-will doctrine. In particular, courts in many states have ruled that employers have negated their ability to treat employees as at-will by making implied promises that the employees will only be discharged for good cause. This can happen, for instance, if your recruiting ads refer to a "permanent position," or if you tell an applicant, "You don't have to worry about having a job here as long as you perform well." Describing the pay for a job as an annual salary ("If you accept this position, you will be paid $25,000 per year") can imply a promise to employ the person for at least a year. Recent court decisions in some states have even ruled that an oral promise to treat employees fairly creates an obligation that an employer prove that any terminations are based on good cause.

Prudent employers need to take steps to protect themselves from these interpretations. Let us be clear that we are *not* suggesting that you treat employees unfairly or fire them on a whim. Fair treatment of employees is a sound basis for effective management and good employee relations. But you can still treat employees fairly without making any promises that force you to defend all of your decisions to employees who may be disgruntled. To minimize your risk of inadvertently promising too much to your new hires, it is a good idea to review your application form and employee manual as well as your interviewing process with a good employment lawyer. Here are additional steps you can take to minimize risks in this area:

- Avoid making promises to applicants. This includes both explicit promises and any statements that might be judged by a sympathetic jury to *imply* a promise. Be particularly careful about promises relating to length of employment or the conditions under which employment may be terminated.

- Be sure that this principle is understood by anyone in a position of responsibility who may be interacting with job applicants. An oral statement, as when a supervisor says, "We've never fired anyone without a good reason," can create a binding legal commitment for the company.
- Review your application materials to be sure they clearly inform applicants that employment is not guaranteed for any specific period of time and that you reserve the right to terminate the employee for any reason (if these are your company policies).
- Pay similar attention to letters or contracts in which you offer candidates employment. For salaried positions, describe compensation in annualized terms (for example, "Should you decide to accept this offer, your salary would be $3,000 per semimonthly pay period, or $72,000 on an annualized basis"). Because offer letters can easily be interpreted as a legal contract, it is best if these letters are reviewed by legal counsel or someone else who understands the legal issues.
- Pay particular attention to your employee manual. Sections describing benefits, conditions of employment, and bases for termination or layoff decisions are particularly likely to contain language that might be considered by a jury to imply that employees are no longer employed at will.

Need to Know More?

We have emphasized the general legal issues involved in hiring decisions rather than going into a detailed discussion of laws, court cases, or regulatory requirements. Our goal has been to strip away most of the legalese and provide you with practical recommendations that are applicable to the most common legal issues.

If you want more detailed information, a number of books on employment law written for the working manager are available; one of our favorites is *Stay Out of Court*.[10] Another good book, more academic in tone, is Sovereign's *Personnel Law*.[11] As a way of keeping up-to-date with changes in the law, you may also find it useful to subscribe to employment law newsletters, such as Rita Risser's *Just Management,* or the state-specific employment law letters published by M. Lee Smith Publishers.[12] Developing a good working relationship with an attorney who specializes in employment law is also a good idea, preferably before a crisis develops.

Summary

The essence of high-impact hiring is to make hiring decisions in a thoughtful, performance-oriented, and systematic manner that treats all applicants fairly. This strategy is consistent with legal requirements to avoid making hiring decisions on the basis of such performance-irrelevant factors as race, color, religion, gender, national origin, or disability. Following are the critical issues from the perspective of both performance-based hiring and legal compliance:

1. Understand the nature of the job and what employee attributes are necessary for the safe and effective conduct of the work, using the work analysis procedures described in Chapter Two.
2. Base your hiring decisions solely on these job-related applicant attributes, not on irrelevant and possibly illegal factors.
3. Use hiring tools that have been shown to validly measure these attributes.
4. Evaluate your hiring procedures for adverse impact (disproportionate rejection of applicants with certain characteristics, such as race or gender). If evidence of adverse impact is found, determine if the hiring procedure is truly valid (job-related) and if other, equally effective procedures will produce less adverse impact.
5. Monitor all your hiring and other employment procedures to ensure that all applicants are treated consistently. The only exceptions are (a) providing whatever accommodations are reasonable and necessary to allow applicants with disabilities to be evaluated fairly on the basis of their ability to perform the job, (b) giving preference to military veterans, and (c) including preferences in bona fide affirmative action programs.
6. Document your hiring (and other personnel) decisions, which will aid in following the systematic and effective decision-making principles of high-impact hiring and will help you to establish, if necessary, that you had a legitimate business reason for every decision.

Chapter Six

Developing a Comprehensive Hiring System

One of the foundations of high-impact hiring is the idea that people are different. Some people are fast learners; others are not. Some people have great memories, while others can't remember the names of people they were introduced to only moments before. Some are great at solving riddles, while others excel at thinking of innovative ways to use everyday objects. Some have extensive vocabularies and others are great with numbers. These are all examples of what psychologists refer to as *mental,* or *cognitive, abilities.*

Of course, people also differ on other dimensions, such as being outgoing and social rather than preferring to be alone. Some people are generally upbeat and positive, whereas others tend to be moody and pessimistic. Of particular importance to employers, people also vary in the extent to which they are conscientious about their obligations, feel committed to a work ethic, or prefer one type of career over another. These "affective" differences among people are referred to as *personality, temperament,* and *interests.*

People also differ in terms of *physical abilities.* One dimension of physical abilities includes differences in various aspects of physical strength or endurance. People also vary on sensory capacities such as vision or hearing acuity and on perceptual abilities, including such things as the ability to visualize objects in three dimensions or to follow the intricacies of a maze or wiring diagram. Differences in applicants' psychomotor skills, such as manual dexterity, can also be important in some jobs.

Just as people differ from one another, so do the employee attributes required for successful performance in different jobs.

That is why we spent considerable time in Chapter Two describing why and how to do a work analysis as the first step in hiring. The goal of high-impact hiring is to use information about differences in jobs and applicants in order to match job seekers with the job and organizational environment in which their capabilities produce the best "fit" with the work to be done and the way it is done.

This chapter will help you to develop an effective system for measuring differences among applicants. In this chapter we outline three key principles that should guide you in developing an effective hiring system:

1. A hiring system needs to begin with a clear understanding of the employee attributes required for success. In this chapter we discuss the Performance Attributes Matrix, an invaluable tool for making sure that your hiring system measures all the relevant attributes identified in your work analysis and excludes any irrelevant applicant characteristics.
2. An effective hiring system consists of a *portfolio* of assessment tools. Rarely, if ever, will a single hiring tool—whether it's an interview, a test, or some other procedure—adequately evaluate applicants' performance potential. In this chapter, we describe how to put together a high-impact package of hiring tools.
3. Each assessment tool should be chosen on the basis of its accuracy, practicality, fairness, and legality. In this chapter you will learn how to evaluate hiring tools based on these criteria.

Once you've developed your system in this chapter, the five chapters that follow will provide in-depth discussion of each of the hiring tools you're most likely to use in your high-impact hiring system. Although you may be tempted to move directly to those chapters, we strongly advise you to read this chapter first so that you have a foundation for selecting among the tools described in the later chapters and bringing them together into a comprehensive system.

The Performance Attributes Matrix: The Foundation for Your Hiring System

One of the critical points we have made about high-impact hiring is that you need to determine *what* attributes you want to look for in applicants before you worry about *how* you're going to assess those attributes. Focusing first on attributes rather than tools avoids the common mistake of relying too much on a hiring tool that you're comfortable with, or one that is sold to you on the basis of its apparent sophistication, even when it fails to measure what's really relevant to work performance.

A technique we've found helpful for choosing hiring tools that effectively assess job-relevant attributes is to develop a Performance Attributes Matrix. The Performance Attributes Matrix begins with the critical knowledge, skills, abilities, and other attributes you identified in the work analysis from Chapter Two. These are listed in the rows of a matrix, or spreadsheet, and the various hiring tools are included in the columns of the matrix. The matrix is then filled in with Xs to indicate which hiring tools will be used to measure each attribute. (In Chapter Twelve we will refine this process by replacing the Xs with weights that indicate the importance of each tool for each attribute.) An example for the job of hotel clerk is shown in Table 6.1.

Advantages of Using a Performance Attributes Matrix

- The matrix provides a simple visual representation of complex information that makes it easy to ensure that you haven't

Table 6.1. Performance Attributes Matrix.

Position: Hotel Clerk

Attribute	App. Blank	Interview	Reference Checks	Work Sample	Personality Inventory	Test: Clerical Perception
Ability to work accurately		X	X		X	X
Ability to work well with customers		X	X	X	X	
Willingness to do repetitious work	X	X	X		X	
Stress tolerance		X	X		X	
Verbal fluency		X		X		

forgotten to measure any of the critical employee attributes identified in your work analysis. Without a matrix, it's easy to focus all your attention on one critical attribute and forget to measure others that you identified as important. Throughout the hiring process, the matrix reminds you of the "big picture" of all the job-related attributes you need to assess, and it structures your entire approach to focus on these attributes and exclude less important or nonjob-related attributes.

- The matrix organizes the process of selecting hiring tools around their real purpose—assessing applicants' job-relevant attributes, rather than irrelevant factors such as your biases or preferences regarding different tools.
- The matrix reminds you that there may be multiple ways of assessing a particular attribute. For example, Table 6.1 suggests that customer service orientation might be assessed in a behavioral interview, by ratings from former employers, by conducting a simulated sales call, or with personality tests that assess traits relevant to customer service orientation. Some of the potential methods shown in the preliminary matrix may be ruled out as you proceed (for example, work samples may be too costly in some circumstances); the matrix provides you with a guide to effective alternatives. Additionally, the matrix shows you where multiple methods can be used to get more reliable information.
- The matrix discourages you from trying to assess too many attributes with one hiring tool. Far too often, hiring managers base their hiring decisions almost exclusively on information from an interview. As you will learn in Chapter Eight, this is both inefficient and likely to lead to serious errors. As another example, managers who become enamored of personality tests often place too much reliance on the scores of a single test. The Performance Attributes Matrix helps you to develop an effective portfolio of tools to enhance your hiring decisions.

Determining What Hiring Tools to Include in the Performance Attributes Matrix

Deciding what hiring tools should be used to measure each of the attributes in the matrix consists of two related steps: (1) determining which *category* of tools is most appropriate for the attribute (for example, determining whether tests, interviews, or background checks should be used to assess integrity) and (2) determining which particular *tool* or *approach* within a category is best (for example, determining which commercially available integrity test is best to use). Choosing hiring tools in two steps simplifies your decision because each category has general advantages and disadvantages that are shared by the particular tools within it. Mental ability tests, for example, are generally accurate at predicting performance, are cost-efficient, are perceived as moderately fair by applicants, and raise common legal concerns that need to be addressed. Knowing these general characteristics can help in determining if tests are likely to be a good alternative or complement to interviews, work simulations, reference checks, and the application form. More detailed information about hiring tools can be found in the next five chapters.

Matching Hiring Tools to Stages of the Hiring Process

In addition to thinking about which hiring tools match the attributes in your Performance Attributes Matrix, it's also useful to think about the order in which hiring tools will be used. Particularly in situations in which you are hiring multiple employees and dealing with a large pool of applicants, the relative cost and time required by different hiring tools can affect your choices.

Assessment of applicants can be thought of as occurring in three stages. In the initial, or screening, stage, the objective is generally to narrow a pool of applicants to a smaller number of plausible candidates. In situations in which a large number of applicants is involved, this phase calls for tools, such as reviews of résumés and application forms, that can quickly and cost-effectively eliminate applicants who are clearly unqualified. However, to meet legal requirements, it is important for these initial screening tools to be accurate and have minimal adverse impact.

The second stage involves more intensive assessment that is intended to sort applicants into three categories: unqualified, minimally qualified, and desirable. (Chapter Twelve provides more detail on how to make these distinctions.) This stage may involve multiple steps, or hurdles, in which increasingly expensive hiring tools are administered to a narrowing pool of candidates. For example, police departments often begin the process of selecting officers with a relatively inexpensive battery of paper-and-pencil tests. This may be followed with physical ability tests and a panel interview, both of which, by their nature, are more labor-intensive and thus more expensive procedures.

The third stage involves a final check on candidates who make your list of finalists. This may involve more expensive and time-consuming procedures, such as conducting reference or back-ground checks or follow-up interviews with upper management. Also included in this category are assessments that are made after a conditional offer of employment, such as medical examinations, if they are relevant to job requirements, and verification of employment eligibility.

Choosing Among Categories of Assessment Tools

For the moment, we'd like you to forget everything you know about hiring employees and consider a very basic question: What are the various possible ways of measuring the differences in applicants' skills, knowledge, abilities, and other job-relevant characteristics? The most obvious approach, though it is rarely used, would be to observe them actually performing the job for which they are being hired. A more practical variation of this approach is to create a simulated work environment in which applicants try out only the critical tasks in a controlled environment. This is the essence of "performance tests" or work samples, which we discuss in more detail in Chapter Ten. Work sample approaches are most appropriate when your goal is to measure developed skills among experienced employees.

If you can't directly observe performance on a task because of time or cost limitations, an alternative is to ask others who have observed the applicant to rate her or his performance. If you're hiring internally, prior performance appraisal information may be useful if it's accurate and relevant to the job the person is applying for. More generally, checking references can be a source of information about an applicant's skills and characteristic approach to work and coworkers. Effective and legal approaches to reference and background checks are discussed in Chapter Seven.

Another approach is to assess an applicant's relevant experience, knowledge, or training. This is less direct than measuring skills, because it assumes that the applicant can translate the experience into effective job performance. In some cases, you can assess experience, knowledge, and training by asking appropriate questions on an application form or with training and experience checklists, discussed in Chapter Seven. Job knowledge tests, which are described in Chapter Nine, can provide a more thorough and standardized assessment of the applicant's understanding of critical information.

Abilities and personality traits are the most general and least observable attributes of applicants. They are particularly relevant when you are hiring applicants who don't have experience doing the kind of work you're hiring for or when the nature of the work is changing rapidly. Since you're looking for a person's potential, rather than his or her past accomplishments, it's difficult to use the kind of assessment approaches we've discussed so far. For that reason, abilities are often measured by standardized tests designed to assess basic mental or physical abilities. As a general rule, tests have the advantage of being reliable and easily quantified, though a test must be matched carefully with a given job to be effective. Some kinds of tests may raise issues of invasion of privacy or unfair discrimination. These concerns are addressed in general terms later in this chapter and more specifically with reference to employment tests in Chapter Nine.

An applicant's personality can be assessed either from the perspective of others, as in reference checks or interviews, or by self-reports from the applicant, such as personality inventories. We describe the appropriate uses of interviews in Chapter Eight and issues surrounding personality testing in Chapter Nine. In Chapter Eleven we discuss the use of specialized tests designed to assess a person's honesty, delinquency, or alcohol or drug use as a means of eliminating trouble-prone job applicants.

A summary of the types of assessment approaches most relevant to each category of applicant attributes is provided in Table 6.2. This is a general guide, and the more detailed discussion in this and the following chapters will help to clarify the reasons for our ratings. Even without this detail, however, the table is useful for illustrating general strengths and weaknesses.

Notice, for example, that Table 6.2 describes interviews as a potential means of assessing all the categories of attributes, but never as the most preferred strategy. Traditionally, interviews have served as many managers' primary hiring tool, yet interviews actually suffer

Table 6.2. Matching Attributes with Hiring Tools.

Attribute	Application Information	Background Checks	Interviews	Tests	Work Samples
Skills		s	s	P	P
Experience	P	P	s		
Knowledge	s	s	s	P	
Training	P		s		
Abilities			s	P	s
Personality		s	s	P	P

Note: P = primary or preferred assessment strategy; *s* = secondary strategy.

from a number of limitations. This is an example of using a tool ineffectively and inefficiently. Our approach to interviewing, described in Chapter Eight, will help you to use an interview where it is best suited. We will describe a particular approach, known as structured interviewing, that helps you to focus on actual examples of an applicant's past experiences and current skills, thus overcoming many of the limitations of ritual interviews.

Once you've identified at least one category of hiring tools relevant to each attribute in the Performance Attributes Matrix, the next task is to locate or develop a good tool *within* that category. Different personality tests, for example, are by no means equivalent in what they measure, or in how well they measure it. Similarly, interviewing and reference checking can range from useless or worse to highly effective. Your choice of a general category of hiring tool—as well as a specific tool within that category—should be based on four criteria that we discuss in the next section: accuracy, practicality, fairness, and legality.

Criteria for Choosing Among Hiring Tools

The most obvious standard for evaluating hiring tools is accuracy, or how well the procedure actually assesses the job-related attributes you're looking for in applicants. Once you've identified procedures that have acceptable accuracy, your final choice among accurate procedures is likely to be based on the additional criteria of practicality of use, perceived fairness, and legality. In the following pages we will consider each of these factors in more detail.

Accuracy

Some of the material in this section is a bit more technical than is typical for this book. Although we have eliminated unnecessary detail, a basic understanding of reliability and validity is necessary to avoid ritual hiring. We've tried to cut through the unnecessary jargon and explain in straightforward terms how the key concepts affect your hiring decisions.

The primary basis for choosing a hiring tool, whether you view it from a performance, ethical, or legal perspective, is its accuracy in assessing differences in job-related attributes among job applicants. Although simple in concept, accuracy is a complex issue that has mired hiring managers, industrial psychologists, and employment attorneys in confusion and debate. Our goal is to avoid these debates and focus instead on the two essential components of accuracy that you need to consider when evaluating hiring tools: reliability and validity. Using tools that are either unreliable or invalid is a common and costly practice in ritual hiring. Promotional materials for different hiring tools also throw these terms around, sometimes accurately, sometimes inaccurately, frequently substituting one for the other in order to mislead you. Your own understanding of these concepts will allow you to cut through this hype and evaluate for yourself how accurate a hiring tool is likely to be.

Reliability

Saying that a measure is reliable can mean many things in different contexts and for different people. In the context of evaluating hiring tools, reliability refers to how much the measurements made with a hiring tool are free of error. Errors of measurement can be *random,* as when applicants interpret an ambiguous test question in different ways. In this case, differences among applicants' test scores may have more to do with random differences in interpretation than with real differences in what the test is supposed to measure. Measurement errors can also be *systematic,* as when an interviewer consistently interprets the behavior of male applicants differently from that of females. For example, the same behavior that is labeled "assertive" in males is often described as "aggressive" when seen in females. In either case, the errors interfere with making good hiring decisions; therefore, it is essential to use only hiring tools that are reliable.

A reliable measure has three characteristics. First, measurements based on it are stable over time and under different conditions. Second, measurements on it will agree with measurements on other reliable tools intended to measure the same thing. And third, all parts of a measuring tool are consistent when measuring the same thing. To help make these concepts more clear, let's discuss how they would apply using a measuring tool with which we are all familiar: the bathroom scale. We can then apply the concepts to hiring tools.

Stability of Measurement. Ideally, a bathroom scale should provide measurements that are consistent over time, people, and conditions. If you're dieting, you want to be confident that differences in measurement before and after your diet reflect the diet, not random fluctuations in the accuracy of the scale. An example from a hiring context is the stability of a person's personality scores over time (assuming that the person's personality has not actually changed). Stability of measurement, technically referred to as *test-retest reliability,* is measured as the statistical relationship, or correlation, between a person's scores on the same measure at two points in time.

Equivalence of Measurement. Suppose the bathroom scale shows that you've lost twenty pounds as a result of your diet, and you want to demonstrate your diligence to your physician. To do so, you need to be sure that the measurements on your bathroom scale are equivalent to those taken on the scale at your doctor's office (which we all know is never the case!). This equivalence of measurement with similar, or parallel, measuring tools is technically known as *parallel-forms reliability.* This aspect of reliability is relevant if you plan to use different forms of a test—for example, to reduce concerns about cheating on the test. Equivalence of measurement is also important when you are evaluating the consistency of different managers' ratings of a person's interview or job performance; in this context, equivalence of measurement is generally referred to as *inter-rater reliability.*

Internal Consistency of Measurement. Finally, let's assume that the bathroom scale is being used by two dieters in the same household, one of whom began the diet weighing 250 pounds and the other who started out at 150 pounds. The two agree to a contest in which the first person to lose 10 pounds will receive a prize. But what if the scale has been designed to be maximally accurate in the "typical" range of 100 to 200 pounds, with increasing errors outside that range? To be reliable and fair, the bathroom scale needs to be as accurate in the range of 240 to 250 pounds as it is in the range of 140 to 150 pounds. This is technically referred to as *internal consistency reliability:* the extent to which measurements are comparable within all ranges of a measure. In hiring contexts, internal consistency usually refers more specifically to the extent to which all questions in a test or interview assess the same attribute. If a test is being used to measure the ability to quickly and accurately add numbers, for example, it should not be influenced by word problems that coincidentally assess a person's verbal fluency.

In summary, a reliable measure provides consistent (that is, error-free) information across time, people, situations, items, or forms. Yet consistency, while necessary for measuring applicants accurately and fairly, is not sufficient for ensuring that a tool will predict job performance. Reliability tells you only that you are measuring *some* characteristic in a relatively error-free manner, but it does not tell you that you are measuring the *right* characteristic. In high-impact hiring, the "right" characteristics are job-relevant characteristics. If you used that bathroom scale to assess job applicants, you would be using a reliable measure that doesn't measure the right characteristic. Because reliability is relatively easy to measure and generally involves more impressive-looking correlations, unscrupulous vendors sometimes try to give the impression that reliability is the only issue in measurement accuracy, as in claims that a test is "95 percent reliable." But all that such claims tell you is that their tool measures the same thing every time, not necessarily the "right" thing at any time. Ensuring that a tool measures the right characteristic involves *validity*.

Validity of Measurement

Validity, or job-relatedness, is the core issue when evaluating hiring tools: it is the key to showing whether and how differences among applicants translate into important differences in subsequent job performance. Validity is also critical from the legal perspective, because group differences in performance on a hiring tool (that is, adverse impact) can only be justified by showing that the tool predicts job performance. (See Chapter Five for more detail.) Understanding validity is critical to choosing hiring tools in an effective and legal manner.

Validity refers to the accuracy of the inferences, or interpretations, you make from the scores on a hiring tool. Notice that we don't refer to the validity of a test or other hiring tool; instead we are talking whether valid inferences can be made about job performance from the scores on a test. For example, the Scholastic Aptitude Test (SAT), an ability test taken routinely by college-bound high school students, was designed to predict performance in college courses. A statistical relationship between SAT scores and college grades helps to support the inference that high school students with higher SAT scores are more likely to be successful in college; in other words, there is an inference that the SAT is a valid predictor of college performance. The relationship between SAT scores and college grades does not directly support an inference that the SAT is valid for other purposes, such as predicting job performance. It *might* be valid for that purpose, but different evidence, such as a correlation of SAT scores with job performance, is needed to support that inference. The lesson here is to be wary of claims that a given hiring tool is "valid." When you hear such a claim you need to ask, valid for what? Validity is not an inherent quality of a test or any other hiring tool. It is a characteristic of the inferences that you make from that tool, and it is always specific to the task for which you draw the inferences.

It's tempting to rely on a test developer or consultant to choose valid hiring tools, but the ultimate responsibility (not to mention legal liability) rests with you. To be sure you're using an effective hiring tool, you need to know enough about the concept of validity to be able to evaluate how well it has been validated for the task you plan to use it for. This applies whether you are using an internal or external consultant or doing the analysis yourself.

There are three basic strategies for establishing whether a hiring tool is valid for your particular uses. The first is to directly assess whether applicants with higher scores on the hiring tool perform better on the job. This is done by statistically relating scores on the hiring tool with scores on job performance measures. This strategy is referred to formally as *criterion-related validation,* because the inference is based on a statistical relationship between test scores and the criterion—in this case, performance—that the test is designed to predict. Both sets of scores are ideally obtained from job applicants, whose job performance can be assessed after they have been on the job for six months or so. As a less preferable alternative, test scores can be obtained from current employees and compared with their scores on performance appraisals. When testing current employees, it is critical to make clear that the tests are not being used in any way to assess *their* job performance. The ideal strategy is to assess all applicants with the hiring tool you are validating, but temporarily not to use this information to make hiring decisions. That is, during the trial period, you would ignore information from the new tool and instead hire people on whatever basis you had been using. Although this approach delays implementation of the hiring tool, it has a variety of statistical advantages, which are beyond the scope of this book to discuss.

While criterion-related validation is often considered the gold standard of validity, it is beset by a number of problems, especially for smaller employers. Two factors in particular, one fundamental to high-impact hiring and one statistical, often make this approach impractical:

1. The approach requires that reliable, valid, and relevant measures of job performance be available for comparison with the test scores. Trying to predict an unreliable performance measure is like shooting at a randomly moving target, and predicting an irrelevant (invalid) measure of performance is obviously a waste of time. Unfortunately, most performance measures, especially those based on supervisory ratings, are seriously deficient.

2. Criterion-related validation also requires that data be collected from large samples of applicants or incumbents, preferably 100 or more. This is an unfortunate requirement of the statistical tests used to confirm the validity of the hiring tool. Although smaller samples are often used, they lower your chances of having meaningful results that show whether the tool is valid for your use.

Fortunately, another validation strategy, called *content valida-tion,* doesn't rest on these problematic assumptions. Content vali-dation is based on showing a *logical* connection between a hiring tool and job performance, rather than demonstrating a *statistical* association between them. This is done by showing that the con-tent of the hiring tool matches the content of the job, hence the name content validation. With this strategy, selection tools can be chosen or developed based on their similarity to actual tasks in-volved in the job. For example, if an analysis of an electrician's job shows that knowledge of the Uniform Electrical Code is essential, it is a fairly straightforward task to develop and defend a test that measures knowledge of the code.

The simplicity of content validation offers many advantages, especially to smaller employers who cannot develop large enough samples to use criterion-related validation. However, content valida-tion can be used appropriately only for relatively tangible, observable performance attributes. It does not offer *proof* that scores on the hir-ing tool actually predict job performance; it offers only a logical argument that the two *should* be related. Therefore, the logical infer-ence must be as direct as possible. It's straightforward to argue that the content of a typing test corresponds with the content of a typist's position, or that a test measuring knowledge of programming lan-guages is necessary for a software engineer. In contrast, arguing that a personality test that purports to measure "dominance" is a content-valid predictor of executive performance is not an effective use of content validation. Content validation will rarely be appropriate when hiring decisions are based on more general abilities or com-petencies such as decision making or persuasiveness.

A third approach to validating a selection system is called *con-struct validation.* A construct is a concept that cannot be directly observed but that is nonetheless believed to exist, such as intelli-gence, motivation, or work ethic. Construct validation uses both logic and actual evidence to support the inference that a measure assesses an unobservable construct. It extends the idea of content validation to more abstract attributes for which content validation is not suited.

Most descriptions of construct validation make this approach sound more complex than neurosurgery. As described in the *Uni-form Guidelines on Employee Selection Procedures,*[1] construct validation involves a complex, lengthy process of specifying theoretical linkages between scores on the test in question and other tests and relevant outcomes to which it should be related, and then systematically testing all these relationships. The more the results of these studies confirm your theoretical framework, the more confidence you can have in the construct validity of your measure. Does this sound confusing—and difficult? That's precisely the reaction of most people, which is why construct validation has so rarely been used in practice.

That's unfortunate, because construct validation is the most important approach to showing validity; in fact, it forms the foundation of high-impact hiring. Thankfully, establishing construct validation need not be as complicated as the *Uniform Guidelines* make it sound. Stripped of the technical trappings, construct validation is the *process of developing a logical argument for why a hiring tool is related to job performance*.[2] Let's consider an example of how this works in practice.

Suppose that you are hiring quality control inspectors for an assembly operation. You've thought carefully about the nature of their work and have concluded that successful inspectors are characterized by a trait you call attention to detail. You've located a personality scale (called FOCUS for our example) that claims to measure attention to detail, and now you're wondering how to establish whether FOCUS is valid for you to use in predicting the performance of the quality control inspectors. That is, you want to determine whether FOCUS is a high-impact hiring tool for this hire and to establish whether you can defend your use of FOCUS in the unlikely event that it should be challenged. Criterion-related validation is not feasible, because you employ only three quality control inspectors, far too few to allow any statistical test of the relationship between test scores and a performance measure. You also realize that even if you had more inspectors, your performance measure isn't as accurate as it should be. Attention to detail isn't specific and observable enough to allow content validation. So you decide instead to establish construct validity through the following steps.

First, you develop a logical rationale explaining why the construct, attention to detail, is needed for the job. This is the reason you conducted the work analysis we described in Chapter Two. Your logic is that the function of the inspectors' job is to identify errors that were overlooked by the assembly workers. The FOCUS scale was designed to assess workers' ability and willingness to focus their attention on details for long periods of time without becoming bored or distracted. Therefore, FOCUS scores should predict how well applicants will perform this aspect of the inspectors' job.

To this point, you've followed the same steps you would for content validation. Given the unobservable nature of the attention-to-detail construct, you must now gather additional evidence that the FOCUS scale really measures attention to detail. A good place to find this kind of information is in the test manual supplied by the test publisher. You look at the FOCUS manual and find that prior research shows strong correlations between FOCUS scores and scores on other measures of attention to detail. If this type of information is not available from the publisher, you will need to collect it yourself from applicants or employees. This can be a difficult prospect for all but the largest employers and is a good reason to purchase hiring tools from developers who invest effort in gathering information on reliability and validity. You also find that people with high FOCUS scores get moderately high scores on measures of compulsiveness and relatively low scores on measures of creativity. The manual also reports that accountants and engineers, people whom you'd expect to be detail-oriented, have higher FOCUS scores than do artists and advertising executives. These findings are consistent with the test developer's "theory" of attention to detail, and they increase your confidence that the scale measures what it claims to.

If it is possible, you would also like to find evidence that the measure predicts job performance in jobs requiring attention to detail. You look further in the manual and, with a little luck, you find that FOCUS scores predicted the success of assemblers in a large manufacturing company. Although the study was done for a different job, the underlying trait of attention to detail is important in both jobs. If attention to detail predicts success for assemblers, it seems reasonable that it will also predict successful performance for people inspecting the quality of the assemblers' work.

At the end of this process you don't have definitive proof that the test predicts quality control inspectors' job performance, but you have built a strong case based on good professional judgment. As industrial psychologist Robert Guion notes, "Professional judgment, unlike hunch or 'play it by ear' decision-making, is systematic, informed, and based on understanding and research."[3] Based on your systematic analysis of the job and of the evidence supporting the FOCUS scale, you should feel reasonably confident that the test is an appropriate measure for you to use. You should also feel confident that you would be able to convince a judge or jury that the test is job-related. However, you should remember that validation is an *ongoing process* of building confidence. It would be wise to begin a process of systematically collecting performance data on people who were hired using FOCUS, so that you can continue to monitor its effectiveness, and so that the data can be used if criterion-related validation later becomes feasible. As a hiring manager, you should never have a stake in using a particular test and always have a stake in making sure that every test you use is accurate and job-related. If ongoing monitoring makes you increasingly confident about the test, you will continue to use it. If, instead, you become less confident, you can use the approach we've outlined to find a more accurate test.

Before ending our discussion of validity, we should also mention an important concept called *validity generalization*. Validity generalization is not so much a means of validating a selection tool as it is a way of justifying the use of the tool by combining information from many different validation studies that have been done by others. Validity generalization is based on the commonsense notion that it should not be necessary to show the validity of a hiring tool each and every time it is used. If fifty different employers have shown that Test X predicts performance in Job X, isn't it reasonable to assume that it will also predict performance in the same job for the fifty-first employer to use it?

The validity generalization solution to the problems of small samples and deficient performance measures is to *estimate* the validity of hiring tools based on existing validation data. This involves locating tools with existing validity data based on large samples of similar jobs; as a practical matter, this often means using paper-and-pencil tests for which the publisher can provide validity generalization evidence.

We should warn you that validity generalization is currently a controversial procedure, and adopting this strategy may involve some legal risk. Although it has its vocal critics, validity generalization is recommended by many selection specialists as a scientifically sound procedure.[4,5] If you take this approach, we recommend that you use your work analysis to determine that the job you are hiring for is the same as the jobs included in the validity generalization study. If your job is different from those in the study, or if the performance measures are different from each other in meaningful ways, then it's far less likely that you can confidently use the results.

Validity generalization is largely untested in the courts. Some legal experts are vehemently opposed to its use,[6] and some courts have not accepted it as a valid legal defense for a charge of disparate impact. Our own assessment is that content validation is a preferred approach when it is applicable, but that validity generalization may be a practical alternative for smaller firms using hiring tools that cannot be content-validated, particularly for hiring tools that do not create disparate impact.

Practicality

Although the primary criterion for choosing selection tools should be their effectiveness in predicting work performance, other considerations may also be relevant, particularly when choosing among comparably valid predictors of performance. One such consideration is practicality, which includes factors such as cost, time, and difficulty of use. There's not much point in using even a valid hiring tool if the costs of using it exceed the benefits it provides.

As a rule, standardized tools that require little or no customization have the lowest direct costs, although they may have trade-offs in their ability to predict the specific performance desired for a given job. For example, standardized ability tests are designed to measure generic attributes of the test taker. Mental ability tests assess such basic cognitive processes as verbal fluency, memory, and problem solving; the same tests can be used for any type of job for which these attributes are relevant. On the other hand, more specialized tests of job-specific knowledge or skills—such as knowledge of banking regulations or skill at flying a plane—may have to be custom-developed. The costs of developing, norming (determining typical scores), and validating custom measures may outweigh their usefulness in some cases.

Costs will also be affected by the manner in which the hiring tool is administered. Paper-and-pencil measures that can be administered to a group of applicants require less administrative support than tests that have to be individually administered. Timed tests are quite common, but they require that you have someone available to monitor the test-taking process. This can impose a significant burden on many employers, particularly if you typically process applicants one at a time rather than in groups. Performance tests, in which applicants do a sample or simulation of the work, involve even more administrative overhead to set up the simulation and to provide raters who observe and evaluate the applicants' performance. However, performance tests have the advantage of being tailored to desired job performance, are well suited to content validation, and have a good track record of predicting performance. Interviews can also be very costly, although the total time invested in developing and conducting them is often overlooked.

In assessing practicality, the key issue is to consider the overall cost-effectiveness and ease of implementation of alternative tools, rather than focusing only on either costs or validity. Good estimates of effectiveness (validity) exist for different categories of hiring tools and are summarized in Table 6.3. Costs and other factors affecting practicality are more variable across both different hiring situations and different suppliers of the same type of tool. Therefore, the ratings of practicality in Table 6.3 should be viewed simply as a starting point for your own assessment of cost-effectiveness for the jobs you hire for in your own organization.

Applicants' Reactions and Perceived Fairness

Another important, and often overlooked, consideration when developing a selection system is how applicants react to the hiring process. As a manager, you naturally think of the hiring process as a way of evaluating potential employees. From that perspective, any hiring tools that can provide accurate information about how the applicant will perform as an employee are worth considering. However, applicants also have a decision to make—whether to accept a job with your organization should a job offer be forthcoming. The decision to accept a job can be as significant a decision for the applicant as the decision to offer a job is to you. Selection procedures that applicants view as unfair, irrelevant, or invasive of their privacy may cause your carefully recruited and screened applicants to decide to reject you just when you've decided to accept them.

Table 6.3. Comparison of Hiring Tools.

	Reliability	Validity	Practicality	Acceptability	Adverse Impact
Background					
Résumés	Moderate	Low	High	High?	Low–Moderate
References	Low	Moderate	Moderate	Moderate	Low–Moderate
Applications	Moderate	Low–Moderate	High	Moderate–High?	Moderate
Biodata	High	Moderate–High	Moderate	Moderate?	Low–Moderate
Interviews					
Unstructured	Low	Low–Moderate	Moderate	High	Moderate–High
Structured	High	High	Moderate	Moderate–High?	Low?
Tests					
Ability	High	High	Moderate	Low–Moderate?	High
Job Knowledge	High	High	Moderate–High	High?	Low
Personality	Moderate	Moderate	Moderate	Low–Moderate	Low
Interest	High	Low	Moderate	Moderate?	Low
Integrity	High	High	Moderate	Low–Moderate	Low
Drug[a]	High	Moderate–High	Low–Moderate	Low–Moderate	Low
Performance	High	High	Moderate	High	Low
Assessment Centers	Moderate	Moderate–High	Low	High?	Low

Note: Evaluations are general summaries for each category. Different measures within each category may vary substantially. "?" indicates that research is inconclusive.

[a]Evaluations of reliability and validity are based on confirmatory tests.

Studies show that many job applicants come to the hiring process knowing surprisingly little about the firm with which they're interviewing. As a result, their decision to accept a job is influenced by whatever clues they pick up about the firm during the hiring process. This is why realistic job previews (see Chapter Four) can be so useful for setting realistic expectations. It also means that you need to think about what impressions you create during the recruiting and selection processes.

Put yourself in the role of a job applicant. You respond to an advertisement by mailing in a résumé and then hear nothing for weeks. Just when you've given up on hearing, and are wondering what you did wrong, you receive a call from the human resources department inviting you for an interview. That's great, but when you ask some questions about the position, you're told that the human resources person doesn't really know the specifics and you'll just have to wait until the interview to ask those questions. How are you supposed to prepare for the interview without more specific information? You do the best you can and arrive a few minutes early for the interview. And wait. And wait some more. Forty-five minutes later you're finally ushered into the interviewer's office and told to sit while the interviewer finishes a call. After some uncomfortable minutes, the interviewer finally makes eye contact with you and begins a rambling set of questions that seem to have little to do with the job. At its end you're told that there are more applicants to talk with, but that they'll get back to you soon. Three weeks later you finally hear from the company, when the human resources department calls to set up appointments for a drug test and an interview with the corporate psychologist. What impression of the company would you come away with? You could hardly be blamed for thinking that the company is pretty cold, impersonal, and disorganized.

Studies have shown that applicants have definite feelings about the hiring process, and that these feelings can affect their decision to apply for or accept a job. Applicants who have few alternatives may take a job despite their concerns, but they may join your firm with a chip on their shoulder that will affect their subsequent morale, productivity, and longevity. More qualified applicants who are left with a poor impression of your organization may decide to work for your competitors, meaning that you not only have lost the opportunity to gain a potentially effective employee, but also have provided a competitor with a valuable resource. If you've aggra-vated an applicant enough, you may also have lost a potential cus-tomer, which is particularly critical if you hire from a tight-knit professional workforce, are located in a small- to medium-sized community, or provide any goods or services that your applicants are likely to purchase themselves.

Research has only begun to explore the factors that affect appli-cants' reactions to selection systems. In general, applicants react more positively to procedures that appear to be job-related. Per-formance tests, work samples, and simulations, for example, are gen-erally well received because they so clearly resemble the nature of the job being applied for. The same is true for job knowledge tests that assess applicants' awareness of information that is needed for a job, such as knowledge of programming languages, accounting principles, or building codes. More abstract tests of mental ability are less obviously related to job performance, and personality inven-tories may bear little or no obvious relationship to job requirements. Note, however, that we are talking only about the applicants' *percep-tions* of job-relatedness. Personality and general ability tests may be effective at predicting job performance without this being obvious to job applicants or other casual observers.

A second important factor in applicants' reactions to hiring tools seems to be privacy. A number of selection procedures, such as integrity tests, drug screening, and personality assessments, are viewed by many job applicants as an unwarranted invasion of their privacy. An important factor affecting privacy is the extent to which applicants feel able to control what information they provide and how it is used. Genetic screening is perhaps the best example of a hiring procedure that violates this principle. An applicant who is asked to provide a urine or blood sample during a preemployment physical exam has little option but to agree or lose the job. As opposed to interviews or tests, the applicant has no control over the information revealed by the specimen. Moreover, the applicant may have little awareness of—or control over—what the sample is being analyzed for, and in fact he or she may assume that it is a normal part of a physical exam or perhaps is being used for drug-screening purposes. If the applicant subsequently learns that the sample was also analyzed for genetic markers of disease suscepti-bility (for example, to avoid hiring employees who are more likely to develop an illness when they are exposed to a particular environmental toxin), would you be surprised if the applicant felt that his or her privacy had been invaded?

Another aspect of control is applicants' perception that they can do something about poor performance on a hiring tool. Applicants react more positively when they can improve poor test results. Studies show that employee acceptance of drug testing is increased by the ability to appeal a positive drug test, for example, by explaining that the applicant uses a prescription medicine that mimics the pattern of an illegal drug in the urine. Similarly, some people believe that applicants feel frustrated by "failing" a personality test. If you fail tests of mathematical ability or expert knowledge, you can always do some reading or take a course to improve your scores. But there's not much chance of "improving" your personality. This same concern can affect applicants' reactions to integrity tests or reference and background checks.

Another factor that affects applicants' attitudes toward a selection system is how *systematic* it appears to be. In a study of a selection system that we helped to design, applicants' attitudes toward personality testing were much more positive when the personality testing occurred as part of a comprehensive testing battery that included standard ability tests than when it occurred alone.[7] Job applicants respond favorably to a hiring system that appears to be well thought out and comprehensive. A systematic hiring approach communicates that the company is serious about hiring good employees, and applicants who "survive" such a rigorous selection process feel justifiably proud about being part of a company with high standards.

In sum, it's a good idea to consider applicants' perceptions of the relevance and fairness of the tools you include in your selection system. Applicants' reactions may not be as directly related to organizational performance as accuracy, nor as externally mandated as legal requirements, but applicants' perceptions and attitudes can significantly affect whether they actually apply for or accept jobs in your organization.

Our recommendation is to use the information in Tables 6.2 and 6.3, first to locate the hiring tools that are best suited to accurately assessing the job-relevant characteristics of applicants. Then select from this pool of valid hiring tools those that are most practical and least likely to alienate applicants. If this results in choosing some hiring procedures that are unpopular with job applicants, special steps to reassure the applicants about the testing may be useful. We discuss examples of these steps in more detail for personality testing in Chapter Nine, and for integrity and drug testing in Chapter Eleven.

Legality

We have left our discussion of legal criteria for last because we believe that legal considerations are largely subsumed under the other criteria, particularly the criterion of accuracy. This is not to suggest that legal requirements are trivial; employers who have been on the losing end of challenges in court can attest to the importance of legal compliance. But by evaluating hiring tools in terms of accuracy and fairness, you have already met most of your legal obligations.

Your primary legal obligation is to make hiring decisions without regard to protected personal characteristics such as age, race, religion, gender, or disability. By conducting a work analysis and developing a Performance Attributes Matrix, you have ensured that your hiring decisions are based on job-relevant factors rather than discriminatory ones. The matrix provides very effective documentation of this.

Your remaining legal obligation is to monitor your hiring process to: (1) ensure that all applicants are treated similarly, with the exception of making reasonable accommodations for applicants with disabilities, and (2) determine if the hiring tools create adverse impact against groups of individuals with protected characteristics. If adverse impact does occur and you are challenged, you will need to show the job-relatedness (validity) of the practice causing the adverse impact. If you follow our approach, you will already have collected this information as part of your process of evaluating the effectiveness of your hiring system.

Two legal points are so widely misunderstood that we want to reemphasize them:

1. There is no legal requirement to validate your hiring system unless a plaintiff has successfully shown that it creates adverse impact. We recommend that you evaluate the validity of your

hiring tools, when it is technically feasible to do so, as part of choosing hiring tools on a high-impact basis, and as part of your ongoing process of monitoring the effectiveness of your choices. However, doing so is not legally mandated unless you find that they are causing adverse impact.

2. Hiring tools that show adverse impact are not necessarily illegal. Two common examples of predictors that create adverse impact are measures of physical strength, for which women as a group often score significantly lower than men, and tests of general mental ability, which often adversely affect members of black and Hispanic groups. Although you should try to find equally valid measures with less adverse impact, it is legally acceptable to use hiring tools that create adverse impact as long as you can show that they are valid for predicting job performance.

Summary

High-impact hiring consists of more than an application form and a hastily assembled set of interview questions. An effective selection *system* consists of an integrated set of selection tools and procedures that have been carefully chosen to validly assess all of the essential characteristics identified in the work analysis of a position. The Performance Attributes Matrix is a valuable tool for relating the performance attributes to corresponding hiring procedures and for having a clear visual picture of how attributes will be measured. Using a Performance Attributes Matrix in conjunction with a thoughtful work analysis provides the foundation for building an effective hiring system that will also meet legal requirements.

Potential measures of each performance attribute should be evaluated on four criteria: accuracy, practicality, fairness, and legality. Accuracy, consisting of the dual standards of reliability and validity, is the ultimate standard on which performance and legal compliance rest. Practicality ensures that procedures fit within the resources of your firm and the practice of your work group in a way that will provide a good return on investment. Fairness ensures that the hiring procedures do not alienate applicants and interfere with your efforts to recruit and retain a committed and motivated workforce. Legality involves the defensibility of your procedures if they are challenged as having a discriminatory effect.

We have attempted to describe some very technical issues in terms that can be understood and used by hiring managers whose expertise is in areas other than industrial psychology. In doing so, we have left out many concepts and perhaps oversimplified others. In the same way that you seek the advice of employment attorneys when dealing with complex legal issues, you may occasionally find it worthwhile to consult with industrial psychologists when dealing with specific issues. In addition to consultants listed in your telephone directory, advice can often be obtained from industrial psychologists in research universities and private sector research organizations.

Chapter Seven

Gathering Background Information

High-impact hiring is based on gathering information that will allow you to make better decisions about applicants' work performance in your company. Gathering job-relevant information about applicants' past experience and background is an important part of this process; it occurs at two points in the high-impact hiring process. At the beginning of each hiring event, basic background information is used to screen out applicants who are clearly not suited for the job. This process, which we will refer to as *screening*, is usually done by reviewing information in résumés and application forms. The first half of this chapter is devoted to a discussion of how to improve this process through the use of job-specific application forms, experience checklists, and biographical information blanks.

Applicants who pass this first cut then proceed to more intensive hiring tools, such as interviews and tests. These tools are used to further reduce the pool to a small set of qualified applicants. At this point, you are likely to explore candidates' backgrounds again through reference checks with previous employers and perhaps other, more in-depth, background investigations. The second half of the chapter presents a high-impact hiring approach to this final information-gathering step before job offers are extended.

The Challenge of Screening

The problem of screening is well described by the story of Mary, an entrepreneur in Boulder, Colorado. Mary had been working as a bored clerk for a large company, but her real joy in life was brewing beer at home. One day she came up with the idea of developing a subscription newsletter for other fans of home- and microbrewed beer. Mary quit her job and began the process of making contacts with microbreweries, gathering recipes, learning how to do desktop publishing, and developing a subscription list. She soon realized that she needed another person to assist her, so she put a small ad for an assistant in the next edition of the newsletter. Much to her delight, she received nearly a dozen application letters in the first week. Her delight turned to chagrin, however, as her mailbox began to fill up with résumés and application letters. Mary had hoped to hire someone to help her meet the deadline for her next issue, but now she had to find time to review and reply to over two hundred applicants. Is it any wonder that her process of screening applicants was haphazard and her first hiring experience a near disaster?

This problem is not unique to Mary. Many large companies receive hundreds of unsolicited résumés every week; staffers had to sort through nearly 100,000 applications and résumés in the first months of the Clinton administration.[1] Faced with that kind of information overload, the goal of hiring outstanding candidates can easily shift to a more immediate goal of winnowing the pile of résumés down to a set that can be more readily processed. The challenge is to find a way to do this that is effective in screening on the basis of performance, fair, and efficient.

Not all employers have Mary's problem of an embarrassment of riches. Some jobs involve work that is less interesting than dabbling in microbrewed beers and locations less desirable than Boulder. In these instances, a much more involved recruiting process may be needed to provide an acceptable applicant pool. But screening and reference checking are still needed to ensure that you are hiring applicants who are at least minimally acceptable. As an overall approach, the key to doing this effectively is to structure your screening process so that you are focusing on the *critical* characteristics described in the Performance Attributes Matrix you developed for the job (see Chapter Six).

Using Résumés and Application Letters

Particularly for professional-level jobs, the screening process often begins with résumés and application letters received from applicants. Résumés provide a particular challenge because they contain whatever information the applicant decides to include in whatever format she or he decides to use. The résumé may or may not include the information you need to determine an applicant's capabilities. Differences in style and content make it difficult to compare applicants to each other or, more importantly, to your hiring needs and standards. This open-ended characteristic of résumés also makes it easier for applicants to overemphasize particular factors (for example, that they studied at Harvard), leave out critical details (such as the fact that they never actually *completed* their degree at Harvard), or embellish a mundane work record with an impressive list of overstated "accomplishments." A résumé, despite appearances to the contrary, only contains information that an applicant deemed to be helpful in securing a job with your organization.

How do you critically evaluate an applicant in the one minute or so that most managers spend on unsolicited résumés? First, you need to remind yourself what you're really looking for. Four years' experience working as an administrative assistant to the chief financial officer of a Fortune 500 company looks pretty impressive—until you remind yourself that all *you* need is a secretary who can type, file, and greet customers. Start by recalling the critical attributes identified in the Performance Attributes Matrix, then scan the résumé looking for past experience that *directly relates* to the attributes required for your job. Underlining or highlighting key terms can be a helpful way of structuring this process. Watch for concrete terms like "audited," "used Excel," or "supervised a sales staff of fifteen." Beware vague descriptors like "innovated," "planned," "coordinated," or, our favorite, "envisioned."

If the highlighted terms in the résumé look a lot like your list of performance attributes, you'll want to encourage the applicant to complete an application form so that you can more systematically evaluate his or her credentials. Other applicants should be sent a polite rejection letter informing them that you don't currently have an opening that fits with their qualifications. If someone looks like a good candidate for a position you may have open in the future, you may want to let the applicant know that you will be keeping the résumé on file for potential future use. Highlighted or underlined terms, as well as other notes written on the résumé, will make it easier to scan the résumé later when you need this information.[2]

Many companies that regularly receive large numbers of résumés have turned to computers to speed up the process of scanning them for key attributes. You may want to consider this approach if you hire regularly and receive a large volume of résumés, or if you receive a lot of unsolicited résumés. You can automate the process by optically scanning résumés or receiving them electronically, and then using software (Resumix is one such program) that searches the résumés for key terms. Automating the process permits you to compare applicants to multiple positions that you may have open, allows you to store résumé information for future job searches, and takes care of tracking applicants. Tracking software can even be used to automate the process of sending letters to applicants.

Using Application Forms

From a hiring perspective, the purpose of an application form is to collect job-relevant information that can be used to screen applicants. Ironically, while application forms are perhaps the most widely used hiring tool, they are also one of the least effectively used and most widely misused hiring tools. One reason is that they often are not treated very seriously by the potential employer. Take a minute to look critically at the application form you are currently using. Ask yourself: How much thought was put into using it as a hiring tool? How many of the questions are directly relevant to the job you're hiring for? How much information that you need is *not* included in the form? How many of the questions are likely to violate the legal principles we described in Chapter Five?

If you're like most employers, you're using a generic form that was intended as much to collect information for use *after* an applicant is hired as to determine the applicant's qualifications. Such a "universal" form probably leaves out much of the information that you need for the specific job you're hiring for now. And it probably includes a number of questions that are likely to be considered illegal if they are challenged. Fortunately, improving application forms is a fairly straightforward process.

The first step is to develop a customized application form for each job or set of related jobs. With modern word-processing software, there is no excuse for relying on the generic forms available from office supply vendors. A master document can be created that includes basic categories of information; you can easily and quickly make whatever minor modifications are needed to customize this form for each particular position. Customizing the form also provides a professional image, which is important because the application form may be the applicants' first contact with your organization.

Basic Information in an Application Form

All application forms will need to include the following information:

- Name and contact information, such as phone number and address, that will allow you to arrange an interview.
- Work experience, including names of organizations and supervisors, addresses, periods of employment, and a description of work responsibilities.
- A record of education, training, licenses, or other credentials related to the job being applied for.
- A list of references who are familiar with the applicant's work performance, along with information about how to contact them.
- A "disclaimer" statement that reserves your right to verify all information in the application and warns that providing inaccurate information can be grounds for not hiring or termination.[3] The statement should also reserve your right to contact references in addition to those listed by the applicant.
- A disclaimer statement concerning employment-at-will, if applicable. Typical disclaimers say something like "I understand and agree that employment is at-will, and that this employment relationship may be terminated at any time, by either the Company or myself, with or without cause." Both disclaimers should be highly visible, so that there is no doubt that the applicant has read and agreed to them. The best strategy is to include them at the end of the application, followed immediately by a space for the applicant's signature and the date.

In addition, applicants need to complete Form I-9, Employment Eligibility Verification, which is available from the Immigration and Naturalization Service, within three days of beginning work. The Immigration Reform and Control Act requires you to verify the identity and employment eligibility of *all* new hires; failing to do so can result in civil or criminal penalties. You may wish to include a statement to that effect on the application form so that applicants who are not eligible for employment are put on notice of the requirement.

Customizing the Application Form

Nearly any other job-related questions can be added to this basic application form that will provide you with the information you need to screen applicants effectively. For example, for many professional positions you may be interested in applicants' professional memberships, patents, or publications. If you are hiring a person who will have access to valuables, questions about the ability to be bonded may be critical, as may questions about related criminal convictions. The high-impact question to ask yourself is whether these questions will differentiate between successful and unsuccessful applicants; questions that don't are a waste of everyone's time and may cloud the later quality of your decision making, regardless of whether they are legal.

What Should Not Be in the Application Form?

Our approach to application forms emphasizes making them effective by ensuring that each piece of information is job-related and helps to differentiate between successful and unsuccessful applicants. This also means that any question that doesn't meet both of these tests should not be included on an application form. Taking this approach pays dividends beyond hiring for performance, because it also minimizes the legal liability that can be posed by unnecessary questions. The EEOC generally assumes that *all* questions on the application form are used for making hiring decisions—why else would they be included? Questions that are included mainly for postemployment purposes, such as age, emergency contact information, and health status, should be asked after the hiring decision has been made.

Suppose that you are challenged for making an unfair hiring decision and the plaintiff points out that you asked a potentially discriminatory question on the application blank, such as a question about age or race. The burden of proof is now on you to show either that you didn't use the information to make the hiring decision, which is generally difficult to prove, or that the question is truly job-related. The moral is clear: ask only questions that you know and can show are job-related!

Studies have repeatedly shown that violations of this simple principle are the rule rather than the exception. One study found that only 2 of 150 Fortune 500 firms had problem-free application forms; 38 percent of the forms had ten or more potentially illegal questions.[4] A more recent study of nearly 500 firms showed little improvement; only one firm's application was problem-free.[5]

While any job-related question can be included in an application form or interview, the EEOC's *Guide to Pre-Employment Inquiries*[6] describes a number of questions that are likely to be looked at particularly carefully by regulatory agencies and the courts. Since states often have regulations that are more extensive than federal guidelines, you should also consult with your state Fair Employment Practices Commission for guidance. Many of these agencies have a brochure describing potentially illegal questions, along with suggested alternative questions that may be more job-related.

In many cases, the difference between acceptable and unacceptable questions is a matter of wording the questions in terms of job requirements. For example, instead of asking where applicants were born, which creates the potential for discrimination on the basis of national origin, you can ask them if they can provide proof of eligibility to work in the United States if they are offered employment. A partial list of the more common areas of concern is included in Figure 7.1.

Federal equal employment opportunity regulations present one particularly tricky "gotcha" on application forms. You are forbidden to make hiring decisions on the basis of race and sex, with the narrow exceptions of affirmative action and situations in which gender may be a bona fide occupational qualification. On the other hand, employers are obliged to keep track of applicants' race and gender so that the EEOC can monitor compliance and detect potential discrimination. Many employers justify asking about race and gender on the grounds that this allows them to meet the reporting requirement, yet the EEOC has expressed particular concern that these questions are often used for discriminatory purposes. The best solution is to ask applicants to indicate their race, sex, and disability status on a separate tear-off form that is immediately separated from the application form. The tear-off form should explain that the information is required by federal requirements, that completing it is voluntary, and that the information will not be used for making employment decisions.

Figure 7.1. Potentially Illegal Preemployment Inquiries.

Gender or Race

- Don't ask unless it's job-related (which is very rare).
- Avoid indirect indicators, such as requesting a photograph, a listing of nonrelevant hobbies or social club memberships, and so forth.

Marital or Family Status

- Prohibited (this may imply discrimination against women): Asking applicants if they are married, if they have children, or what their child care arrangements are.
- Allowable: Asking applicants if they can meet attendance requirements (if this is asked equally of all applicants).

Age

- It's best not to ask, except for minimum age requirements, such as for serving alcohol or working with hazardous machinery. In these cases, indicate that employment is subject to verification that the applicant meets the minimum age requirements.
- Avoid indirect indicators, such as date of graduation from high school.

Religion

- Don't ask any questions that would suggest religious preferences, unless religion is relevant (this is rarely the case except for religious institutions).
- Don't ask about availability to work on holidays and weekends, unless you can show that this requirement is job-related *and* has not unfairly excluded applicants in the past. It's best to simply indicate the regular days, hours, and shifts to be worked and ask applicants if they can comply with them.

Military Service

- It's best not to ask, as it may create adverse impact against women.
- Avoid questions about type of discharge; this may have an adverse impact on minority applicants.
- Acceptable: questions about education or training previously received, whether or not it was in the military.

Criminal Record

- Prohibited: questions about prior arrests, because they presume guilt and may create adverse impact.
- Acceptable: questions about *relevant* convictions, but they should be accompanied by a statement that convictions will not necessarily disqualify the applicant and that they will be considered in the context of the seriousness of the crime, how long ago it occurred, and the applicant's subsequent behavior.

Credit History

- Questions are prohibited unless specifically job-related (for example, if the employee would handle money or valuables, or be exposed to bribes).
- The Fair Credit Reporting Act requires notification to applicants that their credit is being checked. If applicants are turned down because of their credit history, they must be informed of the name of the credit agency that provided the information.

Disabilities and Health Status

- Prohibited:
  - Asking applicants if they have a disability.
  - Asking applicants if they will require an accommodation to perform the job.
  - Asking applicants about job-related injuries or workers' compensation history.
  - Medical examinations prior to a job offer.
- Allowable:
  - Asking about an applicant's ability to perform specific job functions, or asking applicants to describe or demonstrate how they would perform job tasks, if this is asked of all applicants.
  - Asking applicants if they can meet attendance requirements or about their attendance on past jobs. (However, questions about missing work due to *illness* are prohibited, since this might reveal that a person is disabled.)
  - Questions about current or past use of illegal drugs (but not about prior addiction, or about the amount of drugs used, which might reveal an addiction).
  - Asking applicants if they drink alcohol or whether they have been convicted of driving under the influence (but not about alcoholism, which is a covered disability).

Going Beyond the Traditional Application Form: Gathering High-Impact Hiring Information

A sobering thought is that research has not shown application forms, as they are generally used, to be very valid predictors of job performance. This is partly because some information collected on application blanks isn't very job-related. Education, for example, is only weakly related to performance in most jobs. That's probably not because education is irrelevant, but because application forms generally measure education very crudely as years of schooling or perhaps grade-point average. Possessing a high school diploma certifies that applicants attended school for four or so years; it provides no guarantee that they can read or write, much less understand mathematics or think logically. Similarly, college grade-point averages vary according to the institution and the major (engineering students often have GPAs one full point lower than liberal arts students) and have only a tenuous relationship to mastery of particular material that may be important for a hiring decision. For this reason, you should determine whether formal education, training, or qualifications are job-related before asking about them on your application form.

A second, critical, reason that application forms haven't proved very predictive is the informal way in which they are typically used. Research dating back to the early 1900s shows that information about a job applicant's background *can* be among the most valid predictors of future performance. The key is choosing and then using the information in a structured, job-related fashion. We will describe three such structured approaches: training and experience checklists, accomplishment records, and biographical information blanks, known as biodata. Checklists are useful for employers of all sizes, while the biographical information blanks are best suited to employers who hire large numbers of employees in a particular job classification. Accomplishment records, like checklists, can be used by both large and small employers.

Training and Experience Checklists

The simplest approach to structuring application form data is similar to the approach we earlier described for reviewing résumés.

The first step is to clearly identify the performance capabilities you wish to assess from the application form, and then design appropriate questions to assess those capabilities. The second step is to develop a structured way of scoring the answers, such as by underlining and counting the number of references to critical attributes.

One standardized way to do this is to include checklists of critical experiences and accomplishments on the application form. For example, if you were looking for familiarity with typical personal computer software, the checklist might include entries for the specific software used on the job. Applicants can either check off the systems they've used or, better, rate their familiarity with each system on a scale of 1 to 3. Training and experience checklists have been found to be considerably more valid than less structured uses of job application data.

Accomplishment Records

A second approach is to ask applicants to describe their accomplishments in narrative form. For example, you might ask them to take a paragraph or two to describe on the application form their past experiences using PC-based software. Their answers would be scored by you or another expert using a checklist you have developed in advance, similar to the one described in the previous paragraph. This method has the advantage of making the correct answer less obvious, and it may also be more efficient than a lengthy checklist. To further reduce exaggeration, applicants should be asked to provide the name of someone who can verify the listed accomplishments.

Accomplishment records are highly job-related. Their validity is often comparable to that of well-developed cognitive-test batteries, and they are less likely to have an adverse impact on minority applicants. Their obvious job relevance also means that, like training and experience checklists, they are seen as fair and reasonable by most job applicants. However, they take some up-front time to develop and can be time-consuming to score for large numbers of applicants. In addition, accomplishment records should not be used for jobs that do not require writing skill, since they depend on applicants having reasonably good writing skills. Narrative summaries are also more time-consuming and difficult for applicants, although this may be turned to your advantage by using them to indirectly screen out less conscientious applicants or those with less interest in the position.

We strongly recommend that you incorporate skill checklists or accomplishment records into your application forms wherever possible. Once you have made the initial effort to create a customized application form in a word-processing program, as we recommended at the beginning of the chapter, it will not represent a large amount of additional work to create skill checklists or accomplishment-record questions. The effort you put in will pay considerable dividends in allowing you to collect valid, job-related information early in the hiring process.

Biodata or Biographical Information Blanks

The most comprehensive approach to using biographical data, or biodata, involves explicitly scoring and weighting applicants' descriptions of their past experiences. "Scoring" these experiences provides a way to determine which experiences actually predict job performance; it also allows you to develop a formula to combine the information in an optimal manner. This guarantees that the information will be used in way that is fair, legal, and efficient.

Biodata can be collected on a standard application form, but it is usually better to develop special biographical information blanks (BIBs) for this purpose. BIBs are generally intended to assess both an applicant's ability and his or her motivation to work. BIBs may consist of questions that cover everything from personal background (including such areas as demographics, home environment while growing up, and education) to hobbies, likes and dislikes, and specific individual and group accomplishments.[7]

Creating a BIB ideally begins by determining performance attributes, as we described in Chapter Two. Questions are then developed to explore the life experiences that might suggest that an applicant possesses these attributes. For example, if attention to detail is one of the critical performance attributes, you should ask about life experiences that might lead a person to be detail-oriented, or that would suggest that she or he enjoys doing detail-oriented work. The questions are worded in multiple-choice format to allow easy scoring, and the answers of high- and low-performing groups are then compared to determine which items actually predict success on whatever aspect of performance you are trying to assess. Poorly performing items are eliminated and statistically optimal weights are assigned to the remaining items, which can then be used for hiring purposes.

BIBs have repeatedly been found to have excellent validity, among the best of any hiring tools. If they are carefully developed, they also have little discriminatory impact. On the other hand, they have two weaknesses. One is that they may be disliked, since some of the items may not be as obviously job-relevant as those on accomplishment records, for example.[8]

The other disadvantage is that they are not yet practical for smaller employers. The process of testing and weighting the items requires very large samples, preferably in the range of four hundred to six hundred applicants or employees for the same job or job family. BIBs also require "recalibration" every three years or so, which again requires large samples of employees.[9] A second factor is the up-front time involved in preparing good items for the BIB. Because many of the items will not effectively differentiate between effective and ineffective performers, BIB developers often begin with two hundred or more trial questions. Writing that many effective questions is challenging, although collections of "generic" life history items are available to ease this task.[10] A third factor is that BIBs have traditionally been assumed to work only for the specific jobs for which they were developed, making validity generalization (see Chapter Six) uncertain. However, more recent research has suggested that it may be possible to develop more generalizable BIBs that are effective for different employers. For example, London House Publishing sells two "generic" BIBs, one for professional and managerial positions and one for entry-level jobs,[11] and Richardson, Bellows, Henry and Company markets predeveloped BIB forms for managerial, supervisory, and clerical jobs.[12]

Reference and Background Checking

Most of the steps in the hiring process involve gathering self-reported information from applicants, through either application forms, interviews, or tests. This is an efficient and mostly effective approach to gathering job-relevant information. At some point in the hiring process, however, it becomes necessary to seek information from other sources, such as past employers and supervisors, teachers, or other acquaintances of the applicant. Such information provides a different perspective on applicants' qualifications and on their self-reports of their qualifications. We will refer to this generally as conducting reference or background checks. *Reference checks* refer in particular to gathering information on past work performance from former employers or supervisors, or others familiar with the applicant's work. *Background checks* refer to more extensive checking of job-related parts of an applicant's life history, often including checks on possible criminal activity.

Reference checking is one of the more contentious areas of the hiring process. Many managers argue, with good reason, that reference checking is often a waste of time. Applicants are unlikely to seek recommendations from people who will speak about them in unflattering terms, so nearly all letters of recommendation are filled with glowing accolades. This is particularly true of the "letters of introduction" that some applicants carry from job to job. In fact, the rare letter writer who attempts to provide a more balanced perspective on an applicant may be dooming that candidate simply because negative comments are so rare.

Attempts to get a more frank evaluation of the candidate through a conversation with the reference are often thwarted by company policies that prohibit revealing more than the applicant's dates of employment. Even managers who are not censored by company policies are often afraid that saying something negative will cost the applicant a job or even get the manager sued. With all these limitations, reference checking may seem like a waste of time.

Why Bother with Reference Checks?

Although each of these criticisms is often valid, we agree with those who argue that reference checking is an essential part of the hiring process. It serves two vital purposes: verifying information that the applicant has provided and obtaining additional information that the applicant is not well suited to provide.

Purpose 1: Verifying Information
One of the problems with self-reported data is that you have to trust applicants to provide accurate and complete information about themselves, even when doing so is not in their best interests.

Criminal courts don't expect this of defendants, which is why there is a constitutional protection against self-incrimination. Why should we expect it of applicants, particularly in situations in which they have the ability as well as the motivation to present themselves in the most positive light? Job applicants can't make themselves look better than they really are on a test of mathematical skills, but they certainly can—and do—fake their answers in interviews, on personality inventories, and on application forms.

Research suggests that 20 to 25 percent of job applications include at least one major fabrication.[13] Misstatements are particularly common for questions about educational credentials, past salary and job title, and reasons for leaving the last job.[14, 15] One study actually found that 15 percent of the firms that had been listed by nursing aide applicants as their previous employer had never heard of the applicants![16]

A key function of reference checks is to verify relevant information that is likely to be misrepresented by the applicant. If a college degree is essential for the job, you need to verify that the applicant actually received the claimed degree. It is not uncommon for applicants to indicate that they attended a college when they did not receive a degree; they may in fact have been taking only an occasional course as a part-time student. Some applicants have even claimed to have a degree from schools they never attended at all. This kind of problem can be quickly detected by calling the registrar's office at the university, or by requiring that a certified copy of the applicant's transcripts be sent directly to you.

It is also important to verify any necessary licenses or certificates. One large health care provider, pressured by time and staff shortages, hired a licensed practical nurse without verifying her credentials. Imagine the shock of a patient who was under local anesthetic when the nurse fainted in the middle of an operation, leaving the doctor to carry on alone. Imagine the chagrin of the hiring supervisor when it turned out that the person had never been licensed. And imagine the reaction of the hospital's risk manager if the patient had sued. Even worse is the situation of a number of hospitals that have belatedly learned that physicians on their staff had falsified their credentials and, in at least one case, never even graduated from medical school.

Other information that applicants are likely to misrepresent, such as past salary, may not be essential to know. Starting salaries should be based on internal pay structures or current market wages for the job being filled, not on a candidate's past salary. Regulatory agencies have found that questions about prior pay are often used to pay women and minorities less, and they are likely to challenge your use of this kind of question if you are accused of pay inequities. If you are asking about pay because you are concerned that an applicant may not be willing to take a cut in pay, it makes more sense to ask that question directly than to assume that a lower salary will be a deterrent. Differences in cost of living, workload, or other factors may offset lower salaries in many applicants' minds.

Purpose 2: Obtaining Additional Information

In addition to verifying information provided by the applicant, reference checks may also provide additional information that the applicant cannot be expected to provide. No one is asked to list shortcomings on an application form, nor have we ever seen that as a section of a résumé! But you want to make a high-impact hiring decision based on a clear understanding of the balance between an applicant's true strengths and real-life weaknesses. Someone who has experienced both of these first-hand with an applicant in a work environment—an honest reference—can be invaluable to you. If you want to know about a candidate's leadership style or other managerial skills, there may be no better source of information than the applicant's previous subordinates or coworkers.

Careful checking is also important for understanding an applicant's character and how it may be manifested in situations that are difficult to either ask the applicant about or simulate in the hiring process. We can hardly expect an applicant for a child care position to admit being a pedophile, yet that sort of information is clearly critical to the hiring decision. It is similarly unlikely that an applicant will admit to having been fired from a previous position for stalking and threatening a coworker, or for embezzling funds. Background checks of criminal records and checks with previous employers and coworkers may be the only way to obtain this vital information.

Courts have ruled that employers have a duty to adequately protect their employees and customers from applicants who have the potential to cause harm. For example, suppose a hotel hires a maintenance worker who subsequently uses a passkey to enter a guest's room and sexually assault the guest. If it is later determined that the employee had a criminal record of sexual assault that the hotel could have learned about during a background check, the hotel may be found guilty of *negligent hiring*. Negligent hiring occurs when (1) an employee harms a third party during the course of employment, (2) this was as a result of the employee's being unfit, and (3) the employer knew or should have known of the applicant's unfitness. Failing to check references is an invitation to a negligent-hiring lawsuit in this situation. As we'll explain in the next section, you may also be held responsible for creating a negligent-hiring situation if you withhold important information about a past employee when you are asked for a reference.

As critical as it is to use reference and background checks to detect problem behaviors, we don't want to leave the impression that this is their only function. Talking with a previous supervisor or other knowledgeable source may also provide useful information about how to best manage an applicant whom you decide to hire. You might learn, for example, that an applicant responds best to personal coaching from a supervisor, or that she or he is particularly effective at motivating disgruntled workers. This may be crucial information for helping the applicant to quickly become effective in the new job.

Legal Considerations with Background Checking

We hope that we have successfully made a case that references should be checked for all new hires, and that a particularly high standard is necessary for positions of trust. The problem is that many employers are unwilling to provide references, particularly negative ones. A survey of 1,331 human resource managers conducted in 1995 found that although 80 percent claimed to check all applicants' references, only 63 percent would provide references to other employers.

One reason for this reluctance to provide references is a fear of being sued for *defamation of character*. Defamation is a tort liability (meaning that it is a civil rather than criminal case) involving an injury to a person's character or reputation resulting from false statements.[17] In other instances, past employers may be concerned that their statements could cause applicants to be unfairly labeled as problem employees when their behavior might be much different in a different job, firm, or period of time.

Concerns about defamation lawsuits are arguably overblown, since defamation concerns only communications that are false. Sticking to the truth is always a defense against a defamation lawsuit, particularly if you can document the accuracy of your comments. This is especially true of privileged communications, in which "a duty (moral, social, legal) to speak and an interest to hear facts about another's performance are relatively more important than an individual's reputation."[18] The key is to provide information in good faith to someone who has a legitimate interest in the information. Gossiping to neighbors about an employee who is a pedophile is not a privileged communication, but informing a child care center that is considering hiring the former employee most likely would be.

Despite the defense of truth, and such strategies as having candidates give permission for the reference or even waive their rights to review the reference (neither of which necessarily provide much legal protection), many employers feel caught between a rock and a hard place when it comes to providing references. In response to this dilemma, over half of the states have developed what are typically called Quality in Hiring Acts to protect employers who provide good-faith references from being sued. Although the details vary from state to state, most of these laws protect employers from civil liability when they provide good-faith information on the job performance of current or former employees. Many employers are taking a "wait and see" attitude toward this protection until more case law develops, but these laws have the potential to make it much easier to obtain useful references. In the meantime, undertaking a good-faith effort to obtain references will still often provide you with information crucial to your hiring decisions. Even if your effort is unsuccessful, it is likely to provide a defense against negligent hiring claims.[19]

Another reason for employers to provide useful references comes from an emerging legal doctrine known as *negligent referral*. Negligent referral refers to an employer's failure to disclose relevant information about a current or past employee in response to a legitimate request. The concept was central to a lawsuit filed against Allstate Insurance for failing to disclose that a former employee had been discharged for carrying a gun in his briefcase. The employee subsequently shot three coworkers to death after being terminated from his next job.[20] The resulting lawsuit against Allstate serves as a reminder that *not* providing references can pose more legal risk than providing accurate reference information.

Keys to High-Impact Reference and Background Checking

Effective reference and background checking involves seven key points, which are described in more detail in the following paragraphs.

Obtain Reference Information from Knowledgeable Sources

Before seeking references, ask yourself who is likely to be in a good position to know the information that you are seeking *and* be willing to provide it honestly. Many companies have a policy of referring reference requests to their human resources department. Unfortunately, most personnel officers are not likely to have direct information about an applicant's performance or character; at most, they are likely to be able to tell you when the person worked at the company, what the person's job title was, and perhaps the person's reason for leaving. Acquaintances, friends, and coworkers may be in a better position to describe the applicant, but they are likely to be biased, particularly if their names are provided by the applicant. Thus, in most cases, the most useful information is likely to come from an applicant's former supervisor.

Develop an Effective Relationship with the Reference Provider

Reference providers have a number of reasons not to be candid when you ask them for a reference. They may have little or nothing to gain from being honest, and they may feel that there are significant risks. One risk is a fear of being sued, and another is that they don't know how fairly you will use the information they provide. Thus your first task is to establish trust and to clarify the benefit to the reference providers of giving you an honest evaluation. Reminding them that you are facing the same difficult task that they also deal with when hiring may help break through some barriers. It may also help to ask a reference provider to think not so much in terms of the applicant's *past* failures and successes as their likely future success in the job they're applying for.[21] This means that you need to clearly describe the job and the qualifications you're attempting to assess. Doing so has the added advantage of reassuring the reference provider that you are focusing on job-relevant attributes rather than personal traits that can increase the likelihood of a lawsuit.

Ask for Job-Related Information Only

At this point, it should go without saying that references should only be asked about behaviors that are job-relevant. Your Performance Attributes Matrix will indicate what attributes you intend to assess in the reference checks, and we recommend creating a Reference Checking Form similar to the one shown in Exhibit 7.1 to remind you of what to assess. If the reference provider volunteers irrelevant information, a polite "Thank you, but that is really not relevant to the job for which Susan (or John) is applying" should help get the session back on track.

Document Your Procedures and Information

Another advantage of the Reference Checking Form is that it allows you to document with whom you spoke, what questions you asked, and how you reached your conclusions about the applicant's qualifications. This system allows you to quantify the reference information so that it can be more easily combined with other information you've obtained about the applicant. It also provides documentation in the unlikely event that a legal challenge should arise.

Check Multiple References

It is important to check with more than one reference provider. Even in the best of cases, most reference providers are likely to provide only very limited information, partly because each may have only a limited perspective on the applicant, and few will be willing to mention the serious problems you're most concerned about. Asking more people increases the likelihood of learning about any problems. Some authorities suggest contacting three primary references and three secondary references (references that were not suggested by the applicant).[22] The number that is cost-effective for you is likely to depend on the riskiness of the position, your volume of hiring, and your level of resources.

Exhibit 7.1. Example of Reference Checking Form.

Applicant name

Reference check by

Company name

Contact name

Phone

Date

Attributes	Response Ratings (Check One per Attribute)			
	Good	Indifferent	Poor/ Problem	Wouldn't answer
Ability to work accurately on detailed tasks *Comments:*				
Ability to work well with others in a team environment *Comments:*				
Willingness to do repetitious work *Comments:*				
Skill at making oral presentations to large audiences *Comments:*				

Dates of employment verified: Yes ___   No ___
Position verified: Yes ___   No ___
Reason for leaving verified: Yes ___   No ___

Verify Negative Information

Another factor that will affect the number of references you obtain is whether you receive negative information about an applicant. Negative references may signal a problem, or they may reflect such irrelevant factors as a supervisor's irritation with a subordinate's leaving, jealousy about the applicant's upward mobility, or other biases. Try to corroborate negative information with an independent source before it is used to make a hiring decision. You also want to ask yourself how credible the negative information is, given what you know about the applicant and the reference provider.

Use a Background Investigation Agency when Appropriate

Reference checking can be a difficult and time-consuming endeavor, especially if you hire only occasionally and are not practiced at it. Particularly for more sensitive positions where a thorough job-related background check is appropriate, it may be worthwhile to hire a firm that specializes in this work to assist you. These firms are familiar with the procedures for doing criminal and credit checks, verifying educational credentials, and interviewing former supervisors. Fees often represent a worthwhile investment, especially since they are usually incurred only for the few applicants whom you are otherwise ready to hire. If you'd like to see a demonstration of how such background investigations can be done, point your World Wide Web browser to the pages of the Informus Corporation (http://www.informus.com) or the Alexander Information Group (http://www.mhv.net/~alexinfogp).

However, it's important to remember that only background information that is truly job-relevant should be obtained. Driving records may be a matter of public record in most states, but there is no point in checking them if a clean driving record is not critical to job performance. Other information, such as a credit record, is relevant only to a small set of jobs in which employees will be handling money or are susceptible to bribes. Moreover, information that is not in the public domain will require prior permission from applicants. Since these investigations become a matter of public record under the Fair Credit Reporting Act of 1970, applicants have more ready access to the information that is obtained.[23] Thus it is particularly important that you work with a reputable firm with high ethical standards, and that you inform them precisely what job-relevant attributes you wish them to verify. Keep in mind, too, that there may be errors in the data bases used by even reputable firms. As with other types of reference checking, try to confirm negative information before using it to reject an applicant.

Medical Examinations

As part of your verification process, you may also want to determine whether an applicant is physically capable of doing the work. One approach is to use tests of physical abilities, described in Chapter Nine. Another alternative is to have applicants evaluated by a health care professional. As straightforward as this may seem, medical examinations need to be done carefully to avoid discriminating against qualified applicants who have disabilities. In order to be effective and in compliance with the Americans with Disabilities Act:

- Medical examinations should be conducted only *after* a conditional job offer has been extended.
- Medical examinations should be required of all applicants for a particular job, not only those whom you suspect may be unable to do the job.
- The person doing the examination should understand the job—particularly its "essential functions"—and the resulting physical and mental demands. See Chapter Two for more guidelines on how to accomplish this through the work analysis process.
- Applicants who have disabilities affecting their ability to perform the essential functions of the job need to be evaluated for possible accommodations that would allow them to be effective performers (see Chapter Five for more information on the reasonable accommodation requirements of the Americans with Disabilities Act).

Summary

It is a virtual truism that, all other things being equal, a person's past behavior is one of the best predictors of how he or she will perform in the future. An essential component of high-impact hiring is to gather information about applicants' life histories that is relevant to, and predictive of, their performance on the job for which you are about to hire them. Information on résumés and application forms can be used to effectively and legally screen out applicants who clearly do not fit the requirements of the job. The smaller pool of applicants who survive this screening process then move on to the more intensive—and expensive—hiring procedures described in the next four chapters. As we will describe in Chapter Twelve, the goal is to develop a progressively more qualified applicant pool so that the final set of finalists will all be at least minimally qualified to perform the work.

We have described the use of reference checks and background investigations as one of the *final* steps in the hiring process. Like screening procedures, reference and background checks are typically used primarily to screen out undesirable applicants, although both sets of tools can be used to assess levels of competency among acceptable applicants as well. Background checks are your last line of defense against a low-impact hire, and they should be treated as seriously as the other steps in the high-impact hiring process.

Chapter Eight

Understanding and Using an Interview Strategy That Works

Personal interviews are without a doubt one of the most widely used tools for hiring. Would you hire an employee without first conducting at least one interview? Résumés and job applications can convey a good deal of information, but they just don't have the same "feel" as a face-to-face interview. Nor is it likely that many job applicants would accept a job offer without first meeting their new employer. To put it in the terms of this book, interviews are the quintessential hiring ritual. The challenge you face is turning this established ritual into a high-impact hiring tool. Thus, it is not a matter of *whether* to use job interviews as part of your hiring system, but *how* to use them most effectively.

While the use of interviews is nearly universal, it is clearly not the case that interviews are always—or even usually—used effectively. In fact, traditional job interviews have developed a tainted reputation among researchers who study hiring practices. Until recently, interviews were widely condemned for lacking reliability and validity and for being highly susceptible to all kinds of irrelevant biases. More recent research has shown that interviews *can* be an effective hiring tool if steps are taken to minimize their inherent weaknesses and build on their strengths.

The key differences between effective and ineffective interviews are structure and focus. Traditional interviews tend to be unstructured and largely unplanned conversations that may or may not focus clearly on job-relevant factors and that are highly susceptible to imprecision and bias. *Structured interviews*, in contrast, consist of carefully planned, job-related questions that can be systematically scored so as to reliably identify high-potential job candidates. Our goal in this chapter is to help you to develop structured interviews as a key part of your high-impact hiring system.

As a first step in that direction, it's important to understand why traditional, unstructured interviews have persisted as the most popular hiring procedure (and ritual) despite the criticism they have received. It's our experience that many managers resist changing to more structured interviews because they feel so comfortable with the more informal interviews they currently use: unstructured interviews are like those old worn-out shoes that fit so comfortably.

Why Are Interviews So Popular?

If it seems foolish to even ask why interviews are so popular, it is testimony to the ubiquitous role of interviews in hiring, at least in North America. Yet it is often the universally accepted practices that are most in need of questioning. Six basic claims are made for using a traditional wide-ranging job interview as the primary hiring tool. Let's evaluate these claims and see what we can learn about how to make your interviewing more effective.

Claim: Interviews Provide a Personal Touch

Employers and job applicants want to be able to see each other before committing themselves to a long-term relationship. This explains why telephone interviews aren't usually considered to be a replacement for face-to-face interviews. Psychologists tell us that direct, personal experience creates the strongest, most lasting impression of others. Many managers feel that they simply "know" when an applicant is right for the job, based on an overall reaction that they can't articulate—the feel is either right or wrong. Maybe it's the way some applicants won't quite look you in the eye, maybe it's their posture, or the confidence with which they speak. But whatever it is, many managers feel that only a personal interview provides the opportunity to develop this intuitive insight.

Interviews also allow more flexibility than other, more standardized hiring procedures. You can change direction to follow up on an interesting comment, modify questions to fit the specific background of particular applicants, or challenge applicants to defend claims made in their résumés or job applications. Although tests and other procedures seem cold and impersonal, interviews allow people who actually do the work to evaluate the applicant's qualifications. Moreover, the interviewers may be the same people the applicant will eventually have to work with. Isolating the hiring process from the future boss or coworkers may create obstacles to the acceptance of new employees, especially those who will be playing pivotal roles.

Much can be said for these arguments. At the same time, psychologists tell us that our natural confidence in our ability to evaluate people is often unfounded. Some people may have a natural talent for sizing people up; most do not. The problem is that people who are not effective are often unaware of their blind spot. People express similar levels of confidence in their evaluations regardless of whether their evaluations are accurate or not. The tendency to overlook our weaknesses is as naturally human as is our tendency to trust our instincts. The result can be both poor hiring decisions and an unwillingness to face up to the problems created by hiring applicants who turn out to be poor performers. As we will see, interviewing requires careful planning and structure in order to be effective; simply relying on insight tends to be a crapshoot.

Claim: Interviews Are an Efficient Way to Gather Information

This claim has a number of variations. One is that, because of their unstructured nature, interviews can be used to collect a lot of information about a job applicant in a limited time. Tests, as we will see in Chapter Nine, typically focus on one aspect of performance, whereas interviews are often used to assess everything from interpersonal skills and social appropriateness to motivation and common sense. Especially for small businesses or for situations in which only a limited number of job applicants are to be screened, interviews seem ideally suited as a catchall procedure for evaluating a wide range of job qualifications.

Unfortunately, this assumption isn't realistic or accurate. Far from being the informal conversations that they are sometimes treated as, interviews actually place complex demands on the interviewer, not to mention the interviewee. Based on an often vague set of desired qualifications, you must ask questions that lead job applicants, who are motivated to make themselves look as good as they possibly can, to give truthful answers. The answers, as well as any nonverbal cues, must then be interpreted, remembered, and combined into a judgment that is based not only on job requirements, but also on an applicant's standing relative to other applicants (preferably without reliance on non-job-related characteristics such as race, gender, age, the order in which the interviews were conducted, or what the interviewer had for lunch). All of this occurs under time pressure and in the midst of other distractions.

With this complexity, it should not be surprising that research shows that the validity of interviews is enhanced when interviewers are asked to evaluate *fewer* job qualifications during an interview. We are simply asking too much if we expect to reliably evaluate more than a few dimensions during typical interviews. Even doing this effectively requires careful planning and structure.

Claim: Interviews Are the Best Way to Evaluate Certain Job Qualifications

If we accept that we cannot reasonably expect to assess *all* job qualifications in an interview, we can then focus on the claim that job interviews are uniquely suited to measuring certain qualifications that are not well assessed with other procedures. Here research supports the claim that such dimensions as interpersonal skills, verbal fluency, and sociability are assessed effectively by interviews (assuming that these qualities are actually required for job performance).[1] Interviews can be designed to serve as effective simulations of actual job-related demands for these characteristics.

Interviews are also suggested as the best way to assess "chemistry" or "fit" between the applicant and the supervisor or organization. Such claims are far more tenuous. Unless fit is defined clearly in terms of job performance, hiring decisions can easily be based on irrelevant factors. It is critical in high-impact hiring to be certain that selection procedures assess characteristics that are truly important for effective job performance. This is particularly crucial with interviews, which too often are conducted informally and with little explicit attention to job relevance. If fit is defined in terms of specific personality, interest, or ability factors that are job-relevant, interviews can be an effective hiring tool.

Claim: Interviews Provide an Opportunity to Confirm Other Information

Interviews provide a unique opportunity to fill in gaps or inconsistencies in applicants' résumés or application forms. This kind of cross-checking is essential. In some cases, you may want to learn more about specific experiences or skills listed on a résumé to make sure you understand what the applicant actually did in a previous job. For example, if an applicant lists "sales experience" on her résumé, you would want to know whether this means that she made sales presentations or simply operated a cash register. Similarly, it is important to explore any gaps in employment history.

First Impressions Can Be Misleading

Research on interviews presents an interesting dilemma: exposure to information about an applicant prior to an interview creates a first impression that is likely to bias the information collected in the interview. Studies have consistently shown that hiring managers are prone to rapidly forming a vivid initial impression of job applicants; subsequent information that is inconsistent with this impression is frequently ignored, probably unconsciously. Evidence contrary to their first impression is often not sought, and if it is encountered, it may be ignored. The result can be a one-dimensional view of the applicant that's often inaccurate.

Exposure to too much information about a job applicant prior to the interview can create a particular problem with first impressions. When different interviewers review a résumé or application, they emphasize different factors and thus form different first impressions. One interviewer may review a résumé, notice that the applicant is an alumnus of the same Ivy League school that she attended, and immediately form a positive first impression. Another interviewer, seeing the same information, may react negatively to graduates of Ivy League schools, feeling that they don't fit with the company's culture. A third interviewer may not even notice the Ivy League connection but instead may key on the fact that he and the applicant share the same birth date. The lack of standardization makes it easy for the interviewers to form first impressions based on factors that are irrelevant to how well the applicant will perform on the job. These first impressions then can bias how they interact with the applicant during the interview.

Avoiding the First-Impression Problem

The best solution to inaccurate first impressions is to try to ensure that only job-relevant background information is included in an applicant's file. Since this may be difficult to do, a second strategy is not to review all of an applicant's file prior to the first interview.[2] Instead, review only the information that is relevant to what will be covered in the interview, such as the application form or résumé. You don't need to be aware of an applicant's test scores or letters of recommendation prior to conducting an interview, because in the interview you are going to be focusing on different aspects of the applicant, such as interpersonal skills. If the other information in the file is relevant, it can be included later in the decision-making process, when it won't "contaminate" the interview.

In most cases it's quite practical to ignore a lot of this background information in the initial screening interviews and then use subsequent interviews to cross-check information on the résumé or application blank, when, it is hoped, first impressions have already been formed on job-relevant factors. If you are working with a colleague or assistant, you can have your colleague process the application material and provide you with only the necessary information or with a summary of the key qualifications on the résumé.

Claim: Interviews Are a Good Public Relations Tool

Another frequently cited advantage of traditional interviews is that they allow the interviewer to "sell" the job applicant on the company. Selling the applicant may be a critical factor if you really want to hire someone, particularly in a competitive labor market. Even if you don't want to hire particular job applicants, you still want to retain their goodwill throughout your hiring process. After all, job applicants are often potential customers, and they may even encourage others to apply for a job that doesn't fit them. Seen in this way, an interview could serve as much as a recruiting or marketing tool—or even as a realistic job preview (see Chapter Four)—as it does a means for selecting the best candidates.

Studies show that job applicants form impressions about the company on the basis of how they are treated in the recruitment and interviewing process. Considerate treatment, timely processing of their application, and an articulate and well-organized interviewer who asks job-related questions all enhance a job applicant's opinion of an employer. Demonstrating sincere interest in a candidate can increase the likelihood of the candidate's choosing your company over another employer. Certainly, selection interviews should build a positive image of the employer in the eyes of job applicants.

Once again, though, we are expecting too much of the interview if we hope to use it simultaneously for selection and public relations. It's difficult enough to design an interview for gathering information to guide a hiring decision. Adding other functions to the interview creates conflicts that reduce its value for hiring. As an example, it's best for selection purposes to let the job applicant do 80 percent of the talking in an interview. This allows you to obtain more information about the applicant, which reduces the tendency to create premature first impressions based on superficial characteristics.[3] On the other hand, if the purpose of the interview is to provide information about the company, the interviewer will need to spend much more time talking. What the applicant gains in information about the company, the company loses in information about the applicant.

As another example of conflict, when interviewers are trying to sell the company to a job candidate, they are more likely to emphasize the most positive aspects and gloss over the blemishes. As we saw in Chapter Four, this can lead to applicants' taking jobs that they later become unhappy with, resulting in costly turnover. Researchers have also shown that selling the company reduces the likelihood that you'll ask the really tough questions that can help you to select the best employees. It can even lead to unintended— but legally enforceable—obligations to the applicant (see the discussion of employment-at-will in Chapter Five).

The solution is to decide in advance the *primary* purposes of an interview, or, more likely, of a series of interviews. Interviews are among the more expensive selection devices, simply because they take a good deal of your valuable time. A total of six to eight person-hours per candidate is not uncommon for many jobs, and this figure will be much higher for managerial and professional positions. For that reason, decisions to lengthen interviews to allow more time to achieve additional purposes must be analyzed carefully. It's generally more efficient to provide applicants with information about the company prior to individual interviews through brochures, videos, websites, or, especially in the case of campus interviews or ongoing recruiting for large numbers of positions, an informational meeting for all job applicants. Information about the job and company may have more value if it is in written form, so that applicants can read it under less stressful conditions than an interview and also refer back to it when considering job offers, for example, or after they have been hired.[4] Time can then be allowed toward the end of an interview for the applicant to ask questions of the interviewer. This keeps the emphasis on having the applicant do the talking (in this case the questioning) and allows the interviewer to evaluate the applicant in terms of the appropriateness of the questions asked.

The primary purpose of interviews is likely to differ for preliminary and follow-up interviews. The purpose of an initial, *screening* interview should be to screen out applicants who clearly are not qualified for the job; therefore, the principal focus should be on assessing absolutely critical job qualifications.[5] Follow-up interviews explore applicants' qualifications in more depth and breadth. As you narrow the pool of applicants to a small set of desirable candidates, you can then place more emphasis on convincing them that the job is one they want to accept. This sequence enhances cost-effectiveness, because more lengthy and complex interviews are reserved for the reduced pool of finalists.

Claim: Interviews Are Easy to Do

This claim is as important as any in explaining the ubiquity of interviewing in the hiring process. One textbook on employee selection derisively describes the typical employment interview as unplanned (sit down and wing it); quick and dirty, with questions that are casual, speculative, and often obtuse; and done by an interviewer who is unprepared and makes snap decisions about job applicants.[6] This approach to interviewing, unfortunately all too common, is certainly far easier than the procedures we are advocating in this book. It is also far less effective. Let's consider some of the problems that occur with this unsystematic approach to interviewing.

Problems with Traditional, Unstructured Interviews

Many managers are simply not aware of the limitations of typical interviews or the fact that effective alternatives exist. In fact, interviews are perhaps the best example of ritual hiring. They are a ritual because everyone uses them; as we asked earlier, can you imagine making a hiring decision without conducting an interview? They're also a ritual because they serve to make hiring managers feel as though they are in control. Unlike letters of recommendation, résumés, or employment tests, *you* control the interview, or at least you feel as though you do. Finally, they're a ritual because they're generally used without any evidence that they really work, or despite evidence that they often don't work.

The solution to the issues we have identified is not to stop doing interviews, but to take a more structured and performance-oriented approach to them. In the remainder of this chapter we will use the principles we discussed in Chapter One to analyze interviews from a high-impact hiring perspective. Rather than accepting interviews as a ritual, we will describe four fundamental problems inherent in typical unstructured interviews: subjectivity and bias, inaccuracy, legal exposure, and lack of validity. We will then describe a method of structured interviewing that can add impact to your hiring decisions.

Subjectivity and "Gut Feelings"

When we've asked managers to describe the primary weakness of interviews, the most typical answer we get is that interviews are subjective. In truth, subjectivity has been given a bad rap. It simply means making decisions based on your perceptions and judgments. Obviously, you make subjective decisions all the time; making quality decisions with insufficient time and information, as you do in hiring or other business decisions, might be considered the hallmark of a manager's job. Subjectivity itself is not the problem with interviews. It is the *lack of structure* with which the subjective judgments are reached, and a resultant lack of focus on critical outcomes, that can be the downfall of interviews.

The challenge in making decisions based on subjective factors is to structure the decision process so that it is driven primarily by relevant decision factors, and minimally by irrelevant ones. In the case of employment interviews, years of research show that interviewers' judgments are easily influenced by applicant characteristics that are at best irrelevant, resulting in low-impact hiring as well as in illegal discrimination; at worst this leads to hiring less desirable employees than just hiring randomly. As interviewers, we are more likely to give more positive ratings to applicants whom we like, for example. This is natural, and it wouldn't be a problem if we liked applicants solely because they were more qualified to do the job. But life isn't that simple.

One of the strongest biases affecting interview ratings is the physical attractiveness of the applicant, especially facial attractiveness. But how often is physical attractiveness really essential to job performance? In addition, interviewers may have different standards for what is attractive, further eroding the credibility of the interview process. As interviewers, we are also more positive toward applicants who are similar to us. That's a problem if we need to hire someone quite different from us. Once you realize that physical attractiveness and similarity play such key roles in interviewers' decisions, it should hardly be surprising to learn that interviews are susceptible to illegal discrimination on the basis of gender, race, and age.

Other kinds of biases can lead to hiring decisions that are ineffective even if they are perfectly legal. If you tend to like exciting people who always seem to have a million things going on, you may find that you hire people who are ineffective at jobs requiring patience and attention to detail. If a Brooklyn or West Texas accent puts you off, you might lose the benefit of a skilled medical technician because of his or her speech pattern.

The truly invidious problem is that we are often unaware of our biases and how they affect our hiring decisions. Personal beliefs and values lead interviewers to unthinkingly ask different questions of male and female applicants, or to interpret the same answer differently if it is given by a white rather than a black applicant. In fact, studies have shown that interviewers' attitudes affect their *nonverbal* behavior toward an applicant—for example, how close to the applicant they sit, how much eye contact they maintain, and how often they nod in agreement. This subtle rejection or encouragement affects how the applicant acts, often reinforcing the interviewer's preconception of the applicant as being qualified or not. In effect, the interviewer's unintentional nonverbal language *creates* the very applicant behavior that the interviewer is expecting, resulting in a self-fulfilling prophecy.

Unfortunately, bias is one of the most difficult aspects of interviews to correct, probably because we're often not aware of our biases. None of us wants to admit, even to ourselves, that our hiring decisions may be influenced by irrelevant biases. One potential solution is to involve multiple interviewers, so that their biases cancel out. Discussing differences in interviewers' reactions to an applicant could make people more aware of their biases; however, doing so requires time for discussion and an environment in which differences in perspective are valued.

Another approach is to think about our own preferences and whether or not they relate to job performance. An acquaintance of ours once related her method for trying to become aware of unconscious biases. She would start her interviews with a set of intentionally non-job-related questions to help break the ice. But before moving on to job-related questions, she would consciously ask herself what her initial impression was of the applicant and why she felt that way. Since her first impression was probably not job-related (she hadn't gotten to the job-relevant questions yet), she knew that it was probably based on nonrelevant biases. By making herself aware of why she was feeling positive or negative toward the applicant, she could then work to consciously factor this bias out of her evaluation of the job-relevant interview questions.

Inaccuracy and the "Evil Twin"

As many an employer has lamented, the job applicant who looks so good in the interview often doesn't seem to be the same person once she or he has been hired. As one manager put it, "I interviewed Paul for the job, but his evil twin brother showed up for work."

Job applicants often get psyched up for interviews and come across much more positively than they would in normal work settings. At the very least, most job applicants are on their best behavior during job interviews. Some individuals, however, go beyond merely putting their best foot forward and make up whatever answers they think will get them the job.[7] Unstructured interviews, with their speculative and often unverifiable questions, make it easy for applicants who are so inclined to give whatever answers they think the interviewer is looking for.

To make matters worse, an increasing number of job applicants have been through interviewing workshops that train them to look good in an interview. Thus it is not only devious job applicants who may "work" the interview, but also the diligent ones who are looking for an edge in a competitive job market. These training programs give job applicants a preview of what is likely to be asked in an interview, including descriptions of most interviewers' favorite questions, and coach them on how to present themselves and how to respond. For example, the book *Knock 'em Dead*[8] includes over two hundred common interview questions, along with suggested answers. As a result, it is increasingly hard to determine if interview questions are telling you as much about the applicants' qualifications as they are about the coaching they have received.[9]

What is often not apparent is that the opposite may also occur: the applicant who doesn't have it together in the interview might have turned out to be a star performer on the job, and might now be the star working for your biggest competitor. In many cases interviewees are so anxious about the interview that they freeze up and don't perform as they would in a more natural job setting. This apparent lack of social skills may cause an otherwise well-qualified applicant to fail the interview (this assumes, of course, that making a good impression under pressure is not a requirement of the job). In fact, it's often the most motivated applicants who get overly anxious in interviews.

Structured interviews offer a number of strategies to help you avoid these problems. One is to focus on job-specific qualifications and questions and to eliminate the generic questions that are most likely to have been rehearsed in a training session. Another is to avoid being influenced by the applicant's presentation, since it may say more about exposure to interviewee training than about typical behavior or personality. It also helps to be skilled at putting job applicants at ease, especially those who may have been out of the job market for a while or those who feel alienated by the selection process. Structured interviews help you to feel confident, which in turn can help put the applicant more at ease.

Job Interviews Can Lead to Lawsuits

If interviews are so subjective and susceptible to bias, can't they cause employers to run afoul of legal guidelines on discrimination? (If you are not sure what these guidelines require, Chapter Five will be helpful.) Yes, they certainly can, although to date there has been less litigation concerning interviews than concerning other selection procedures such as tests. Some experts have even suggested that interviews are low-risk, despite all their problems, simply because everyone accepts them as common practice.[10]

For a long time, employers retreated from tests and other selection procedures because of a mistaken belief that interviews were not subject to the same strict standards as tests. They assumed that subjective procedures like interviews were not amenable to scientific scrutiny and that as long as the *intent* of the questioning was not discriminatory, they need not worry about discrimination lawsuits. This belief encouraged some employers to stick with unstructured and unscored interviews so that they would not have to validate them if they had an adverse effect on minority or female applicants.

In reality, various courts have handed down judgments against employers that were based at least in part on identified weaknesses in their interviewing procedures. The legal liability of interviewing was increased in 1988, when the U.S. Supreme Court ruled in *Watson* v. *Fort Worth Bank and Trust* that employers must be able to prove that subjective selection procedures like interviews are job-related if they have adverse impact (see Chapter Six for more details).

An analysis of case law suggests a number of steps you can take to minimize the legal risks involved in using interviews.[11] Notice that each of these are also good procedures for conducting performance-based hiring:

- Interview questions should be based on the knowledge, skills, and abilities specified in the Performance Attributes Matrix you developed for the job (see Chapter Two).
- Applicants should be evaluated solely on the basis of these critical attributes; other factors should be ignored. Resist the temptation to add new hiring criteria in the middle of an interview.

- Interview questions generally should ask about job-relevant behaviors rather than abstract traits.
- A structured interviewing format should be used.
- Interviewers' ethnicity and gender should reflect that of the applicant pool; judges and juries are more likely to suspect bias if all interviewers are white males.
- Interviewers should be trained, or at least experienced, in conducting interviews.
- Questions should be avoided that might lead a reasonable person to suspect discriminatory intent. See Figure 7.1 for a list of suspect questions.

Interviews Often Lack Validity

Researchers have long noted that interviews, particularly typical unstructured ones, have about the lowest validity of any selection procedure. However, this need not be the case if you take steps, like those we'll describe in the next section, to avoid the problems with interviewing we've discussed. Recent studies have shown that structured interviews are far more valid than unstructured interviews—as much as twice as valid.[12-14]

A recent Bureau of National Affairs survey found that only 33 percent of responding companies reported using structured interviews.[15] The strategic implication should not be overlooked by any business concerned about competitiveness: by being one of the relatively few companies to use structured interviews, you can use high-impact hiring as a way of gaining a competitive advantage by hiring employees who perform better and stay longer.

Structured Interviewing: The High-Impact Hiring Strategy

What, exactly, is a "structured" interview? Structured interviews have three critical characteristics that distinguish them from traditional unstructured interviews: a standardized format, job-related questions, and a method of scoring applicants' responses.

Standardizing Interview Questions

The most obvious characteristic of structured interviewing, in contrast with unstructured interviews, is the use of preplanned questions. Unstructured interviews are often little more than an informal conversation in which the interviewer relies on instinct or habit to decide what questions to ask. Often, different questions are asked of different job applicants, making it difficult to compare the applicants fairly. Structured interviewing, in contrast, protects the integrity of the hiring process by ensuring that the critical questions are asked in the same way for all job applicants.

Experts disagree on whether interviews should be totally structured, so that the procedure is *exactly* the same for all applicants, or whether the interviewer should be allowed to follow up with "probe" questions to clarify job applicants' answers. Our experience in training hundreds of people in structured interviewing is that it is often difficult to get a fully satisfactory answer with an initial question. With most applicants, follow-up questions are necessary to get the information you need to make a good hiring decision.

Some flexibility in the order and style of questions is also likely to make the interview more enjoyable for both you and the applicant. An overly structured interview may give applicants the feeling that they're being interrogated. Your goal in conducting an effective structured interview is to give the impression that the interview is a planned, yet extemporaneous, conversation. If you find a high level of standardization appealing, you can always write a set of optional probe questions in advance.

Using Job-Related Questions

The job relevance of the interview questions is at least as important as their standardization. Unstructured interviews too often result in questions that are ambiguous, hard to evaluate, and questionably job-related. One of our students provided an excellent example of what we mean. During an interview for a position as a management consultant, she was asked the gem, "If you could be any animal, what would it be?" After a couple of seconds of thought, she decided to answer that she'd be a dolphin, reasoning that they are intelligent and sociable, characteristics she judged to be relevant to the job, as well as graceful. Interestingly, she confided to the class that her truthful answer would have been an eagle, but she was concerned that it might provide a less favorable image to the interviewer. Although a number of students agreed that a dolphin was a good answer, she was crestfallen when others in the class mentioned that an article had just appeared in the local newspaper describing some distinctly antisocial characteristics of dolphins, including the tendency of males to sexually assault their trainers. It is anybody's guess what the interviewer was looking for when he asked the question, but it *is* clear that different interviewers might interpret her answer in very different ways. Interview questions developed to assess specific job-related characteristics are unlikely to create such problems.

Structured interviews involve asking only questions that are based on an analysis of critical job requirements. A common mistake with unstructured interviews is to ask questions based on characteristics of the *applicant,* rather than characteristics of the *job.* When answering the question, "What should I ask in an interview?" many interviewers review the applicant's résumé or application for ideas. In contrast, structured interviews focus first on the job description and on critical performance attributes for question content.

As we described in Chapter Two, the first step in developing a selection plan should be to determine the necessary qualifications to do the work, using work analysis. At the least, you should always take the time before interviewing to ask yourself what attributes you want to assess in the interview and how they are related to job performance. This essential step needs to occur before any thought is given to developing specific questions.

You should also ask yourself which qualifications are most appropriately measured in an interview and which are better assessed through other approaches that may be more valid or less costly, as we discussed in Chapter Six. Most experts feel that interviews are best suited for measuring applicants' verbal and interpersonal skills. Interviews can also be an appropriate medium for assessing job knowledge, particularly if there are a small number of applicants, if you can write a set of valid questions assessing job knowledge in advance, and if knowledge of the job can be explained verbally, rather than needing to be shown. On the other hand, if the questions are easily scored and there are a lot of applicants, a simple written test may be a more efficient way to measure applicants' knowledge. A performance test (see Chapter Ten) will be better if verbal explanations of job knowledge aren't useful.

Remember, too, our earlier discussion of the problems of trying to measure too much in an interview. A rule of thumb is to allow five to ten minutes for an answer to each question and to ask two to three questions for each attribute you want to assess, allowing another five to ten minutes to begin and end the interview. This suggests that assessing four characteristics in a sixty-minute interview is a reasonable goal, particularly if you're just getting used to this form of interviewing.

Once you've determined the characteristics to be assessed in the interview, the next step is to formulate questions that will assess these qualifications in applicants. There are four basic types of interview questions: closed-ended, open-ended, behavior-description, and situational. Effective interviews involve a balance of open-ended, behavior-description, and situational questions. (Examples of each type of question are shown in Figure 8.1.) Closed-ended questions, such as "Are you proficient in the use of Lotus Notes?" are generally not very useful. Interviews are more effective when applicants spend most of the time talking, whereas closed-ended questions encourage short, direct answers. If you really want a yes-or-no answer, why not ask the question on the application form?

Open-ended questions are designed to get applicants to expand on their job-relevant knowledge, skills, or experiences. Open-ended questions can be particularly effective at the beginning of an interview. They allow you to break the ice by asking nonthreatening questions that give an overall view of the applicant's background. However, it is still important that these questions be focused on the critical attributes identified in your Performance Attributes Matrix.

Situational and behavior-description interview questions can help to ensure that interviews are focused on job-related qualifications. Both develop interview questions that focus on highly specific job requirements. Their primary difference is in how the questions are posed. Figure 8.2 provides examples of both types of questions.

Situational interviewing develops "what if" questions based on actual job situations. The preferred way to develop these questions is to use examples of actual job behaviors that are critical to success. These incidents are then used to develop hypothetical scenarios that applicants are asked to imagine themselves experiencing; applicants are evaluated on their description of how they would handle each situation.

Behavior-description interviewing asks applicants how they have actually behaved in similar situations in the past. Behavior-description

Figure 8.1. Examples of Structured Interview Questions and Sample Answers for Bar Manager.

Behavior-Description Question: Ability to control difficult situations

- Question: Can you give me an example of a time when you had to refuse service to several customers because they were intoxicated? (What was the situation?) (What did you do?) (What was the outcome?)
- Evaluation criteria:
  - Good: Took an authoritative stance; remained in control; helped customers relax; got customers away from other patrons; did not give in to customers.
  - Acceptable: Asked for help because he or she did not know how to deal with customer; agreed to let customer stay.
  - Poor: Got into fight or used physical force; lost control; kicked customer out without an explanation; served customer alcohol.

Situational Question: Ability to resolve conflicts

- Question: A customer complains that he was short-changed. The customer claims that he gave the bartender a $50 bill, whereas the bartender claims that he was given a $20 bill. What would you do?
- Evaluation criteria:
  - Good: Determines whether there is a $50 bill in the register. If not, explains to customer that since there is no $50 bill, customer must have been mistaken. If there is a $50 bill, asks bartender how he handled transaction (to see if bartender kept the customer's money off to the side while counting change). Unless bartender is certain he kept the customer's money aside, apologizes and refunds $30 to customer. Otherwise, explains situation to customer; if customer is upset, offers gift certificate. Speaks to bartender afterward about correct change-making procedures.
  - Acceptable: Determines whether there is a $50 bill in the register. If there is, provides apology and refund if it's a regular customer or if customer does not appear to be intoxicated.
  - Poor: Makes snap decision without evaluating situation. Fails to talk to bartender about how to avoid errors in future.

Open-ended Question: Prior experience

- Question: Describe your prior experience managing a restaurant or bar. What type of establishment was it?

- Evaluation criteria:
  - Good: Minimum one year of experience. Worked in popular bar, with a young crowd, that was crowded at least three nights a week (assuming that this is the type of bar for which the person is being interviewed). Managed both day and night shifts.
  - Acceptable: Less than one year experience. Worked in a quiet bar, with older customers and few large, boisterous crowds. Worked only day shift.
  - Poor: Did not have experience closing bar or performing inventory control. Only worked as assistant manager.

Figure 8.2. Examples of Situational and Behavior-Description Interview Questions.

Situational Questions

- "What would you do if an irate customer demanded a cash refund but did not have a receipt for a product he or she no longer wanted?"
- "How would you respond to an employee who accuses a fellow employee of theft?"
- "It's 3 P.M. and you have a report due to your manager at 5 o'clock. Suddenly a major client calls and says that they have a crisis and need your immediate help. What do you do?"
- "You're working a skeleton shift when you discover smoke coming from an electrical generator. What steps do you take, and in what order?"

Behavior-Description Questions

- "Think of a situation in which you were part of a team and another team member refused to pull his or her weight. Describe the situation. What did you do? What was the outcome?"
- "Please describe a situation in which attention to detail was very important. What did you do to focus your attention and minimize errors? How effective was it?"
- "An important part of this job is selling people on your ideas. Can you describe an example of how you persuaded someone to accept your point of view? What, exactly, did you do to accomplish this?"
- "Think of a case in which you missed a deadline. What caused you to miss the deadline? What happened as a result?"

interviewing is based on the commonsense notion that past behavior is generally a good predictor of future behavior. Job applicants who can describe specific instances of having solved difficult customer service problems on prior jobs, for example, are likely to do so again in the job for which they're being hired.

Behavior-description interviews usually include questions that pertain to:

- Prior work experience that is either directly or indirectly related to the job being recruited for
- Job-relevant interpersonal experiences
- Educational experiences

Separate questions are usually developed for applicants who have not had prior relevant work experience. For example, if you wish to determine the applicants' ability to work with irate customers, you might ask those who have had retail experience to describe a situation in which they had to work with a customer who was angry about the quality of a product. Applicants who have never worked in a retail setting might be asked to describe how they dealt with a friend who was angry because the applicant had not followed through on a commitment.

So far, research has not determined whether situational or behavior-description interviewing is better. Advocates of behavior-description interviewing contend that it is more difficult for applicants to lie about *specific* past behaviors than to make up favorable descriptions of what they would do in a hypothetical situation. Proponents of situational interviewing counter that behavior-description interviewing is too rigid. Because people can learn from their mistakes, examples of past behavior may not tell you how the applicant would handle a similar situation in the future. Moreover, some applicants may never have experienced a situation comparable to what you're asking, but they can still role-play how they would respond if they found themselves in that situation.

Our recommendation is to use a mix of open-ended, behavior-description, and situational questions in most interviews. Open-ended questions can be useful to open an interview, but they should be used sparingly—perhaps one or two in an interview. We suggest that a majority of the remaining questions be of the behavior-description type, to focus on the applicants' past success with similar performance requirements. Finally, you may want to add one or two situational questions, both to allow for a change of pace and to see how well applicants can think on their feet (assuming that this ability is relevant to the job).

Using Standardized Rating Scales

Most structured interviewing methods use a rating scale to score job applicants' answers to the interview questions. Giving applicants a separate score on each dimension assessed in the interview has the following advantages over the more common approach of forming an overall, subjective impression of a candidate and then using that "gut reaction" to decide whether or not to hire the applicant:

- Developing the rating scales provides another opportunity to think carefully about what you're looking for in a candidate. This is particularly true if you develop sample answers to guide your ratings, because it focuses attention on the behaviors that are essential to job performance, rather than on vague traits.
- Numerical ratings allow you to develop a formula to combine all the information you've obtained from interviews, tests, letters of reference, and other measures into an overall score for each applicant. As we discuss in Chapter Twelve, this increases both the efficiency and the effectiveness of your decision making.
- Numerical scoring systems make it easier to evaluate the effectiveness of the interview process. Aside from any legal requirements to validate hiring procedures (described in Chapter Five), you may want to determine how effective interviews are relative to other procedures. If you follow the principles of structured interviewing and maintain normal records, this should not be hard to do. By contrast, validating the simplistic "hire-reject" evaluations inherent in most unstructured interviews poses more formidable statistical obstacles.
- You can use the scored interviews to evaluate *interviewer* performance, too. If you use multiple interviewers, and if you hire enough people, you can use scored interview data to determine which of your interviewers are doing a good job of selecting high performers and which may need additional training.

Developing effective rating scales isn't a complicated process. The first requirement is a clear description of what attributes should form the basis for scoring an applicant's answers. For example, one of our clients wanted to hire sales representatives who exhibited a customer service orientation. They defined customer service as "listening to and understanding customers' needs and wishes in order to match these with [our services], rather than talking a customer into a standard package of [services]. A 'Customer Comes First' mentality."

The second requirement is some basis for assigning a numerical score to an applicant's answers. Some approaches use simple rating scales in which scores are labeled with adjectives like "excellent," "good," "fair," or "poor." Others involve rating the applicants' answers relative to those of others—for example, those in the top, second, middle, fourth, or last 20 percent of all candidates. The most widely recommended strategy is to include sample answers and their associated scores. With any of these approaches, you'll want to take notes about what the applicant says, and the rating forms should provide space to include examples or quotes to support the ratings assigned.

In sum, structured interviews provide the core of a high-impact hiring approach to employment interviewing. Figure 8.3 provides a summary of the advantages of structured interviews compared to more traditional approaches to interviewing. However, structured interviews are not the only step toward increasing the effectiveness of your interviews. In the remainder of this chapter, we discuss the importance of well-trained interviewers and the use of multiple interviewers.

Interviewer Training

Studies show that experienced job interviewers are not consistently better than inexperienced interviewers. This suggests that informal, on-the-job training in doing interviews isn't sufficient for high-impact hiring. Nor are run-of-the-mill interviewing workshops that emphasize universal approaches likely to be much help, for all the reasons we have already described. (Where do you think the "favorite animal" question came from?) Research-based training programs, which we recommend, typically emphasize five key principles in addition to using structured interviews.

Figure 8.3. Advantages of Structured Interviews.

- *Emphasize job-relevant qualifications.* This not only creates more reliable assessment but also enhances validity and provides a defense against discrimination charges.

- *Standardize treatment of applicants.* This ensures that all critical job requirements are assessed and that no nonrelevant (and illegal) factors are minimized.

- *Ensure that interviewers are aware of job requirements.* Often interviewers don't fully understand the performance requirements they are looking for in applicants.

- *Reduce the effects of coaching.* Most interviewing workshops coach job applicants in how to answer "generic" questions, whereas it's difficult to preplan answers to job-specific questions.

- *Reduce effect of biases.* This is done by focusing attention on job-relevant factors.

- *Encourage note-taking and use of rating forms.* This facilitates assessment of specific performance dimensions rather than overall judgments.

- *Encourage delay in making judgments.* This reduces reliance on first impressions and permits more careful analysis of all information about the applicant.

Principle 1: Make the Interview Process Comfortable

It is important to establish a comfortable environment for the interview, so that the interviewee is put at ease. "Stress" interviews, in which applicants are intentionally pressured, are rarely necessary and are likely to create strong feelings of resentment in most interviewees. Extra efforts may be needed for applicants who have little experience with the interviewing process, such as those who are just entering or reentering the workforce or who have been laid off from jobs that they've held for a long time, or those who may feel awkward because they are of a different gender, ethnicity, age range, or socioeconomic group than you are. Remembering how anxious you were at your last (or first) interview may help you to develop empathy for the applicant.

Learn the applicant's name and use it during the interview, making sure to pronounce it correctly. Introduce yourself and describe what you do and what your role is in the hiring process. It may also be helpful to describe the overall hiring process, including who else will be interviewing the applicant and how and when the final hiring decision will be made.

Some casual conversation to break the ice can be helpful. Try to pick a neutral, nonthreatening topic, such as a comment about the weather, the applicant's drive to the interview, or an item from current events, but avoid contentious topics like politics, religion, or sports. A follow-up icebreaker dealing with something from the applicant's résumé may be useful for making a transition into the "business" of the interview.

Giving applicants a preview of what the interview will involve can also help put them at ease, especially if they are not accustomed to structured interviews. If you plan to use behavioral interviews, let the applicants know this by explaining to them that you will be looking for answers that describe *actual examples* of past experience or behavior on the job. You will need to remind most applicants to describe examples from their past experience a number of times during the interview as they get used to what is probably a new type of interview for them. It may be helpful to explain how this approach is different from what they may be used to and why you find it to be effective. Also let them know that you will be taking notes to help jog your memory.

Let the tone of your voice and your body language communicate your interest in the applicants. Applicants are more likely to open up in interviews if you express sincere interest in what they're saying. Make the transition between questions sound as natural as possible, so the applicants don't feel as if you're mechanically following a checklist of questions.

Principle 2: Allow Plenty of Time

Plan to ask at least *two* questions relating to each of the performance attributes you hope to assess in the interview. More complex attributes may require more questions before you feel that you've really assessed the applicants' qualifications. Asking for examples of past behavior can also require a good deal of thought on the applicants' part, so be patient and allow them time to think of appropriate examples. Remember that the time spent interviewing is an investment in your company's success. You want to be sure to cover each of the qualifications you have targeted for the interview, as well as leaving time for questions the applicant may have and allowing at least ten minutes for opening and closing the interview. Studies show that interviewers who feel pressed for time make poorer hiring decisions, at least in part because they rely more on first impressions than on using the interview as a way to get new insights into an applicant.

Principle 3: Develop Good Listening Skills

Effective listening involves not only hearing what applicants say, but also how they say it and what they don't say. One key requirement for good listening is letting applicants do most of the talking. If you ask good questions that get applicants talking about their past work-relevant experience, this should be easy. For many of us, the hard part is *not interrupting the applicants.* You can't learn much about them if you don't let them talk! Really concentrating on what they're saying and how what they say relates to the requirements of the job doesn't leave you much time to talk, beyond asking follow-up questions. Effective listening is tiring, so it's wise not to schedule too many interviews and to allow enough time between interviews for scoring and for mentally recharging yourself.

Principle 4: Avoid Judgment Errors

A fourth key topic is how to avoid bias and judgment errors when evaluating an applicant's performance in an interview. Interviewer training usually involves a description of several types of judgment errors that are frequently found in interviews. These include:

- *Halo error:* rating an applicant similarly on all performance dimensions rather than recognizing areas of strength and weakness. An example would be noting that an applicant has good interpersonal skills and then assuming that she or he would also be highly motivated and conscientious.
- *Leniency, severity, and central-tendency errors:* ignoring differences in interview performance and giving *all* applicants high, low, or average ratings, respectively. This is mostly a problem if different interviewers have different standards.
- *Contrast effect:* giving an applicant higher-than-deserved ratings when he or she is interviewed immediately after a weak

candidate, or lower-than-deserved ratings when he or she is interviewed after a strong candidate.

- *Similarity effect:* giving higher ratings to applicants who are like you.
- *First-impression error:* forming a lasting overall reaction to job applicants based on first impressions.
- *Stereotyping:* assuming that all members of a group share characteristics thought to be typical of that group. For example, assuming that all engineers are poor communicators or that all accountants are introverted will frequently lead to poor hiring decisions.

Awareness of these errors may have some effect on reducing them, but the most effective strategy is to emphasize the interviewees' job-related behavior and to have a consistent, standardized scoring system for evaluating answers. Halo error is perhaps the most pernicious of the errors. It may help to remember that most people are better at some things than others, and that few people are all good or all bad. If you find yourself getting a one-sided view of an applicant, probe to see if there's another side of the person that you're missing.

One way to think about rating applicants is to use an analogy to an accounting balance sheet. All companies have both assets and liabilities. What's crucial is the net balance between them, the company's net worth. In hiring, you want to hire applicants who have higher, rather than lower, "net worths." This means that you need to get an accurate assessment of their job-related assets and liabilities; everyone has both. When you are interviewing, you need to be like a good accountant or auditor and focus on making a fair and accurate assessment of assets and liabilities. The time for toting up the balance sheet is not when you are in the midst of doing your valuation.

Principle 5: Practice and Receive Feedback

As with any skill training, gaining knowledge through methods like reading this book is only the first step. To become proficient at interviewing, you need to practice the key skills and get feedback on how well you're doing. Plan some time for practice and feedback as part of your next round of interviews. Start by working with your colleagues in developing the structured interview for the position. Then, if several people will be conducting interviews, practice interviewing each other. After the practice interview, the interview "subject" should provide feedback to the interviewer. If you are the only person doing the interviewing, practice interviewing and getting feedback from a current incumbent of the position or of a similar position. If you are the sole professional or owner of a small business, ask a colleague outside your organization to help you, and return the favor.

Group Interviews and Multiple Interviewers

When the topic of bias comes up, whether in selection interviews or performance appraisals, one of the first suggestions is usually to use multiple raters. Averaging the judgments of multiple interviewers is assumed to cancel out errors, including the effects of individual biases. A second assumed advantage is that it will be easier for multiple interviewers to remember what interviewees have said. The result should be a more thorough assessment of the interviewees. On the other hand, using multiple interviewers increases costs and extends the time required to make a hiring decision.

Whether or not group interviews are effective depends on how they are used. Research shows that individual interviews are more accurate than "board" interviews, in which multiple interviewers simultaneously interview an applicant.[16] But there may be advantages to having multiple interviewers conduct *separate* interviews and then pooling their information. This may be particularly beneficial if the interviewers divide the set of interview questions so that each interviewer has a particular domain to cover, as well as including some common questions to allow comparisons.

Pooling of information from multiple interviewers is only effective if each person brings a unique contribution to the final hiring decision. For instance, group interviews should be more effective when interviewers are diverse in their perspectives and experience. As an example, the unique contributions women can make to a male-dominated profession are more likely to be noted if at least one of a group of interviewers is a woman.

Another important consideration is how the information from the multiple interviewers is combined. Two common approaches are:

1. Multiple individual interviews followed by a group meeting to discuss and then vote on the applicant
2. Multiple individual interviews in which interviewers make an independent evaluation of the applicant prior to or without a group meeting

We recommend using the latter approach. (A third potential alternative, a single interview session attended by multiple interviewers, is probably the prototype for the "board" interviews that, as explained earlier, have been found to be no more valid than individual interviews.) Having interviewers make independent decisions *before* meeting as a group should result in less conformity and more useful integration of the different perspectives. For example, we know of one company that uses multiple interviewers for many hiring decisions. After all the interviewers have had time to talk to the candidate, a group meeting is held and the first step in the meeting—before any discussion is allowed—is a "thumbs up, thumbs down" test. This requires people to independently evaluate the information they collected in their interviews and commit themselves to a position. The information is used, not as a formal vote, but as a starting point for a discussion, in which people are allowed to change their evaluation based on information shared by the other interviewers.

The key to effective group decisions is ensuring that the unique insights of individual decision makers are included in the final decision. When a group will be involved in a hiring decision, then, the following techniques should all help to improve both interviewing and the subsequent hiring decision:

• Using multiple, individual interviews
• Having interviewers rate applicants *prior* to meeting as a group
• Having the person in charge of the group meeting ensure that every participant's ideas are given attention and that no one, including the leader, dominates the group meeting
• Asking one person to act as a devil's advocate
• Holding a secret ballot following the discussion

We don't know at this time if the increased cost of holding a formal group meeting is justified by a significant improvement in the quality of the hiring decision. It may be that a more cost-effective approach is to simply average each interviewer's individual ratings without having the interviewers meet as a group, particularly if the interviewers substantially agree.

Summary: Increasing the Effectiveness of Interviewing

The effectiveness of your interviewing can be increased in the following ways:

1. *Determine the purpose of the interview.* Is your primary purpose to assess the qualifications of applicants, provide a realistic job preview, sell the job to the candidate, or tell the world more about your company? While each of these may be worthwhile activities, they require different emphases in the interview. If your primary purpose is to assess applicants' qualifications, emphasizing other functions will interfere with good hiring decisions.

2. *Ask about only a few key job qualifications.* Make a list of the necessary job qualifications before you start planning the interview. From this list, choose only the qualifications that are best assessed in an interview; the remaining requirements can be assessed with other hiring tools. Plan to ask at least two questions about each job qualification being targeted in the interview, but no more than ten questions in a one-hour interview.

3. *Use a structured interview format.* Limiting yourself to your list of qualifications to be assessed in the interview, develop interview questions that pertain to job-related attributes. The questions should ask either about past behavior that is relevant to the job or about how applicants would behave in hypothetical future job situations. Avoid questions that ask about broad traits, that give applicants too much latitude to fake a desirable answer, or that are not directly related to key job requirements.

4. *Limit use of preinterview information.* To minimize the creation of first impressions that may "contaminate" the initial interview, limit your review of applicant information before the interview to information that is absolutely necessary in order to conduct

a thorough interview. Be particularly careful not to form any initial impressions on information that is unreliable or piecemeal; this information, if it is critical and job-related, can always be verified after you form an impression of the applicant based on job-related interview data.

5. *Create a relaxed interviewing environment.* Put the applicant at ease initially with small talk, followed by an overview of what the interview will entail. Allow plenty of time for the interview, and let the applicant do as much of the talking as possible. Convey the message that you are willing to invest time and effort to find employees who will be a good match for your firm.

6. *Develop a system for scoring interviews.* Be clear in your mind what you are looking for in your questions and then allow time during or after the interview to evaluate the applicants' answers. Formal rating scales based on the qualifications being assessed are most effective, especially if they include sample answers.

7. *Evaluate applicants' strengths and weaknesses on specific dimensions, not their overall suitability.* Overall impressions are too vulnerable to bias and are often affected by factors that are irrelevant to job performance.

8. *Don't make hiring decisions during the interview.* These should be based on a thoughtful analysis of all the information about applicants, not just the information from the interview.

9. *Train interviewers.* If it is appropriate to your situation (for example, if you have multiple interviewers or do a lot of hiring), consider a training program that provides interviewers with information and practice, as well as feedback, concerning structured interviews and the effects of bias. If your resources are more limited, work with another person, such as an incumbent of the position you're interviewing for, to practice developing and conducting structured interviews and making ratings.

10. *Evaluate the success of your interviewing.* While a formal validation program may not be necessary, keeping track of the success of your hires, and of the specific predictions you made as a result of your interviewing, can help you to determine if you need to work further on improving your interviews. Tracking the relative performance of multiple interviewers can also be an effective quality assurance tool, as can periodic postrecruitment surveys of job applicants to gain their insights into the hiring process.

Chapter Nine

Using Employment Tests Effectively

People—both job applicants and employers—have mixed feelings about tests. One of the reasons that testing during hiring is so popular in the United States is that it fits well with our culture's emphasis on fairness and recognizing accomplishment. Most employers pay homage to the notion that hiring should be based on competence or potential for performance, and that hiring decisions should be unbiased and fair. Tests are frequently proposed as an ideal means for providing accurate, objective data, untainted by the personal biases of interviewers or decision makers, to guide these decisions. Applicants and managers alike should benefit, according to testing advocates, from the objectivity and precision of employment tests.

On the other hand, most people have had at least one bad experience with tests—in school, if not when applying for a job. One of us (Rosse) remembers being turned down for one of the first jobs he applied for as a teenager because of the score he received on an employment test. Many of us may harbor personal doubts, or even animosity, toward testing. These doubts are sometimes confirmed by blatant misuse of tests in selection systems.

One of our colleagues recently related an excellent example of how testing can be misused, even with the best of intentions on the part of the employer. In this case, a printing company had been using a test that assessed each applicant's ability to make accurate measurements, add fractions, do mental division, and so forth. Since the tests were being used to hire typesetters, whose work involved these skills, there was a sound rationale for believing that the test would be job-related. After a few years, a secretary with no experience or training in human resources and hiring began administering the hiring process. A persuasive test salesman of dubious ethics convinced her that what she really needed for hiring was a personality test, which had little validation data for any job, much less for this job. She began administering the test to applicants, and gradually it replaced the math test altogether.

After a few years, managers began to notice a decline in the quality of the typesetters and an increase in turnover, so they called in our colleague to validate the personality measure. What our colleague found was fascinating. Among the various dimensions of the inventory, only one dimension was predictively valid, and because of the way in which it was being used, it possessed *negative* validity: people who scored high on the test left the company more quickly. Not only did the company lose the value of the test that measured job-related math ability, but it actually would have been better off hiring randomly rather than hiring based on the scores from the personality inventory.

The important point of this story is not merely that tests can be misused. That is true of all kinds of hiring practices, although the apparent sophistication of tests may make it easier to overlook the mischief. Had the company continued to use the test of job-relevant mathematical ability, all would have been fine. The key, as with any other set of tools, is to pick the right kind of tool for the right job, select well-designed and well-made tools, and learn to use them effectively and appropriately.

Employment tests are certainly among the most effective hiring tools available to employers. Properly selected and wisely used, tests can be an important part of your high-impact hiring system. We want to take the mystery out of choosing and using tests, as well as to dispel the notion that tests are only for huge organizations with sophisticated testing operations. In this chapter you will learn more about different kinds of employment tests, when each may be appropriate, and how to use them as one component of your high-impact hiring strategy.

What Is a Test and Why Would You Want to Use One?

Testing experts Moshe Zeidner and Robert Most define a test as "any systematic procedure in which a person is presented with a uniform set of . . . tasks, questions, or problems intended to solicit particular responses, which are then scored and interpreted according to a specified criterion or performance standard."[1] Let's consider three key elements in this definition and why they are important to using tests according to high-impact hiring principles:

1. *Tests are systematic, or standardized.* Unlike traditional unstructured interviews or reference-checking questions, all applicants are treated alike by a test. The test and its scoring key neither know nor care whether the test taker is white or black, young or old, male or female; there is no room for idiosyncratic bias when evaluating the results of such a test. (We will discuss in a later section of this chapter the possibility that tests are biased against racial minorities.) Unlike interviews, tests produce results that aren't affected by an interviewer's being tired, sick, or grumpy. Well-designed tests that are administered properly provide essentially the same experience to all applicants, time after time. As long as tests are both developed and chosen to assess job-relevant attributes, standardization should increase your odds of making good hiring decisions by eliminating sources of unreliability in your information.

2. *Tests consist of a carefully selected set of items.* The process of developing an employment test begins with carefully defining what the test is supposed to measure and then writing items that provide a representative sample of this content domain. Substantial work goes into both defining and sampling what the test is supposed to measure and refining the items into the smallest number of questions that will provide a reliable, valid, and unbiased measurement. The resulting test must then be administered to samples of people to determine typical scores, called *norms,* and to verify that it actually predicts the criteria it was designed to predict, such as job performance. With all this work, the development time for a quality commercially published test can easily take three to five years. The payoff is a high degree of confidence that the test actually measures what it was designed to measure. You can't have the same confidence in a test when corners have been cut in this process. That's why a key foundation for selecting and using tests effectively is understanding how to differentiate well-designed tests from the rest.

3. *Tests are scored according to some standard.* As we describe in Chapter Twelve, explicit scoring of hiring tools provides a number of advantages. Scoring is particularly easy with tests, since well-developed tests include scoring keys that have been designed and tested to provide the optimal scoring of each item. In many cases, standardized tests also include norms that can be used to interpret scores.

These three characteristics of effective tests are important characteristics of any high-impact hiring tool. You will find it worthwhile—and enlightening—to compare all of your hiring tools to these three characteristics of tests. The *Guidelines on Employee Selection Procedures,* used by the EEOC and the courts to evaluate hiring procedures, consider all employment procedures to be tests, so the comparison is a useful one. Structured interviews, as we describe them in Chapter Eight, meet all the standards that define a test: they are relatively standardized, use a set of questions designed to sample a particular job-related content domain, and are systematically scored according to some standard. That's precisely why the validity of structured interviews is so much better than that of unstructured interviews and so near that of employment tests. Remembering the care with which good tests are developed and trying to apply a similar level of diligence to other hiring tools is a key to high-impact hiring.

Types of Employment Tests

All sorts of tests have been written for all kinds of purposes. In this chapter we focus on the tests that are most commonly used in hiring contexts. These include tests of:

- Mental and physical abilities
- Job knowledge
- Personality
- Occupational interests

The next two chapters describe aspects of high-impact hiring in which other kinds of tests play a role. Performance tests, including work samples and simulations, are described in Chapter Ten.

As part of helping you to "select out" candidates with "negative performance," we will discuss the use of integrity, honesty, and drug tests in Chapter Eleven.

It's important to understand the different types of employment tests in the context of building a comprehensive system of hiring tools. You sometimes will hear claims made that one kind of test can solve all your hiring problems by predicting everything you need to know about an applicant's performance. We prefer a more balanced approach that fits the right tool to the right job, and that recognizes the importance of developing a well-rounded understanding of job applicants.

Tests of Mental Abilities

Mental ability—also commonly referred to as cognitive ability, intellectual ability, or simply intelligence—describes a person's capacity to learn, reason, and problem-solve. Mental ability tests were originally developed to measure students' ability to learn in school, though research has subsequently shown that they can be effective for predicting performance on jobs ranging from extremely simple assembly tasks to intellectually demanding professional and managerial jobs. The National Football League even uses cognitive ability tests to help select football players.[2] It's not surprising that mental ability is important for performance in school, but why should it be so relevant to job performance?

Industrial psychologist Jack Hunter argues that there are two reasons for this.[3] One is that knowledge is as relevant to job performance as it is to academic performance, and people who score highly on mental ability tests also tend to have a better understanding of job-relevant knowledge. Being familiar with all the nuances of Plato's *Republic* may not be essential for many jobs, but being able to read quickly and accurately and then make reasoned judgments based on your understanding of what you read often is. Similarly, mail clerks need to know enough geography and history to realize that New Mexico is part of the United States, not Mexico. (Many don't!)

The other reason that mental ability is important has to do with on-the-job learning and performance. Employees with greater mental ability are quicker and more accurate on cognitively demanding tasks, are better able to prioritize, can more readily innovate and adapt rules to unexpected circumstances, and can more effectively learn new material as changes occur.[4] Don't these sound like things you've been looking for in your employees?

As testing specialist Gerald Rose points out, it really shouldn't be surprising that ability tests predict job performance.[5] Cognitive ability tests measure what is taught in schools: the Three Rs of reading, writing, and arithmetic, plus reasoning. Schools around the world emphasize these skills for a good reason: they're fundamental to success in life and work. Therefore, measuring differences in applicants' skills in these basic life competencies is a fundamental part of most hiring systems.

General Versus Specific Mental Abilities

There has been a great debate over whether mental ability should be thought of as an overall ability or as sets of specific abilities. Do you want to hire generally smarter employees, or those with strengths in particular abilities? Nearly a century's worth of research clearly shows that intelligence is made up of many different components; a simple breakdown includes verbal, mathematical, memory, and reasoning components. People who are good on one dimension tend to be good on the others as well; this also applies to those who do poorly. As a result, tests of cognitive ability often include items from many different dimensions, but then report only an overall score, such as the widely known IQ score.

Which approach is best when using mental ability tests in making hiring decisions? So far, research suggests that overall measures of cognitive ability are most efficient in the majority of cases.[6, 7] They seem to work as well as or better than composites of tests measuring specific abilities, and they rest on research showing that basic cognitive ability is necessary for nearly all jobs. For example, the Wonderlic Personnel Test is a widely used employment test that provides an overall general mental ability score.

On the other hand, many authorities feel that all the evidence is not in on this issue. Many employment tests focus on more specific abilities, and we will be describing some of these tests and how to use them effectively. Along with having the capability to select tests specific to a job, you may find it much easier to explain the use of more specific tests to other people, including job candidates and juries who are skeptical about the use of employment tests. It should not be difficult to justify the use of numerical aptitude tests for cashiers or drafters, tests of verbal comprehension for editors, or tests of memory and deductive reasoning for detectives. Multiple-ability test batteries such as the Basic Skills Tests and the Employee Aptitude Survey, both published by Psychological Services, Inc., or The Psychological Corporation's Differential Aptitude Tests include measures for these and other specific cognitive abilities.

Testing Other Critical Abilities

Purely mental abilities are by no means the only focus of effective employment tests. Industrial psychologist Edwin Ghiselli categorized ability tests as either intellectual, perceptual, psychomotor, or spatial-mechanical. He found that the importance of each type tended to vary among different occupations.[8] Although general mental ability was relevant to nearly all jobs, the following abilities were often equally or even more predictive of success for particular jobs.

Perceptual ability involves the capacity to accurately detect and interpret "environmental stimuli." An example of a perceptual ability that has long been found to be critical for clerical jobs and jobs in crafts and the trades is perceptual speed and accuracy, which describes the ability to see details quickly and accurately. It is measured by a number of specific ability tests, such as the Forms Checking test from the Basic Skills Test, the Visual Speed and Accuracy test from the Employee Aptitude Survey, or the Name Finding Test from the Hay Aptitude Test Battery.

Tests of *psychomotor abilities* measure bodily movements that involve close coordination of muscular and brain activity. Hand-arm steadiness, reaction time, and manual dexterity are common examples of psychomotor abilities. They are somewhat akin to tests of *physical abilities,* such as measures of physical strength or sensory acuity (for example, vision and hearing). Tests of psychomotor and physical abilities often require both special equipment and individual assessment; as a result they have not been as widely used as paper-and-pencil tests of mental or perceptual abilities.

Another example of a specific ability with extensive use in employment testing is *mechanical ability*. Mechanical ability reflects an understanding of how basic mechanical and physical forces affect everyday life, for example, how gears, levers, and pulleys work. Some tests of mechanical ability, such as the Bennett Mechanical Comprehension Test, measure only this basic understanding of principles, whereas others also measure such psychomotor and perceptual abilities as manual dexterity, visual acuity, and spatial relationships. As you might expect, mechanical ability is a particularly good predictor of performance in trade and industrial occupations.

Tests of Job Knowledge

Tests may also assess a person's *knowledge* of specific information needed for a job; this is the same type of test most of us recall from our school years. The key distinction between ability tests and knowledge tests is that the former measure very general knowledge, which is used to estimate an applicant's ability to learn and apply knowledge in general. An employer hiring an English major to be a sales representative probably doesn't care about the applicant's knowledge of English literature. Rather, the employer hopes that the applicant's ability to learn about literature indicates a similar ability to learn about the company's products and sales techniques.

Knowledge tests, on the other hand, are designed to measure applicants' familiarity with specific information they will need on the job. Unlike ability tests, knowledge tests are appropriate when applicants must possess a particular body of knowledge at the time they are hired, rather than learning it on the job. Licensing exams are an example of knowledge tests, as are standardized tests of basic literacy. Similarly, "trade tests" assess the specific knowledge expected of journeymen plumbers, electricians, machinists, and the like. We will have more to say about these kinds of assessments as we discuss performance tests in Chapter Ten.

Personality Inventories

Personality can be thought of as the set of personal characteristics, or traits, that explain why people behave fairly consistently in different situations. For example, some people are generally pleasant, helpful, and tactful in their interactions with others, whereas other people tend to be rude, inattentive to others' needs, and cranky. Psychologists refer to this trait as *Agreeableness*. Similarly, some people are generally calm and even-headed even in the face of stress, whereas others are moody and chronically anxious. This reflects differences in the trait of *Emotional Stability*. As you might expect, these differences in ways of approaching life also show up as differences in job behavior, and they can sometimes make a huge difference in the work effectiveness of two workers with the same level of ability and knowledge. For example, work researchers have found that Agreeableness and Emotional Stability affect employees' ability to work in teams, provide customer service, and tolerate stress.

How important is personality compared to factors such as ability and knowledge? Recent studies have suggested that it depends on what aspects of work performance you're talking about. Technical task performance—how well a person welds, writes code, or conducts an audit—is usually best predicted by abilities and experience. But for more interpersonal tasks, such as providing leadership or working with customers, personality factors play a more important role. Personality differences are also a more significant factor than cognitive abilities when it comes to indirect contributors to work performance, such as going out of your way to help a customer or being a good team player. Finally, personality is also particularly important for predicting counterproductive behaviors, such as workplace violence, theft, or on-the-job substance use, which we will discuss in more detail in Chapter Eleven.

Like cognitive abilities, personality has many dimensions. Unlike cognitive abilities, however, there may not be a general personality dimension that is relevant for all jobs. Therefore, it is essential to give some careful thought to what kinds of personality dimensions are relevant for predicting performance in the particular job for which you are hiring.

Thousands of personality traits have been proposed, and different personality inventories measure different subsets of these traits. However, recent research shows that most of these traits can be summarized in about five (some would say up to eight) basic dimensions. These dimensions are briefly summarized in Table 9.1. Because personality traits are named with words that are also used in common speech, psychologists follow the practice of capitalizing the title of a trait (such as Conscientiousness) to differentiate it from more general use of the same word. We'll follow that practice here.

Table 9.1. The Five Factor Model of Personality.

Dimension	Descriptors
Conscientiousness	Organized, systematic, thorough, practical, neat, efficient, careful, hardworking, achievement-striving, persistent
Emotional Stability/ Adjustment	Not being anxious, moody, temperamental, emotional, nervous, depressed, touchy, fearful
Agreeableness/ Likability	Kind, cooperative, sympathetic, warm, trustful, considerate, pleasant, helpful
Extraversion	Talkative, assertive, verbal, energetic, bold, active, daring
Openness to Experience/ Intellectance	Unconventional, open to new ideas, questioning, curious, creative, imaginative

Research most consistently links work performance with the *Conscientiousness* dimension of personality.[9] This makes sense when you consider that some experts prefer to think of this dimension in terms of two underlying factors, called Achievement and Dependability. Achievement is the tendency to work hard, set performance goals, and persist—what might be termed a positive work ethic. Dependability refers to being disciplined, organized, and accepting of authority. Achievement tends to be correlated with task performance, while low scores on Dependability often predict problem behaviors at work.

A number of experts feel that *Agreeableness* and *Emotional Stability* are also relevant to most jobs.[10] Some have even argued that the combination of Conscientiousness, Agreeableness, and Emotional Stability represents a general personality factor that is equivalent to general cognitive ability in its relevance to all jobs.[11] While that may overstate the case, Agreeableness and Emotional Stability seem reasonably related to performance in many jobs. Team-based work, for example, depends on at least minimally acceptable levels of agreeableness and cooperation, and Emotional Stability is a reasonable requirement for jobs involving stress. Anxious, whining, fault-finding, or generally cranky employees not only are likely to be ineffective, but may also inhibit the performance of others with whom they work.

The job relevance of *Extraversion* is more controversial. Although it does not appear to predict job performance in general, it may be relevant for sales and managerial positions.[12-14] This is particularly true if Extraversion is defined in terms of being appropriately forceful, persuasive, and energetic rather than simply in terms of being outgoing and friendly.[15] (This is an example of the importance of testing job-related characteristics. Persuasiveness is more job-related for such positions than mere friendliness.) Extraversion—in combination with Emotional Stability and Conscientiousness—is a component of most measures of customer service orientation.[16]

The final dimension of personality, *Openness to Experience,* is less clearly related to job performance. Employees who are high on this dimension are more open to new ideas and may thus fit better in jobs requiring creativity and an open mind. Being tolerant and nonconforming also seems to play at least a minor role in predicting success in sales positions.[17] Employees who score low on Openness to Experience may be better suited to tedious and detail-oriented work.

It's important to realize that all of these are dimensions of so-called normal personality. They describe different styles that people use in responding to life situations, rather than the neurotic or dysfunctional personality styles measured by clinical psychologists and psychiatrists. One style may be more effective in some situations and another more effective in others.

Measures of Occupational Interests

People also differ in the types of work they are attracted to. Occupational-interest inventories ask about the kind of work and leisure activities you prefer, rather than asking about how you generally behave. Occupational preferences predict what kinds of jobs people choose and how satisfied they are with their occupations. When combined with measures of what a person is capable of doing, interest inventories can help to produce a better fit between applicants and jobs.

Interest inventories have generally not played a significant role in hiring, mainly because they measure what people *like* to do rather than what they *can* do. A person may very much want to be a musician, but that is of little consequence to a symphony orchestra if the person has not had musical training. Instead, interest inventories have typically been used for career counseling. Students who are unsure of their occupational plans may find it helpful to know that their interests are very similar to the interests of accountants, artists, or entrepreneurs. Knowing that they are likely to enjoy a particular occupation, they can then plan to acquire the necessary skills to be competent as well as satisfied in their career.

This same approach can be used for selection or placement decisions. You generally want to hire an employee who not only is technically competent but also will be satisfied and not quit prematurely. Effective performance is a function of both abilities and motivation, and interest inventories may be one way of assessing motivational fit. For example, Robert Hogan and his associates studied two jobs for which technical fit was very carefully screened: U.S. Navy explosive ordnance disposal divers and police officers.[18] They found that mismatches in employee interests and occupational demands were responsible for most of the attrition from the diver training program and for performance problems among the police officers.

A practical problem with using interest inventories for selection is that most of the questions are transparent: applicants can determine which answers would make them look most suitable for a particular job. Transparency is less of a problem if the interest inventory is being used for *placement* purposes. For example, seasonal employers must hire large numbers of applicants at a particular time. This kind of hiring often involves hiring any applicant who meets the very general guidelines for employment, rather than the more typical matching of applicants to a particular job. In fact, in many cases employers in a competitive labor market cannot afford to turn down any "qualified" applicants. Here, the critical task is deciding which of the many jobs needing to be filled is best suited to each applicant. Turnover is often a problem in these jobs, partly because the placement and matching process is generally done on a haphazard basis. Assessing new employees' interests after they have been hired, when the employees have less motivation to respond untruthfully, may be an effective technique for improving the quality of job matches.

Tests You Don't Want to Use

So far we've described four categories of tests that are widely used to help guide hiring decisions. Within these categories of tests, you are likely to find a range of quality; we'll present guidelines at the end of this chapter that will help you to identify the tests that are more likely to be effective. But some categories of tests are uniformly poor in quality, and we recommend that you avoid them. We refer to these tests as "Black Magic" hiring tools because they rely on superstition and anecdotes rather than scientific evidence of effectiveness. Current Black Magic favorites include tools that base hiring decisions on graphology (handwriting analysis), astrological projections, and "face analysis," though other wacky ideas spring up on a regular basis.

One common characteristic of Black Magic hiring tools is a reliance on pseudoscientific jargon and "theories." Astrologers, for example, have developed an extensive lexicon and convoluted explanations for why the alignment of heavenly bodies affects our daily lives. Graphologists often speak with equal certainty about the way that various arcane characteristics of people's handwriting can provide insight into their psyches. The first step in evaluating these techniques is to strip through the jargon and ask yourself if the underlying explanations make any sense. In many cases, they don't.

Another common characteristic of Black Magic hiring tools is that they provide very general descriptions or predictions. These "Barnum statements," named after the famed showman who proclaimed that a sucker is born every minute, are purposely designed to be almost certainly true of everyone who reads them. Take a minute to look at today's paper and read your horoscope; it's probably pretty "accurate," right? Now look at the horoscopes for the other signs. The odds are that they are at least as descriptive of you—and of everyone else. The same technique is used when vendors invite you to take a personality test, have your handwriting analyzed, or have a numerological analysis performed. The report is likely to be written in such a way that you have to agree that it sounds a lot like you, but that tells you little or nothing about whether the tool will be useful for making hiring decisions.

The key high-impact hiring issue is whether the information from a hiring tool is really valid for predicting success on the job.

Proponents of Black Magic procedures cite "evidence" that is based on personal testimonials or anecdotes rather than scientific studies. These anecdotes are often so vaguely described that it is impossible to determine what other factors were at play that might explain the positive results, or even to determine if the results were really as positive as they are portrayed. For example, the apparent validity of polygraphs (lie detectors) is due more to the stressful interviews polygraphers use and the fact that these interviews are structured than to the fancy machinery. Well-designed experiments control for alternative causes and use large, random samples to provide credible results. These kinds of studies have so far failed to provide evidence that such Black Magic hiring procedures as astrology, graphology, or polygraphy predict job performance at any better than chance levels.

To Test or Not

Tests are probably the most controversial of hiring tools. Few managers even think about whether or not to use application forms or interviews (though we hope you will now think considerably about how to use them most effectively), and about the only debate regarding reference checking is whether the information you obtain is worth the time and effort required to get it. But when it comes to testing, opinions are varied, and often strong. A brief review of the history of employment testing will show that interest in testing has waxed and waned over the years and may also illustrate why testing has been so controversial.

A Brief History of Employment Testing

The application of testing to employment can be traced to military uses in World Wars I and II. The military services were faced with the daunting task of sorting through vast numbers of enlistees in a very short time, in order both to screen out those who were unsuitable and to place enlistees in the positions for which they were best suited. They turned to industrial psychologists for help, and the result was the development of some of the first standardized tests designed for large-scale group administration.

Following both wars, employers faced a situation similar to that faced by the military only a few years earlier: an influx of former soldiers returning to jobs in a quickly expanding economy. It is hardly surprising that they learned from the military's experience and turned to testing specialists for help. Especially with the more specialized test batteries developed during the Second World War, the use of testing to select and classify new hires grew exponentially.

Testing began to receive more criticism in the late 1950s and 1960s. Tests were accused of measuring only superficial characteristics and of being unable to represent the "whole" individual. With their emphasis on standardized scoring and single correct answers, tests were challenged as screening out creative people. Those that measured applicants' personalities, in particular, were argued to represent unwarranted invasions of applicants' privacy. Perhaps the most damning criticism was that testing was overused, often with little thought to why the testing was necessary or whether a particular test was appropriate for the use to which it was being put. Such criticisms began a trend away from the use of testing in hiring.

Contributing to this trend was the passage of the Civil Rights Act of 1964. The employment-related sections of the Civil Rights Act were not intended to be "antitest"; in fact, the Act included an exemption for "professionally developed" tests used for hiring. The reason for the Act's effect on testing can be traced to regulatory agency and court challenges brought under the Act that happened to focus for many years on the inappropriate use of tests.

The most dramatic example was the landmark *Griggs* v. *Duke Power Company* decision, in which the Supreme Court ruled against the employer's use of an intelligence test on which minorities scored much lower than whites. The Court decided that the mere fact that a test was "professionally developed" was not sufficient if its use had a disproportionate effect on a particular demographic group. Rather, the Court required a *clear business justification* for the test, including evidence that the test was job-related. Duke Power had neither established a clear rationale for using an intelligence test, such as by conducting a job analysis, nor shown that the test improved their hiring decisions. The test may have been appropriate and effective, but the company had no evidence to prove it. The only hard evidence was that the test had an adverse impact on black applicants.

The quarter-century since the *Griggs* decision has seen a continuing line of litigation and debate over extremely technical issues concerning the fairness of tests and how to prove their job-relatedness.

As a consequence, many employers, and their attorneys, have assumed that using tests is an invitation to be sued. Many employers also assume, incorrectly, that showing the validity of employment tests is more necessary or difficult than showing the validity of other hiring tools. The result has been a significant decline in the use of tests and, ironically, a corresponding increase in the use of more subjective hiring tools.

In recent years, however, testing has seen a resurgence of interest. A 1992 survey of nearly five hundred human resource directors found that 30 percent anticipated further growth in the use of employment tests.[19] A number of factors explain the increased interest in test use.

Realization That All Employment Tools Should Be Validated

Tests are not treated any differently from other hiring tools in the *Uniform Guidelines*. In fact, the *Guidelines* consider all hiring procedures (interviews, reference checks, prior performance records, work samples, and so forth) to be tests, and the same requirement to show job-relatedness applies if—and only if—any of the procedures have an adverse impact on applicants with protected characteristics.

Evidence That Tests Are Generally Job-Related

Once the Supreme Court affirmed that all hiring tools must meet the same standards of job-relatedness, the advantages of tests became more clear to employers. First, standardization of tests reduces inconsistent and biased treatment of job applicants. By contrast, a number of court decisions had blasted interviews that lacked consistency, demonstrated blatant bias, or failed to include balanced panels of majority and minority interviewers.[20] Second, researchers had begun to amass evidence that tests show considerable validity for predicting job performance across a wide variety of job, and that tests were generally among the most valid of hiring tools (see Table 6.3).

Evidence That Most Tests Are Fair to Minorities

The most crucial, and still controversial, change is evidence that tests are not intrinsically biased against applicants who are not middle-class whites. We can summarize this very technical debate with two key conclusions.

First, not all tests have an adverse impact on minorities. Adverse impact does not generally occur with use of personality, performance, drug, or integrity tests, or physical ability tests, except that women are likely to score lower as a group on many tests of physical strength, but it does occur for black and Hispanic applicants on cognitive ability tests.

Second, most tests that are valid for white applicants are also valid for nonwhite applicants, particularly the cognitive ability tests that have adverse impact. In other words, minority applicants who score lower on tests also tend to receive lower evaluations of job performance; therefore, using the tests to make hiring decisions is performance-related. Note, however, that these statements apply only to group averages. *Individual* members of different demographic groups may score much higher or lower than other members of their own or other groups. We will have more to say about the fair use of tests at the conclusion of this chapter.

Frustration with Alternatives to Testing

After years of relying almost exclusively on interviews, which are often poorly conducted, hiring managers have grown frustrated with their limitations. Managers know that they haven't been getting the quality employees they need, and successful managers are setting aside their preconceptions about testing to see if tests can provide an effective complement to interviews and other hiring tools. Tests are not the only answer, but they often represent the most reliable and cost-effective means of providing *part* of the information that goes into high-impact hiring.

Concerns with Testing

Up to this point, we've focused mainly on the advantages of including tests as part of your high-impact hiring system. Managers also have some legitimate concerns about using employment tests. We will discuss five of the most serious of these concerns: overreliance on test scores, discrimination, invasion of privacy, faking, and cost and efficiency.

Overreliance on Test Scores

One of the primary concerns is that the apparent objectivity and accuracy of tests may lead hiring managers to place too much reliance on them. Properly developed tests that are well matched to the needs of a job can be effective, but they are no more infallible than any other hiring tool. No test can predict a specific individual's future performance with complete certainty. Inflated claims by a test vendor that a test can do so are a sure sign of snake oil. If tests are used, they should be included as one part of your overall hiring plan, and the information from them should be evaluated in the context of all the other valid information you have about an applicant. Placing undue confidence in tests can be as bad as relying solely on interviews or any other hiring tool.

Mental ability tests, for example, measure some part of a person's previous exposure to and capacity for dealing with intellectual tasks. By themselves, they can't tell you what one candidate will actually do with that capacity on your job, compared with another candidate. By using such tests together with other tests and selection tools, you can get a more complete picture of what capabilities a candidate can bring to a job, and how and whether those capabilities will be used effectively to achieve performance. Job knowledge, interest, training, personality, and career and life changes all affect how someone performs on a job over a period of time. The more complete picture you get, the better job you can do at predicting what this performance is likely to be.

It is particularly important not to overemphasize scores on personality inventories. Personality guides behavior and therefore performance, but it does not determine it. For example, introverts can be as effective in social situations as extraverts; it just takes more effort on their part. Personality is more likely to affect behavior when external influences on behavior such as work rules, social expectations, and monitoring systems are less powerful. Only people with the most extreme personality styles will act inappropriately during job interviews, formal sales presentations, or other events in which social norms are clear and readily enforced. Personality is more likely to be relevant for predicting differences in behavior when employees have choices about how to behave, or when they feel that their behavior is not being monitored. Thus, even though Conscientiousness is relevant for both outside salespeople and bank tellers, it is more likely to predict the job performance of outside salespeople who work on their own from day to day.

It's also useful to remember that more is not always better when it comes to personality. For example, job applicants who are high on Conscientiousness may turn out to be too conventional and rule-bound for jobs requiring creativity.[21] Even in a job in which Agreeableness is important—for example, the job of sales manager—people with extremely high Agreeableness may find it difficult to set direction and quotas for the sales force; correct errors with salespeople, other managers, and customers; or even close a sale. Before interpreting the scores from a personality test, you need to ask yourself if there is a level beyond which more of a trait is no longer productive, or is even counterproductive. This is one of the reasons that it is important to validate your testing program to verify that the scores predict job performance in the manner you expected.

Discriminatory Effects of Testing

One of the most frequent concerns about testing is that it may be discriminatory. This is primarily a problem for tests of cognitive ability, not personality inventories or tests measuring specific skills or job knowledge. Racial differences in mean scores create a dilemma for employers who are concerned about turning away large numbers of nonwhite applicants. The "solution" used by many employers has been to avoid tests and instead use other hiring tools with less adverse impact, but also less validity. While this avoids one problem, it creates another: the potential for low-impact hiring.

Perhaps this can be seen more clearly when it is looked at from the perspective of the adverse impact against women created by physical ability tests. As a general rule, women have less physical strength than men. (Again, it is important to remember that there are plenty of exceptions, which is the reason for making hiring decisions based on careful analysis of individual, not group, characteristics.) Suppose that physical strength is important for the job; what might happen if you ignored differences in physical strength between men and women in order to avoid creating adverse impact against women? AT&T found out the answer to this when they instituted a special hiring program designed to recruit more women into the historically male-dominated telephone lineman's job: women failed the training program at much higher rates than men, and work injuries soared.

The high-impact hiring solution is to (1) recruit the highest-quality applicants, who are likely to be qualified applicants regardless of their ethnicity or gender; (2) use cognitive ability tests only when they are appropriate; and (3) use tests as only one component in the overall hiring decision. Other components with less adverse impact, such as structured interviews, personality inventories, well-designed background checks, and work simulations, will enhance the validity of the selection system and lessen the overall adverse impact of the ability tests. Adverse impact can also be reduced by using cognitive ability tests primarily to eliminate clearly unqualified applicants rather than to make fine distinctions between more qualified applicants. In other cases, it may be possible to reduce adverse impact by changing the way the work is done. For example, AT&T was able to redesign the lineman's position so that it required less physical strength.

Invasion of Privacy

Another concern—one that is particularly relevant to personality testing—is that testing is invasive of privacy. Modern inventories of normal personality designed for employment use no longer ask extremely invasive questions about toilet habits or sexual fantasies. Nevertheless, the whole purpose of personality testing is to learn about applicants' characteristic ways of thinking and behaving, and some applicants see such probing as unfair and illegitimate. As one upset job applicant put it, "You're hiring me for what I can do, not for what's in my mind."

From your perspective as an employer, you probably *are* hiring people for what's in their minds. Increasingly complex work requires employees to have the abilities and personality to grow and adapt as your business changes. The challenge is to convince applicants that the information you're gathering from the personality inventory, honesty test, reference checks, drug tests, and so forth is actually relevant to their work performance. A few key steps can go a long way toward this objective:

1. Make sure that personality inventories or any other hiring tools are used to measure only job-relevant traits. The Performance Attributes Matrix described in Chapter Two provides a sound basis for determining which personality traits are likely to be related to successful work performance.
2. Select personality inventories from developers who can document their test's ability to validly assess the critical traits.
3. Select personality inventories that will appear reasonable to applicants. Try to avoid tests with threatening titles, or those that include offensive or strange-sounding questions.

4. Explain that the purpose of the test is to match applicants with the jobs to which they are best suited, not to screen out "undesirable" people. No one benefits when applicants are placed in jobs where they are unproductive and unhappy. Job applicants need to be reassured that the testing is in their best interest as well as yours.

Cheating and Faking

One of the disadvantages of using standardized hiring tools is that applicants have the potential for obtaining the answer keys, or otherwise cheating. Labor unions, for example, have been known to coach their members on how to pass ability tests. Books are also available that provide hints on how to give the correct answers to personality tests and employment interviews.[22, 23] A number of steps can be taken to minimize the effects of cheating on ability, skill, and knowledge tests:

1. Provide a secure testing environment. Be sure that the person taking the test is really the applicant and not a "ringer." Most ability tests require an administrator to explain the test and monitor time; this person can also make sure that applicants are not involved in blatant forms of cheating.
2. Store test materials, particularly scoring keys, in a secure, locked location. If tests are administered on a personal computer, be sure that all relevant files are password-protected. Applicants' and employees' scores should be similarly secured to protect their privacy.
3. When available, use alternate forms of the test so that word of mouth from prior test takers will be less likely to influence a person's scores. Alternate forms are also useful if an applicant needs to retake a test for any reason.

Faking is generally a more serious issue than cheating for personality inventories and other measures of noncognitive abilities. If you are applying for a clerical position and are asked to complete a series of mathematics problems, your answer depends on whether or not you can add, subtract, multiply, and divide quickly and accurately. A much different situation occurs if you are applying for a job in public relations and are asked on a personality inventory if you prefer to be around people or to work alone. Since there is no easy way for the employer to verify your answer, you can choose whichever answer you prefer. And is there any doubt what the "correct" answer is for this job?

Not all questions on personality inventories are that obvious, but it's usually not hard to figure out which answer will make a job applicant more attractive. In fact, people often choose more "socially desirable" answers without even consciously trying to make themselves look good. It's perfectly natural to think of ourselves in positive terms and to want others to see us that way, too. This kind of normal self-enhancement isn't a serious problem, since most personality inventories are designed to take it into consideration. The problem comes when certain applicants intentionally distort their scores in a conscious attempt to provide the answers they think will get them a job. Fakers can thereby gain a big advantage over other applicants who are being more honest, and you're likely to find yourself with a far different set of new hires than you expected.[24, 25]

Faking is a difficult problem to avoid, but it may not be insurmountable. Here are some steps you can take to lessen the problem of faking:

1. Prevent faking by explicitly warning applicants that the test includes measures designed to detect faking, and that faking will affect their chances of being hired. Even a simple warning like this seems to reduce the incidence of faking.[26]
2. Control faking by using personality inventories that include built-in measures to detect and control for faking. These may be called validity, lie, social desirability, response distortion, or faking scales. Look particularly carefully at *all* the application materials of applicants who receive high scores on these scales.
3. You may also be able to reduce faking by using personality inventories with less transparent questions that make it more difficult to determine the correct answers. However, this is a tricky issue, because questions that are too subtle may backfire. Since the purpose and job-relatedness of subtle questions is not evident, applicants may consider them unnecessarily invasive of their privacy. Extremely subtle items also tend to be less valid for measuring the relevant traits.[27]

Cost and Efficiency

Many managers have concerns about the potential costs and efficiency related to testing. We understand this concern. You may have heard of detailed personality profiles that can cost several hundred dollars for each applicant. As in many other situations, though, the cost of an instrument has no necessary relationship to its value. The important consideration in deciding whether to use tests, and which tests to use, has to do with choosing tests that are effectively developed and valid for the job. We don't want to suggest that you need to make an extensive or expensive commitment to testing in order to realize benefits. Using the approach outlined in this chapter to add or improve testing in your selection process is almost certain to improve the quality of your hiring. You can begin by working with a small number of tests for selected jobs and use your experience and the results to determine how you want to use tests in the longer term.

As a general rule, tests provide a very favorable cost-benefit ratio, especially when compared with other selection tools. Measuring basic abilities that are common to many jobs allows economies of scale for test publishers; particularly for group-administered tests, the result can be extremely inexpensive hiring tools. Many basic ability tests cost less than five dollars and require less than ten minutes to administer. Personality inventories are often more lengthy and expensive, particularly if expert scoring and interpretation is provided. However, many inventories are still quite inexpensive compared to other hiring tools.

Using Tests Effectively

Tests are among the most difficult hiring tools for managers to work with on their own. Knowledgeable consultants can be invaluable in helping you to develop and successfully implement a testing program. The use of more specialized tests (usually measures of personality) may be restricted to psychologists or other testing professionals. In most other cases, you will probably not need to use the consultant on a regular basis once your testing program is established. Thus consultants, particularly those who are not specifically associated with a particular assessment tool, are often a cost-effective means of adding a testing component to your high-impact hiring system.

If you decide to work with a consultant, the knowledge of testing you gain from reading this book will help you to select a qualified one and work with him or her effectively. If you decide not to work with a consultant, you need to determine which of the critical performance attributes are appropriately measured with tests and select specific tests to use, as well as determining how to interpret and use the test scores. The remainder of this chapter is dedicated to covering these issues in enough detail to allow you to do this on your own. If you have decided that testing is not relevant to your situation, you may wish to skip the remainder of this chapter.

Identifying Potential Tests

Chapter Two described in detail the process of determining critical performance attributes for a job, and Chapter Six provided guidelines for determining which categories of hiring tools are most likely to be useful for assessing particular attributes. If this process indicates that tests should be included in your hiring system, the next step is to identify which particular tests are most appropriate. An expert consultant can be helpful in tackling the task of reviewing tests and matching them to the critical attributes for the job. If you prefer to do this on your own, a number of books are available that describe specific employment tests. *Tests: A Comprehensive Reference for Assessments in Psychology, Education, and Business*[28] provides a cross-referenced guide to more than three thousand tests, including information on what the tests are designed to measure, how much time they require to complete, how much they cost, and where they can be obtained. What *Tests* does not provide, however, is a critical review of the effectiveness of the tests. This kind of critical analysis can be obtained from *Test Critiques*[29] or the *Mental Measurements Yearbook*,[30] a volume of objective reviews published biennially and available at most university libraries. For more general information, *Practical Issues in Employment Testing*[31] provides a readable description of many of the issues involved in evaluating tests.

Another option for choosing tests may be to work with one or more of the major test publishers listed in Table 9.2. Although this list is nowhere near inclusive of all the publishers of testing materials,

Table 9.2. Selected Major Publishers of Employment Tests.

Publisher	Examples of Tests
Consulting Psychologists Press 3803 Bayshore Road Palo Alto, CA 94303 415-969-8901	Myers-Briggs Type Indicator Inventory Personnel Reaction Blank Strong Interest Inventory Wesman Personnel Classification Test
Hogan Assessment Systems, Inc. 2622 East 21st Street, Suite 14 Tulsa, OK 74114 800-756-0632	Hogan Personality Inventory
International Personnel Management Association 1617 Duke Street Alexandria, VA 22314 703-549-7100	IPMA Clerical, Library, Business Tests IPMA Fire Service Tests IPMA Police Service Tests
Psychological Assessment Resources P.O. Box 998 Odessa, FL 33556 800-331-8378	NEO Personality Inventory Self-Directed Search Dictionary of Holland Occupational Codes
The Psychological Corporation P.O. Box 839954 San Antonio, TX 78283 800-228-0752	Bennett Mechanical Comprehension Test Career Interest Inventory Minnesota Clerical Test Short Employment Test
Psychological Services, Inc. 100 West Broadway, Suite 1100 Glendale, CA 91210 818-244-0033	Basic Skills Tests Employee Aptitude Survey Professional Employment Test
Saville & Holdsworth, Ltd. 575 Boylston Street Boston, MA 02116 800-899-7451	Automated Office Battery Critical Thinking Test Occupational Personality Questionnaire Selling Skills Inventory Technical Test Battery Work Skills Series
Wonderlic Personnel Test, Inc. 1509 North Milwaukee Avenue Libertyville, IL 60048-1387 800-963-7542	Wonderlic Personnel Test Wonderlic Basic Skills Test Hay Aptitude Test Battery Employee Reliability Inventory Personal Characteristics Inventory

it does represent the larger houses that are more likely to have the experts on staff who can help you to determine which tests are most appropriate for your purposes. These in-house experts can be helpful, but always remember that (1) they must rely on you to conduct the work analysis that provides the rationale for selecting tests and (2) they have a vested interest in selling their own tests.

Evaluating Potential Tests

In Chapter Six we described four standards—accuracy, practicality, fairness, and legality—that form the basis for choosing or developing *any* hiring tool. These standards are particularly appropriate for purchasing tests or other standardized hiring tools. When you are purchasing a test, the publisher or developer of the test should be expected to provide information on how well the test meets these four criteria. Your choice among vendors should be primarily influenced by how well they score on these standards.

One of the key elements you are paying for in a hiring tool is the research and development that went into the instrument. A well-developed test has undergone years of work in which the test items were written carefully to measure particular dimensions, tested on various groups to eliminate or revise poor items, checked for reliability, validated against different outcome measures, checked for unfair discrimination, and "normed" to provide typical score ranges. Competent and ethical test developers have this information available and are more than willing to share it with you. Test developers who cannot provide this information should be avoided.

When you are evaluating vendors, the first thing to ask for is a technical manual. Don't be put off by the jargon and statistics that you may find in it; Chapter Six explained the key factors you need to be concerned about and the meaning of some of the technical terms used in test manuals. Armed with the technical manual and other sales material, check for the following elements.

Reliability

Most often, reliability will be reported in terms of internal consistency. Internal-consistency reliability is usually measured by a statistic called Cronbach's Alpha, which indicates the average interrelationship among all the items in a measure. Internal-consistency coefficients should generally be .85 or higher.[32]

If test-retest reliabilities are reported, coefficients should be above .80 and the interval between testing should normally be six months or longer, unless there is a good reason for scores not to be stable over time. Extremely short intervals provide artificially high estimates of reliability.

Parallel-forms reliability is only relevant if you plan to use more than one form; this might be a good idea if you're worried about people reapplying for the job or talking to their friends about the content of the test. If so, parallel-forms reliability should be .80 or greater.

Validity

For most tests, validity will be reported in terms of associations between test scores and performance scores. The most common problem here is with the performance measures used; a high correlation with a performance measure that is not relevant to your use is meaningless. Assuming that a relevant and reasonably reliable performance measure was used, validities should be described as "statistically significant" and will generally be .25 or greater.

Norm Groups

Just as an irrelevant performance measure is useless, you also want to make sure that the groups on which the measure was developed and tested are relevant. College undergraduates are often used to norm tests; their scores may be meaningful if your typical applicants are college graduates, but not if you are hiring research scientists or day laborers.

Test Fairness

Hiring tools should be validated using samples that are culturally diverse and gender-diverse, so that the developer can determine if the test shows adverse impact or test bias. As you are now well aware, adverse impact is not illegal, but you will need to show a compelling reason for using the instrument. All else being equal, it is better to use selection tools that do not create adverse impact. Test bias, also known as differential prediction, in which a test does not predict the job performance of minorities or women as well as it does that of white males, is a more serious problem. Tests that show either adverse impact or bias should not be used without consulting with an independent expert in testing.

Time Requirements

Some tests require only ten minutes, while others require an hour or more. Will the test take more time than it's worth? Does the test have a time limit? Timed tests will require someone to serve as a test administrator; this can be costly, particularly if you cannot arrange to test applicants in groups.

Scoring Options

Some tests can be scored on-site, either by hand with a scoring key or with a special scanning device. Others can be administered and immediately scored on-site using personal computers. Computerized tests often have the additional advantage of automatically creating a data base that can be used for both record keeping and validation, and some multimedia tests offer surprisingly realistic interactive tests. Of course, these also require that you have computers available to use for the testing, which may be a particular problem if you have large numbers of applicants. A final scoring option is to mail or fax score sheets to the test publisher, who scores them and sends back a report. This option minimizes your labor and capital costs, but it may result in unacceptable delays.

Special Versions

The Americans with Disabilities Act requires that applicants with disabilities be accommodated during the application process. Some popular tests have audiotape or large-type versions to accommodate applicants with visual disabilities. Alternatively, you may be able to supply a magnifying glass or read the test to the applicant. Publishers may also be able to offer advice for adjusting the time limits for applicants with learning impairments or physical disabilities.

Another example of special forms are tests that have been translated into other languages. Native-language tests may be a good idea even if proficiency in English is a job requirement, since they are more likely to give an accurate assessment of the characteristic being assessed (unless that characteristic is English-language fluency, of course).

Cost

Direct costs of a test usually include a set of reusable test booklets, one-time-use answer sheets, and an administrator's manual. Hand-scored tests often include a scoring template to increase the speed and accuracy of scoring, while computer-based testing generally includes software that is valid for a prepaid number of uses. Tests with scannable forms require an investment in the scanner; sheets that are mailed or faxed to the publisher are also charged for according to use. In addition, evaluation of costs should include consideration of the time spent by your employees who are administering the tests.

Testing fees generally need to be considered to be an ongoing expense, since few test publishers will license a test for unlimited use. While this can create a temptation to write your own tests, you need to remember the substantial investment of research and development the test author and publisher have made. Unless you have the resources to spend years developing, revising, and validating your own tests, with limited ability to put them to operational use during that time, you are better off paying the use fees.

Summary

Employment tests are a powerful tool in the high-impact hiring process. Carefully developed tests tend to be extremely reliable and often demonstrate quite useful levels of validity if they are carefully matched with the requirements of the job. They are generally low in cost and require relatively little time, making them one of the more efficient hiring tools available. Because of their standardization, they also avoid many of the personal inconsistencies that plague other hiring tools. Properly chosen tests meet legal requirements, although some may not be perceived by job applicants as being as job-related and fair as other employment procedures. Testing, then, is not a substitute for a well-developed hiring system, but making testing part of your hiring system is likely to have positive payoffs.

Chapter Ten

Sampling Performance Through Job Tryouts, Work Samples, and Performance Testing

A scientist of our acquaintance loved to tell of an exam question he gave to a college biology class. "Suppose you are an astronaut on the first mission to Mars," he queried, "and you have just landed on the red planet. Explain how you would determine if life exists, and what it would be like if it did exist." Most students filled pages in their exam books with explanations of complex tests. But the scientist gave full credit to one student who simply wrote, "I'd ask."

Performance sampling, also known as performance testing, can be the "I'd ask" solution to selection for working managers. Managers have the closest access to the most powerful and direct indicator of work performance: work. Performance testing involves sampling candidates' *actual performance* on tasks that are part of the job. Performance tests have the advantages of being clearly job-related and highly valid, and of providing an effective preview of the job, all of which combine to provide impressive results in work performance on the job after selection.[1] By providing applicants with a realistic job preview (see Chapter Four), performance tests can also reduce turnover.

Many organizations utilize assessment centers to administer certain varieties of performance exercises. Frequently, they are used in selection for internal management development or for key hires. But you don't need to use an assessment center to bring the power of performance tests to your high-impact hiring system. You can design your own performance tests that are practical, good predictors, and tailored to jobs in your work group and can draw on your knowledge, as a working manager, of the important aspects of work performance for the job. In this chapter, we will look at principles that underlie effective performance testing and provide you with guidelines you can use in developing performance tests to use in your own work unit.

Effective Performance Testing: Samples Instead of Signs

In Chapter Six we asked you to imagine that you had no experience with hiring and then to think about how you'd go about assessing an applicant's knowledge, skills, abilities, and other characteristics (KSAOs) for a job. We suggested that the most obvious route might be to see if the applicant could actually do the job, or at least the critical components of the job. This approach, which we are now more formally calling performance testing, has the advantage that it provides applicants with an actual *sample* of the work to be performed. By contrast, most other hiring tools are merely *signs,* or indicators, of their *potential* ability to do the work.[2] Some of the signs described in the preceding chapters are very good indicators, and they can sometimes be more effective and practical than a sample. But a work sample has a directness, an immediacy, and, especially, a specificity that gives it special power.

It may be helpful to think of different types of performance tests as existing on a continuum ranging from pure work samples to more indirect signs of future work performance. We will first describe how you can develop highly specific work samples; we will then generalize our discussion to include more generic performance simulations, as well as the use of internships and assessment centers to realize some of the benefits of performance testing.

It is important to remember that performance tests are most effective when they are combined with other kinds of testing as part of a comprehensive selection system. Matching performance testing to the right role is important.

The "life on Mars" exam question at the beginning of the chapter probably helps us to understand where performance testing fits into high-impact hiring as well as anything could. It's amusing to picture a group of earthling astronauts diligently peering at soil samples while their colleague is over behind some rocks asking the natives, "How's life?" But any mission to Mars would involve many kinds of tests. The mission would be the result of literally millions of tests conducted from a distance: from Earth, from space, and from Martian orbit. When these tests are well designed, they yield information that you can't get by just "asking." When they are poorly designed, they yield erroneous information that leads to serious and costly misguided decisions.

In your high-impact hiring system, the results you get from most of your testing and information gathering are "signs": information gathered from indicators that are designed to predict performance. You can think of personality tests, ability tests, interviews, and reference checks as telescope observations from the Earth, from the Hubble Space Telescope, and from satellites. Performance testing comes when you are ready to "get closer" to understanding the applicant's past and future performance. To test for performance effectively, we need to know, first, what performance we are testing for and, second, how to design a test of the desired performance. A fundamental issue for performance-test design is the principle of specificity.

Principle of Specificity

The *principle of specificity* is usually used in describing training and performance and can be summarized in the simple phrase, "You get what you train for." It states that learning is specific; people will perform what they have specifically learned. This means that it's important to develop training that is highly specific to the job to be performed.

The principle also applies to performance testing. A performance test is a specific test of whatever work performance is sampled—whether it's the performance you wanted to sample or not. It's critical for the performance being sampled to be closely related to the job to be performed. If it is, performance on the sample should be essentially the same as performance on the job. If it's not, you will be taking a highly specific sample of performance on something that's different from the job, so the conclusions you will reach about candidates' performance will be faulty.

Specificity Versus Narrowness

It's common to mistake specificity for narrowness. Specificity signifies an accurate representation of the task or tasks to be performed on the job. If the tasks are simple, a narrow test may be adequate to test performance on them. If the tasks are complex, the test needs to reflect this complexity appropriately. As with other tests, it's important to focus a performance test on the most important components of the job: it is not effective to narrowly single out a minor task for performance testing, nor to broadly sample every aspect of a job in a shotgun approach.

Specificity Versus Fidelity

When we ask you to match performance tests closely with job performance, we don't necessarily mean that the test should always be an exact reproduction of the work. Specificity refers to a close match in the performance required to do two tasks, the actual task and the test, while fidelity refers to how good a copy one task is of another. Fidelity isn't always necessary, or even desirable, to developing a test that's reflective and specific. For instance, Charles Hulin and other researchers at the University of Illinois' Institute of Aviation have shown that flight training using a simple computer program was approximately as effective as using a flight simulator.[3]

Performance Testing from a High-Impact Hiring Approach

Essential components for developing performance tests are an accurate understanding of the required KSAOs, identification of the most important work tasks that should be the specific focus of the performance tests, and a description of the desired performance. If this sounds like the work you did in conducting your work analysis and developing your Performance Attributes Matrix, it is!

With this information as your base, how do you select the attributes that are best suited for a performance test? Look for the tasks that you rated as most important for successful performance. Ask three critical questions to evaluate whether each task is a good candidate for performance testing:

1. Is this a task for which there are important differences in performance among current workers, or among applicants in your pool?
2. Is this a task for which you expect competency when a successful applicant *begins* work?
3. If the answer to the first two questions is yes, is this a task for which it's possible to conduct a realistic sample of work that will demonstrate accurately the ability of candidates to perform this task?

Once you've identified a group of tasks for performance testing, here are some questions that will help you to design an effective performance test.

What does successful performance of this task look like on the job? What will a sample of work and working conditions that's a good match with performance on the job look like? Will you be able to accurately use results from the test to draw conclusions about desired performance?

What are the individual components of the task? How can you design a work sample that tests components individually when this is appropriate, and that tests them independently? For example, you might ask candidates for a marketing position to conduct a market analysis for a hypothetical product, analyze your organization's current materials, and develop a marketing plan. You can evaluate their performance of the market analysis independently of their analysis of your organization's materials. However, their development of a marketing plan would be dependent on their marketing analysis, so you wouldn't be able to evaluate them independently. You could make them independent by providing candidates with a sample market analysis from which to develop the marketing plan. As another example, you could ask a computer programmer to conduct an end-user analysis, develop a plan for a product that met end users' needs, code some of the product, and make the code usable by an entire group of programmers. To develop an effective performance test, however, it would be important to structure each of these exercises to be independent of the others.

What is an appropriate scope for the test in time, complexity, and expense? As a rule of thumb, use the shortest, simplest, most practical, and least expensive test that accurately and specifically mimics real work conditions. You also need to make sure that the length of the test and the amount of work required by the candidate is appropriate for the job at hand. The performance tests just described, for example, would be most appropriate for a small number of candidates being strongly considered for critical jobs. The same tasks could be tested more simply by providing specific and realistic starting points for each task, for instance, by asking candidates to perform a shorter portion of the critical task or by providing them with an appropriate starting point part of the way through a more complex task.

When you design the test, continually ask, "Is this really getting at the most important parts of this job? Is this testing the way the job is really done? Has the test become too narrow or too broad?" A typing test, for example, was at one time an excellent specific test of a typist's ability, and entering data by quickly and accurately typing on a keyboard is still a key component of many jobs. But for an administrative assistant's job in a computerized office, it would be more specific and provide a more accurate sample to test an applicant's skill and speed in producing a high-quality document from a combination of written notes and E-mail messages than it would be to find out how fast the keystrokes can be banged out. The performance test you design should involve the tasks the assistant will be likely to perform.

Are you testing just performance or are you inadvertently testing other things that make the test inaccurate? In the example of the administrative assistant's job, a test of typing and document creation would be appropriate if an applicant was expected to have developed skill at operating common word-processing packages before taking the job. A publishing company, similarly, might expect that its graphics and production staff were familiar with certain page layout programs. On the other hand, if knowledge of a specific computer program isn't essential (for example, if employees learn to use the program on the job), the test above would contaminate skill at document creation with knowledge of a particular word-processing program.

Be sure that all important parts of the job have been adequately included and appropriately weighted in the selection system as a whole. Don't get so enamored of performance tests that you ignore important components of the job that aren't as effectively measured by these tests. As an example, performance tests involving physical activities specific to fire fighting would be one appropriate test for a fire department captain or fire management officer. But such tests would make the hiring system deficient by ignoring those positions' management and supervisory duties. Attributes critical to those duties are likely to be better tested by other components of your high-impact hiring system.

We suggest that you design your performance test according to these guidelines: devise a test that is an accurate sample of the work that's done on the job, is easy to administer, is practical for the candidate to perform, and is set up to facilitate evaluation and scoring. Scoring should be done in a simple and objective manner. The best way is to write out a scoring sheet in advance, listing the performance dimensions to be scored and the way they will be scored. Proofreaders, for example, are often given a point for every error they catch in a manuscript that has a known number of errors.

Other tests can be scored on a simple scale of unacceptable, acceptable, and desirable levels of performance, similar to groupings of scores we will recommend in Chapter Twelve. When using such broad scores, it's essential to write out a scoring key in advance that defines each category. Every item in the scoring key should be specific to an aspect of desired job performance. Scores should be based on each task component that is being tested, not on overall impressions. For example, a ski school that rates instructor candidates on technical proficiency, teaching skill, and safety might score an applicant as having desirable technical proficiency and acceptable teaching skill, but unacceptable safety skills.

Candidates can also be scored on a point scale of 1 to 5 or 1 to 10 for each task component. As in the discussion of interviewing in Chapter Eight, the numbers on such scales should be accompanied by words that are clear and tied to performance outcomes.

Industrial psychologist David Robinson developed a test that is a good example of a performance test that brings together close matching with critical performances, good specificity, and effective scoring built into the test. The test was for a construction superintendent's job, though it could have been used for a variety of related jobs. To construct the test, Robinson took blueprints from actual projects and had an architect insert errors into the plans. The candidates were then asked to review the plans as they would on the job and to mark up any errors they noted. Since the company knew the number and location of the created errors on the plans, scoring was a simple matter of counting up correct markups of each error.[4]

Administering Performance Tests

Think through how you will administer your tests to candidates. In particular, make sure that:

- All candidates are tested under similar conditions and evaluated similarly. Otherwise, comparisons of the results will not be valid.
- The test is safe for the candidates to perform. Be particularly cautious about tests involving physical performance or operation of equipment.
- The test does not exclude candidates on any basis that is unrelated to the job itself. In fact, performance tests generally have low adverse impact and high validity. A well-designed test should be able to meet the job-relatedness test of the Americans with Disabilities Act, although you would need to make the same sort of reasonable accommodations for an applicant that you would for an employee. But a poorly designed test that measures something other than a job-related task, and that becomes an unfair barrier to employment, would not be as likely to pass muster and would be more likely to generate claims.
- The way that timed tests are used makes a reasonable match with the real-time demands of working conditions on the job. Timing a test can be a good way to make sure that all candidates work under similar conditions, but unless the tasks are performed on the job under timed or short-term, time-critical conditions, you may want to consider de-emphasizing or even forgoing timing. First, many people do significantly worse on the same test under timed conditions. If the job does not involve timing, you are contaminating the desired work performance with the unrelated ability to perform a timed test. People with learning disabilities may have particularly large differences between results under timed and untimed conditions and at the same time are often superior performers in

the workplace. Second, all tasks involve trade-offs between the two components of speed and accuracy. A timed test emphasizes speed components, sometimes inappropriately, over accuracy components. Again, if you do time the test, the time constraints should be similar to those on the job.

- You are not asking candidates to perform work for your organization without compensation under the guise of a performance test. This would potentially violate the Wage and Hour Law, and it generates resentment and ill-will among potential employees.

Internships

You can use the high-impact hiring approach to performance testing to get performance information from other settings, such as internships. These can be turned into effective opportunities to attract, screen, and performance-test potential candidates. Your organization may use paid or unpaid internships, such as those structured in cooperation with a high school, college, or job development program. You can use the guidelines above to make sure that the internship experience closely matches the work that would be performed in a regular employment setting. In contrast to pre-employment performance testing, it's generally appropriate to ask interns to perform work that benefits your organization. Making the internship a close match to regular employment and involving the intern in work that's useful to your organization have the added benefit of making the internship more meaningful to the intern. Thus, your assessment of the internship can be structured to be an effective and highly specific performance test.

Assessment Centers

Assessment centers are elaborate selection systems designed to measure a wide range of KSAOs, generally for executive or other complex jobs. Candidates typically spend three or more days interacting with each other in a variety of exercises and other assessment procedures, all the while being observed by trained raters, either line managers or psychologists. At the end of the three days, the raters provide evaluations of each candidate on each of the dimensions being assessed, which typically include such factors as leadership, written and oral communications, problem solving, planning, and decision making.

Assessment centers are included in this chapter because they often have performance tests as one of their components, along with interviews, paper-and-pencil tests, and biodata measures. Although the expense of designing and running assessment centers generally limits their use to high-level managerial positions in larger companies, many of the exercises used in assessment centers would be analogous to the performance tests you might use in other contexts. If your organization utilizes assessment centers, you can apply the performance-testing guidelines in this chapter to decide how relevant the information provided by the assessment exercises is to the hiring that you do. You may be able to help shape either the exercises or the scoring so that you realize great benefits from your organization's extensive investments in such centers. And if your organization doesn't use assessment centers, have no fear: you can develop your own assessment center for your work group by using the guidelines in the first part of this chapter to develop your own set of performance tests. Following are examples of assessment-center exercises:

- *In-basket exercises* are generally used to measure such attributes as planning, problem solving, and delegation. In these exercises a candidate is presented with a simulated in-basket of material similar to what is experienced by incumbents in the position being filled. Operating under a time constraint, the candidate is expected to prioritize the material effectively and then respond to the material by making phone calls, writing memos, and planning meetings.
- *Leaderless group discussion* is generally used to measure leadership, teamwork, and communication skills. Candidates are assigned to work as a group on a problem similar to one that might be faced in the position they are seeking. Raters observe the group interaction and evaluate each candidate on his or her ability to work effectively with others and provide leadership.
- *Case analysis* involves giving candidates business situations for which they are expected to provide an analysis and

recommendations. In addition to demonstrating their problem-solving and decision-making skills, candidates are often asked to demonstrate their communication skills in providing written and oral presentations of their analyses.

Studies have consistently shown assessment centers to have a number of advantages as a hiring tool. They seem to be quite predictive of candidates' success in an organization, and they don't appear to show adverse impact against women or racial minorities. Because of their apparent job relevance, applicants are generally quite accepting of them as well. However, critics have pointed out that assessment centers have the potential to create a self-fulfilling prophecy that may make them appear to be more effective than they really are.[5] Assessment-center ratings seem to be much more predictive of career progression (that is, the number and speed of promotions) than of performance ratings.[6] Because assessment center ratings are typically subjective evaluations made by line managers who are acting as assessors, it may be that high-scoring candidates are simply those who fit the corporate mold. You need to be sure that the assessment results don't simply promote the people who have the best skill at getting promoted rather than the people who can perform best.

A related caution is that executives with extensive experience in large organizations are often familiar with assessment-center exercises and skilled at performing them. As one executive told us, "I can do the 'in-basket' exercise in my sleep by now. And I'd never really do my job the way I know you have to respond on the exercise to be successful."

Most of the exercises in assessment centers are somewhat generic, representing a midpoint on the sign-sample continuum described at the beginning of the chapter, rather than being highly task- and organization-specific as our prior discussion suggested. In fact, some of them, particularly in-baskets and business cases, can be purchased from vendors. Alternatively, by designing your own performance tests specific to the demands in your work group, you can realize many of the benefits offered by assessment centers and ensure that the performance tests are truly related to how candidates would do real jobs in your work group.

Summary

The best way to identify a good employee is to observe someone actually doing the job. Performance tests and work samples allow you to sample candidates' actual performance before you hire them. The power of performance testing comes from designing and administering the tests so that they sample the skills needed on the job. Performance sampling is made most effective by basing your sampling on an accurate knowledge of required performance and skills and by making your tests match closely with the work done on the job. You want to administer performance samples and interpret their results with the same focus on what really matters in performing a job. Performance tests, assessment centers, and well-structured internships allow you to sample performance long before, instead of after, you decide who to hire. High-impact hiring is performance-based hiring, and performance testing can be a great capstone of your testing system.

Chapter Eleven

The Dark Side of Performance

Identifying and Assessing Counterproductive Behavior

As you learned in the previous chapter, directly testing for performance can be a particularly effective tool. But as managers know all too well, performance isn't just the presence or absence of positive contributions to a work group. There is also such a thing as "negative performance," actions and behaviors some employees may perform that are detrimental to the output of a work group or an entire organization, and that are often also detrimental to other employees and to themselves. The ability to perform job tasks well is certainly a key component in hiring a good employee, but it is not the whole story. As an employer, you need to be concerned as well about what your current and future workers do *not* do, as in not stealing from you, not engaging in violence or harassment, and not using alcohol and other drugs in a way that interferes with job performance.

In the next chapter, which discusses decision making, you will find that a critical step in making an effective hire is determining who *not* to hire and eliminating them from further consideration. Every working manager knows that counterproductive behavior in workers who are already employed is disruptive and destructive, difficult to deal with, agonizing to get a handle on, and often seemingly impossible to stop. Reducing the number of employees you hire who later engage in counterproductive behavior won't put an end to such problems, but it will certainly reduce the number of these problems your organization has to deal with.

Counterproductive Behavior at Work

From a strictly economic viewpoint, work is about the production of goods or services, and the workplace is simply a setting in which this production occurs. In addition, though, the workplace is a microcosm of society in which all sorts of psychological and sociological dramas unfold. Workers bring with them not only a set of values developed over a lifetime, but also personal and family issues that are on their minds and affect their work positively or negatively. While some employees have a strong work ethic that emphasizes hard work, honesty, and loyalty to an employer, others' experiences have led them to view employers—and perhaps coworkers—as opportunities for exploitation and personal gain. Some have misused alcohol and other drugs for years; others are having short-term difficulties adjusting to a divorce, problems with their children, the death of a family member, or other personal crises. Still other employees are dissatisfied with work that's boring or stressful, lacks opportunities for growth, or pays poorly, and they decide to take out their dissatisfaction on the employer.

All of these situations, and others that you have probably seen as a manager, can lead to the problem of counterproductive behavior at work. Stealing money, goofing off, not meeting responsibilities in a timely way, doing sloppy work as a result of drug use, being uncooperative with colleagues or customers, and harassing fellow employees are all examples of behavior that is detrimental to organizational performance. In some cases, such as chronic misuse of alcohol or other drugs, this behavior is also counterproductive to the employee. But for the most part, we consider behavior to be counterproductive when it interferes with the company's primary purpose, which generally is to produce a particular good or service in a way that results in a profit for owners or shareholders.

What Is Counterproductive Behavior?

Researchers suggest that counterproductive behavior at work falls into one of three categories.[1, 2] Most employees become at least temporarily dissatisfied at some time or another. Employees who engage in solving the problem that led to their dissatisfaction return to being satisfied and don't proceed to counterproductive behavior. But those who can't, won't, or don't solve the problem leading to dissatisfaction tend to engage in three categories of counterproductive behavior: *retaliation* (against coworkers, customers, or the organization), *neglect* (of their work and of standards), and *exit* (looking for ways to leave the organization).

These counterproductive or "deviant" behaviors can be directed against the organization or individuals.[3] *Production deviance,* a form of neglect directed at the company, consists of working slowly or taking excessive breaks, leaving work early, or wasting resources. *Property deviance* represents a more costly category of organizationally directed retaliation that includes such behavior as stealing from the company, lying about hours worked, or sabotaging equipment.

Counterproductive behavior may also be directed at individuals rather than the organization, usually in the form of retaliatory behavior. *Political deviance,* for example, takes the form of showing favoritism, gossiping, blaming coworkers for things they didn't do, and other forms of backstabbing. *Personal aggression* describes even more serious forms of interpersonal deviance, such as verbal abuse of customers or fellow employees, sexual harassment, or violent behavior.

What Causes Counterproductive Behavior?

Explanations abound as to why some people act in these ways while others do not. In general, explanations tend to trace the cause either to the individual employee or to the situation in which the employee works. These two approaches are fundamentally different in their views of people, and in their implications for hiring.

Person-based explanations place blame squarely on the individual. According to this view, people vary in their moral character just as they vary in knowledge, abilities, or skills. Some people wouldn't steal a dime even if there was no chance that they would be caught; to them, such a behavior just wouldn't be right. Other people will engage in the most heinous of behaviors despite clearly stated rules and the threat of being punished, and sometimes without even feeling guilty. Often this behavior occurs even as other people—experiencing the same situation—are dutifully conforming to social expectations. The only reasonable conclusion, according to individual-focused theories, is that deviant behavior is the result of some sort of character flaw within certain individuals. This inherent weakness may be blamed on either innate traits or upbringing, but the important point for our purposes is that in this point of view some people are "bad apples" that must be eliminated at the time of hiring. Background checks, integrity tests, and drug tests are advocated as means of screening out these individuals.

By contrast, *situation-based explanations* assume that workplace conditions are the key factor. From this perspective, people are neither inherently good nor inherently evil; rather, the situation can push or pull a person into counterproductive behavior. One form of situation-centered approach can be seen in what might be termed the "security consultant" approach to dealing with workplace deviance. The underlying assumption of this approach is that everyone is corruptible. Therefore, rather than trying to screen out dishonest employees, it makes more sense to design the workplace so that rule-abiding behavior is inevitable, regardless of the moral character of the employees. Based on this logic, the security approach emphasizes:

- Reducing the temptation to engage in counterproductive behavior by making the behavior more difficult or less rewarding. For example, surveillance cameras, audits, and other security measures make it difficult to steal money or supplies.
- Increasing the costs of being caught if you engage in deviant behavior. Zero-tolerance policies on drug use, for example, are assumed to act as a deterrent.

A similar view sees deviance as a more or less rational response to workplace norms or organizational conditions, rather than as a sign of bad character. A prime example is role modeling: new employees look to their supervisors and coworkers for clues as to what is acceptable behavior. If they see that stealing or goofing off is the norm, they are likely to join in, partly as a way of becoming part of the group.

Another example is when frustration and dissatisfaction with unfair treatment lead workers to think about evening the score, particularly when they feel that they have little power to correct the injustice. A number of studies have shown that theft is often due to workers' feeling that they are underpaid or otherwise being treated unjustly.[4] In other cases, dissatisfaction may lead to sabotage, goldbricking, or personal violence.

This view suggests that reducing counterproductive behavior has less to do with hiring than with managing people once they're on the job. Two key steps help to accomplish this:

1. *Create a favorable work climate.* Workers who are reasonably satisfied with their work climate and who feel that they are treated with courtesy and respect have less motive to retaliate against their employer or coworkers.
2. *Eliminate deviant role models.* Role models have far more influence on employee behavior than do policy statements. Managers are particularly important in this regard, as studies have shown that when supervisors steal or tolerate theft, employees are much more likely to steal as well.[5]

Realistically, both individual and situational factors probably affect employee deviance. While some people are uniformly either "saints" or "sinners," most people's behavior is greatly influenced by the situation.[6] Deviance is simply behavior that is not in conformance with social norms, and many of those norms are created by the people with whom we work. Even honest employees would probably find themselves taking a few office supplies home or occasionally taking a "mental health day" off if their coworkers did and if their supervisors condoned such behavior.

A High-Impact Hiring Approach to Counterproductive Behavior

Although it's important to remember that many of the causes of counterproductive behavior occur *after* a person is hired, you nevertheless want to do all you can to avoid applicants who are predisposed to such behavior. Moreover, dealing with the situation in job applicants is different from dealing with job incumbents. Once people are on the payroll it can be difficult to change the way they act, or to terminate them if they don't change their behavior. There are fewer social or legal constraints on your actions with applicants. While you definitely owe all applicants a fair shake, you don't owe any applicant a job. This means that you may be able to deal more easily with "problem" applicants—by not hiring them—than you can with problem employees who are already in your workplace.

There are several ways of identifying applicants who may engage in counterproductive behavior. We'll begin by discussing the use of integrity and drug tests, and we'll finish the chapter by alerting you to red flags that can show up in your more standard hiring tools, such as structured interviews, application forms, résumés, and reference checks.

As we present these tools for detecting dishonesty or other counterproductive behavior, it's important to remember that they are primarily targeted at the small group of people in an applicant pool who are predisposed toward (and often have a recent history of) counterproductive behavior at work. Removing this small group can have a disproportionately large effect on reducing later workplace problems. But doing so is not a replacement for good management practices that reduce the opportunities and motives for counterproductive behavior on the job. The bottom line is that integrity tests, background checks, and drug testing, as well as thoughtful attention to interviews, reference checking, and résumés, can be a useful part of the hiring process, but they are not a magic wand that will solve all your problems with counterproductive behavior.

Integrity Testing

The integrity-testing field has become a boom industry by nearly anyone's standards. Every year untold millions of job applicants are given tests that ask about their attitudes toward, and past experience with, theft and other counterproductive behavior. At least fifty different integrity tests are in use in the United States.[7] The PDI-Employment Inventory alone has been administered to over sixteen million applicants in the last eight years, and other popular tests are not far behind this figure.[8]

One reason for the growth of integrity testing is that crime has become a serious concern for most Americans, and all the evidence suggests that crime is at least as important at work as at home. Estimates of the cost of workplace deviance range from $20 billion to $400 billion dollars, or at least ten times that of street crime. It has been estimated that three-quarters of employees steal from their employers at least once, and that 30 percent of business failures can be attributed at least in part to employee theft.[9] Managers and employees alike are concerned about reports of increased workplace violence, and lawsuits alleging *negligent hiring* (see Chapter Seven) have left employers scrambling to find better ways to screen job applicants. Managers are increasingly concerned with other kinds of counterproductive workplace behavior, too. Sexual harassment is a particularly ugly form of retaliation against fellow employees. Abuse of alcohol and illegal drugs leads to safety problems, quality problems, and worse.

Growth in integrity testing has been further spurred by the demise of the polygraph, or lie detector. The polygraph, as well as the more recent voice stress analyzer, is based on the assumption that lying produces a specific set of physiological responses that a person is unable to voluntarily control. By measuring these responses—changes in breathing, heart rate, and sweating in the case of the polygraph, or subtle changes ("microtremors") in a person's voice for the voice stress analyzer—proponents claimed to be able to detect when people were lying. However, numerous studies raised serious doubts about the assumption that lying leads to a unique and identifiable set of physiological responses. In 1988, Congress passed the Employee Polygraph Protection Act, which prohibited most employers from requiring or requesting preemployment polygraph examinations. Although an exemption was included for security firms and manufacturers of controlled substances, preemployment polygraph examinations have for all practical purposes been replaced by paper-and-pencil integrity tests.

Types of Integrity Tests

Integrity tests have generally been divided into two categories, depending on what kind of questions they include. One category, referred to as *overt* or clear-purpose measures, are easily identified as measures of honesty. They generally include two sections, one that directly asks about past theft or deviant behavior and a second that assesses the applicants' attitudes about how common theft is and how people who steal should be treated, how often the applicants think about stealing, how easy they think it is to steal on the job, and whether they agree with common rationalizations for theth.[10] Examples of tests described in this chapter are listed in Table 11.1.

Integrity tests in a second category, known as *personality-based* measures, take a more indirect approach to assessing deviant tendencies. Tests in this category include personality scales that have been selected for their ability to predict theft and other counterproductive behavior. Although different tests use different items, most assess applicants' dependability, conscientiousness, social conformity, thrill seeking, attitudes toward authority, and hostility. Because these items are fairly general, their purpose often is not obvious to the applicant, which is why they are also referred to as *disguised-purpose* integrity tests.

Are Integrity Tests Valid?

Researchers and employees alike have long viewed integrity tests with skepticism. Many have doubted that a paper-and-pencil test can really determine which applicants are more likely to become problem employees. However, recent large-scale studies, including a white paper issued by the American Psychological Association

Table 11.1. Types of Integrity Tests.

Type of Test	Examples
Overt integrity tests	Employee Attitude Inventory
	Employee Reliability Inventory
	Personnel Selection Inventory
	Phase II Profile
	Reid Report
	Stanton Survey
Personality-based inventories	PDI-Employment Inventory
	Inwald Personality Inventory
	Reliability scale from the Hogan Personality Inventory
	Personal Outlook Inventory
	Personnel Reaction Blank

(APA), have concluded that integrity tests can be valid and are useful hiring tools for most employers.[11, 12] Both overt and personality-based inventories have been successful in predicting a wide range of counterproductive behaviors, including disciplinary problems, tardiness, absenteeism, turnover, violence, substance abuse, property damage, rule breaking, and theft.[13]

Interestingly, this research also showed that integrity tests are quite effective at predicting applicants' job performance as well as their counterproductive tendencies. The reason for this seems to be that integrity tests are an indirect way of measuring a person's Conscientiousness, among other things. As we discussed in Chapter Nine, Conscientiousness is a personality characteristic that assesses both dependability (which is why conscientious people don't engage in deviant behavior) and achievement (which explains why conscientious employees tend to be better performers). Thus applicants who do well on integrity tests are likely to be effective both because they don't get in trouble and because they are more task-focused.

Integrity tests have two other advantages that can make them a useful part of a preemployment testing battery. The first is that scores on integrity tests and mental ability tests are unrelated to each other, even though both predict job performance. So while intelligence tests can get you employees with better reasoning and problem-solving abilities, there's no assurance that they'll be honest and hard-working, and vice versa. Using an integrity test along with the ability test gives you a better chance of hiring good employees than using either test alone. Second, integrity tests don't pose problems with discrimination: all racial groups score about the same, women score slightly higher than men, and older applicants generally do better than younger ones.[14] Not only is this a benefit in itself; it also means that hiring decisions that are based on a combination of integrity and ability test scores will have less discriminatory impact than those based on ability test scores alone.[15]

Controversies Regarding Integrity Testing

As positive as these results are, a number of controversies remain. Two particularly serious issues are the susceptibility of integrity testing to faking and concerns about the perceived fairness of integrity tests.

Can Integrity Tests Be Faked?

Integrity tests are vulnerable to the same concerns about intentional faking that we described in Chapter Nine. Faking is a particular concern with overt integrity tests, since the purpose of the questions is even more obvious to test takers than with more subtle personality-type items.

Publishers of integrity tests argue that the problem of faking isn't as serious as it might seem. They point out that dishonest employees who seek to make themselves look good are often thwarted by their distorted frame of reference for what a "good" answer should be. Consider a question that asks how much money or property you've stolen from your employer in the last year. A dishonest employee who has stolen a thousand dollars may figure that "Five hundred dollars" is a good answer, assuming, probably correctly, that giving too low an answer would trigger concerns that he or she was faking. An honest employee, by contrast, adds up the value of a few pens and paper clips he or she has taken home and says, "Fifty dollars." Even after underrepresenting the true theft by 50 percent, the dishonest employee stands out clearly from the honest employee.

As comforting as this example is, the problem is that we really don't know how much integrity test scores are affected by faking. Particularly serious is the potential problem of applicants who are *coached* on how to fake. Even proponents of integrity testing fear that coaching could make most integrity tests useless.[16, 17] As a general rule, personality-based measures with more subtle content seem least susceptible to faking. One study found that even subjects who were coached were unable to raise their scores on the Personnel Reaction Blank, which is probably the most subtle of all integrity tests.[18]

Are Integrity Tests Fair?

A number of different concerns have been raised about the fairness of integrity tests. Perhaps the most pervasive is the concern that integrity tests misclassify many honest individuals as being dishonest. While we don't want to minimize this concern, it's important to remember that all hiring tools make mistakes in classifying individuals. The real issue is the *relative* accuracy of various techniques; more valid tools make fewer classification errors than less valid tools. Compared with other approaches to detecting dishonest employees, integrity tests in general are about the best tools available.

Fairness also involves treating applicants with dignity and respect, and many people feel that integrity tests violate this standard by invading applicants' rights to privacy. Disguised-purpose tests, in particular, are designed to keep applicants in the dark as to what is really being measured and, perhaps, how the information will be used. As we discussed with personality tests, the line between the employer's right to know and the employee's right to privacy is open to much debate. High-impact hiring is grounded in the importance of making hiring decisions based on job performance. Since logic and research show that integrity tests predict behavior that is relevant to most jobs, our position is that well-designed integrity tests are generally not an undue invasion of privacy.

Using Integrity Tests

Note that we said that *well-designed* integrity tests are defensible. Unfortunately, reports by both the APA and the U.S. Office of Technology Assessment were highly critical of the marketing and test-development practices used by many integrity test publishers. The APA report in particular criticized many publishers for making false and misleading claims and failing to follow accepted standards for validating tests. You need to pay particularly careful attention to the standards we described in Chapter Nine, possibly with the assistance of a technical consultant, before choosing to use a particular integrity test.

The APA report also recommends against using "cut scores" to categorize test takers as either failing or passing the integrity test. Although such labels are convenient in decision making, the report criticizes many test publishers for not doing their homework when setting these passing scores. The result can be that many trustworthy applicants receive failing scores, leading to both frustrated applicants and a waste of talent. In fact, 40 percent of applicants typically "fail" integrity tests, and probably one-third or more of this group would actually be effective employees.[19]

As with other hiring tools, integrity tests should not form the sole basis for rejecting an applicant. For candidates who receive unusually low scores, you should try to get a better understanding of the reasons, particularly if other information such as conviction records and references are not consistent with the scores. Keep in mind that some people simply don't test well. In particular, people who are not very punitive in their attitudes toward counterproductive behavior tend to receive low scores on integrity tests. In most cases this is because the applicants doesn't feel that such behavior is serious. Research shows that this kind of lenient attitude is characteristic of employees who engage in such behavior themselves, so for this group the test scores should be taken seriously and the applicant rejected. However, in a few cases, low scores may reflect unusually forgiving people who simply don't believe in harsh punishment. They agree that the behavior is wrong and wouldn't do it themselves, but they are more inclined to turn the other cheek than to mete out severe punishments, such as reporting a thief to the police or firing a troublemaker. These people may still be perfectly acceptable employees, though they might not be well suited to many supervisory positions.

With an applicant whose scores are low—perhaps in a category the test publisher calls "risky"—you should treat the integrity test results as a red flag. Be sure to ask the applicant questions during your interview about how she or he would act in situations in which counterproductive behavior has been, or might be, a problem in your organization. You will need to be particularly careful that you conduct thorough reference and background checks, and that you specifically ask whether the applicant has had any history of counterproductive behavior. If the test results are accompanied by any of the other red flags described at the end of this chapter, you're probably better off not hiring the applicant.

Drug Testing

Drug testing refers to a variety of tools that are intended to identify workers who have used certain types of drugs. Most often, drug testing is targeted toward the use of illegal drugs, particularly marijuana, opiates, amphetamines, barbiturates, and cocaine. At the same time, alcohol—the most widely abused drug in our society and the drug widely recognized as having the most significant effect on the workplace—is much less often targeted by drug-testing programs.

In many cases, drug testing is used to determine whether *current* employees are using drugs. This type of testing may be "for cause," as when testing is mandated following an accident or when a supervisor has reason to be suspicious of an employee's behavior. "Fitness for duty" testing may be required to ensure that employees who have undergone drug rehabilitation are no longer using drugs. A third type of testing program for current employees involves ongoing, and generally random, testing, which is assumed to act as a deterrent to drug use. Although these types of testing programs are quite prevalent, our focus in this chapter is on *preemployment* drug tests used to screen out applicants who are likely to use drugs on the job.

Should You Drug-Test?

One of the first issues you need to consider is whether drug testing should be a part of your hiring system. Three basic arguments have been made for drug testing: (1) the argument that drug testing will increase organizational effectiveness by increasing performance and decreasing absenteeism, accidents, and health costs; (2) the philosophical argument that employers and other employees have a right to a drug-free workplace; and (3) the more defensive argument that companies that don't screen applicants for drugs become the "employer of last resort" for drug-using applicants who couldn't get a job elsewhere.

Drug Testing and Organizational Effectiveness

The most fundamental argument is that drug use adversely affects organizational performance. This effect may be direct, as when employees' on-the-job substance abuse affects their efficiency or safety. The effects may also be more indirect: drug users may be more likely to engage in illegal behavior at work, including theft as well as dealing drugs to other employees. Abusers of alcohol and other drugs may also miss work more often and incur higher health care expenses. How valid are these claims?

Surprisingly, research shows that the link between drug *testing* (rather than drug or alcohol use itself) and job performance or accidents is much more tenuous than most people assume.[20] One reason for this probably has to do with the way drug testing is performed. Urinalysis, the most frequently used type of drug testing, cannot distinguish between chronic and occasional drug use, nor between drug use during working hours or away from work. Thus some people who receive positive drug test results may not have been using the drug in a way that directly interfered with their job performance. A second consideration has to do with the type of work being performed. Even on-the-job drug use may have minimal effects on simple, easily learned, low-risk tasks.[21] For other, safety-sensitive positions such as surgeons or pilots, even residual amounts of drugs used well before a work shift might have critical consequences for job performance.

By contrast, credible research has linked drug testing with reduced absences and health care costs. For example, a carefully controlled study of U.S. Postal Service workers found that applicants who tested positive for drug use had 41 percent greater absenteeism and were 39 percent more likely to be terminated than applicants who tested negative.[22] The Georgia Power Company found that employees who used drugs or were problem drinkers used more medical benefits ($1,377 annually) than a matched group of nonabusing employees ($163 annually).[23] Thus, while drug testing may not directly increase performance in all work settings, it is at least likely to reduce health-related costs.

Drug Testing Is the Right Thing to Do

Some employers simply don't want employees who use drugs to be working for them. It's not necessarily a matter of drug users being less productive, incurring greater health costs, or creating safety hazards. Drug use is illegal and inappropriate, the argument goes, and it will not be condoned or allowed at work. Though this position may be admirable, it does raise questions about the appropriateness of using tests that cannot distinguish between behavior at work and behavior off the job. Moreover, emphasizing the illegality of drugs sometimes creates a double standard regarding the on-the-job abuse of legal drugs, especially alcohol.

A stronger version of the "testing is the right thing to do" argument applies to companies doing business with the U.S. government. If your company is receiving federal contracts or grants, you are obligated to comply with the Drug Free Workplace Act's mandate to provide a drug-free working environment. This requires that you establish drug education and awareness programs and take action against employees who use drugs at the workplace.

Defensive Drug Testing

Employers who have concerns about the accuracy or fairness of drug testing are finding themselves backed into a corner by the pervasiveness of applicant drug testing. If most of your competitors have a drug-testing program and you don't, you may end up attracting drug-using applicants who cannot get jobs elsewhere. It's a disturbing prospect to risk becoming the employer of last resort for drug users, and to end up with a disproportionately high number of drug users. If you find yourself in such a situation, you need to find a way to clearly inform drug abusers that they are not welcome. Having a very visible policy of testing all applicants for drugs seems to be one effective way of deterring drug-using applicants from applying for a job.[24]

Types of Drug Tests

There are currently three categories of drug tests. One, integrity testing, was introduced earlier in this chapter in the context of detecting theft and other counterproductive behavior. A second, more widely recognized, approach involves biochemical analysis of blood, urine, or hair specimens. A third approach attempts to assess performance impairment more directly by measuring employees' performance on complex computer-based tasks. The three methods take significantly different approaches to assessing alcohol and drug use as a counterproductive behavior and have different benefits and drawbacks. Before you decide to implement drug testing as part of your hiring system, it is important to understand how the differences between these types of tests can affect hiring decisions.

Integrity Tests

As we described earlier in this chapter, drug use is one of the deviant behaviors predicted by most integrity tests. Unlike biochemical drug tests, which are based on more or less direct "proof" of *past* drug use, paper-and-pencil tests are primarily intended to predict *future* drug use as one form of counterproductive behavior. Overt integrity tests typically do this by asking applicants about their attitudes toward drug use, their associations with drug users, and the extent to which their attitudes toward drug use are permissive versus punitive. Personality-based integrity tests inquire about the way applicants cope with stressful situations, their attraction to risk-taking behavior, and their commitment to conventional norms of behavior.

Because they assess *predisposition* toward drug use rather than actual drug use, integrity tests can be useful for predicting which applicants may later turn to drug use or other counterproductive behavior, as well as for detecting current drug users. On the other hand, since integrity tests don't provide hard evidence of actual drug use, they're less suitable for investigations of accidents or incidents in which alcohol or drug use is suspected. The indirect, or predictive, evidence from integrity tests may be adequate for making hiring decisions, but it would probably not be sufficient for taking disciplinary action against employees accused of substance use.

Biochemical Drug Tests

The most common approach to drug testing is based on the fact that drug use leaves behind a chemical trace in the body. The most direct application of this can be seen in the techniques used by police for detecting alcohol use among drunk drivers. After being consumed, alcohol enters the bloodstream, and until it is metabolized it diffuses through the lungs into exhaled air. An effective and generally reliable measure of alcohol use is therefore made possible by measuring the presence and proportion of alcohol in breath or blood samples. A unique advantage of these tests is that they provide a quantitative measure of the level of alcohol in the body at the time of testing. This makes the tests particularly appropriate for verifying recent use of alcohol, and it has also made possible the conversion of alcohol concentration into estimates of performance impairment, such as the common designation of a blood-alcohol concentration of 0.10 percent as the cutoff for being able to drive unimpaired.

While blood- or breath-alcohol levels have become the standard for detection of alcohol use while driving, they are rarely used in employment contexts other than investigation of transportation accidents. One reason is that alcohol use has not traditionally been the focus of drug-testing programs. Another is that it is difficult for employers to arrange this type of testing, since alcohol is rapidly burned off (metabolized) by the body. Direct analysis of blood-alcohol levels is not appropriate for preemployment testing, because it is regarded as a medical examination, and the Americans with Disabilities Act stipulates that medical examinations can be required only *after* a job offer has been made. Employers who are concerned with preemployment screening related to on-the-job alcohol abuse would want to explore examples of integrity test–based screening tools, like those described above, that include alcohol abuse in the screened behaviors. In addition, at the end of the chapter, we will note ways in which a small number of applicants may disclose serious counterproductive-behavior problems, including alcohol abuse, during the application process.

A second class of biochemical drug tests involves analysis of drug metabolites found in urine or hair samples. As drugs are processed by the body, they leave behind by-products, or metabolites. Urinalysis detects these metabolites through sophisticated analysis of an employee's urine. Depending on the drug and the frequency and intensity of its use, metabolites can be detected in urine from as few as two or three to as many as thirty days after use. Because urinalysis is by far the most widely used form of drug test, most of our discussion of controversies will relate to it.

An alternative is to analyze drug metabolites that are contained in samples of a person's hair. In addition to being less invasive, hair samples require no special storage and provide a more extensive record of drug use compared to urinalysis. Some argue that hair samples retain traces of drug metabolites almost indefinitely, although there is a period of five to seven days before the drug metabolites show up in hair. However, because of a lack of research on standards and validity, the National Institute on Drug Abuse does not recommend hair analysis as a drug-detection method.[25]

Impairment Tests

One of the limitations of urinalysis is that it measures only past use of drugs, not a person's *current* level of performance impairment. Suppose, for example, that you decide to require drug testing as one strategy for reducing accidents in your warehouse operations.

Although a urinalysis program may be effective in screening out past drug users, it provides no defense against a forklift operator who (1) is experimenting with drugs for the first time, (2) had a couple of beers with lunch, (3) doesn't realize that prescription medicine can interfere with performance, or (4) is exhausted from staying up all night with a sick child. Integrity testing might help to reduce scenarios 1 and 2, but it would be useless for scenarios 3 and 4. This is where impairment testing can be a useful complement to preemployment drug testing.

Impairment testing focuses directly on an employee's ability to perform the job at the time of testing, generally by having the employee perform some form of complex, computerized task. One example of such a task is similar to the old Pong video game, in which the employee moves a control in order to hit a moving cursor on the computer screen. Employees perform the task before every work shift, and that day's score is compared to his or her typical performance. If the performance is well below the employee's typical performance, he or she is judged to be impaired and is either sent home, assigned to less safety-sensitive work, or referred to counseling if the problem seems to be severe or chronic. Because the computer task measures basic psychomotor performance, it is presumed to be relevant to most jobs in which some level of attention and coordination are necessary.

From a high-impact hiring perspective, the key advantage of impairment testing is its focus on job-relevant performance rather than on the use of particular substances. Performance impairment may be caused by the use of legal or illegal substances, emotional strain, or physical fatigue. While the causes (and solutions) may differ, they become important to you for a common reason—their impact on job performance. However, while impairment testing can be useful for daily screening of current employees, it is not intended for use as a preemployment screening tool.

Controversies Regarding Drug Testing

In its relatively short existence, drug testing has been the center of numerous controversies. Most of these pertain to urinalysis, although we previously described some controversies surrounding personality and integrity testing used to detect substance abusers.

Among the most contentious debates are questions about the accuracy, legality, and fairness of drug testing.

Are Drug Tests Accurate?

We've all heard stories about the model of sobriety who fails a drug test because of eating poppy-seed bagels or using an over-the-counter medicine that mimics the chemical marker of an illegal drug. Critics argue that false-positive errors, where people are incorrectly identified as using drugs, are common and represent a fundamental flaw with drug testing. Advocates of testing respond by saying that these stories are little more than urban legend, and that drug tests are 99 percent accurate. How should these claims and counterclaims affect your decision about whether or not to test?

Drug testing can be very accurate, but in practice it is susceptible to a variety of factors that often cause significant error rates. However, you can use procedures that will substantially reduce errors. The accuracy of biochemical drug tests depends on the type of analytical process used, the accuracy and care with which the drug sample is collected and analyzed, and professional interpretation of the results of the analysis. Let's consider each of these factors in turn.

Urinalyses can be divided into two basic categories: screening tests and confirmatory tests. Screening tests, such as those based on thin-layer chromatography, enzyme immunoassay, or radioimmunoassay methods, are quick and fairly inexpensive (approximately ten to twenty dollars). Unfortunately, they are also surprisingly error-prone. Carefully controlled studies of screening tests have shown that as many as 37 percent of applicants may be incorrectly identified as using amphetamines, and 66 percent as using methadone. These false-positive errors are often the result of the screening test's inability to discriminate drug metabolites from similar-appearing metabolites or from innocent substances such as the infamous poppy-seed bagel or cold and pain medicines like decongestants or ibuprofen. What is too often overlooked is that these tests also fail to detect many applicants who have used drugs; false-negative rates can be as high as 100 percent.[26]

One way to avoid these errors is to use more sophisticated analytical techniques, such as gas chromatography/mass spectrometry (GC/MS). These techniques are extremely accurate, with overall "hit rates" approaching 99 percent.[27] GC/MS tests used to be much more expensive, but prices have now dropped to little more than those of basic screening tests. Federally certified laboratories that are required to use these tests often offer bundled prices of twenty-five to thirty dollars; at that price, there is hardly an argument for *not* confirming positive test results.

However, while confirmatory tests reduce false positives, they do not solve the problem of the drug users who aren't caught by inexpensive screening tests. If you're serious about detecting drug use among job applicants, you should probably skip the inexpensive screening tests and use GC/MS analysis for *all* samples. About the only time when a two-stage, "screen first and then confirm positives" strategy makes sense is in situations where few of the people being tested are likely to be using drugs, such as ongoing testing of current employees in a company with historically low levels of substance abuse.

Even accurate methodologies depend on well-trained and conscientious staff to collect the urine samples, conduct the analyses properly, and maintain accurate records. Studies have shown that testing laboratories vary considerably on each of these dimensions. Since you don't have the time or expertise to evaluate laboratories yourself, the best approach is to have all the work—including collection of urine samples—done by laboratories that have been certified by the National Institute on Drug Abuse. Lists of certified laboratories are regularly published in the *Federal Register,* and they can also be obtained directly from the National Institute on Drug Abuse or from the Internet at http://www.ctaa.org/resource/drug-alc/hhs-labs.htm.

Interpretation of results is also a critical factor affecting the accuracy of drug tests. You will probably need expert assistance in determining what drugs to screen for and what threshold levels to set to minimize false positives. A good testing laboratory should be able to provide this information as part of its service. It is also important to have positive test results reviewed by a medical review officer, or MRO. In addition to ensuring that the procedures were conducted accurately, the MRO can determine whether any extenuating circumstances, such as the use of substances that mimic the chemical profile of an illegal drug, might have affected the accuracy of test results. In the case of drug tests of current employees, the MRO can also design and monitor a drug treatment program for employees with substance abuse problems. MROs are often provided as part of a full-service laboratory or an Employee Assistance Program.

The bottom line is that drug tests can be extremely accurate indicators of prior drug use if they are implemented properly. Unfortunately, many drug-testing programs do not follow National Institute on Drug Abuse recommendations regarding the use of certified laboratories, confirmatory tests, or MROs. In these cases, claims of unfair treatment may be quite justified and can lead to expensive legal challenges. If you decide to implement preemployment drug testing, we strongly urge you to follow these recommendations. This leads us to the next area of controversy.

Is Drug Testing Legal?

The simple answer is yes, at least for private sector employers, although restrictions vary a lot in different states. Most legal challenges have dealt with federal constitutional protections, which apply only to government employees or employees of private sector organizations that are directly regulated by federal statutes, such as firms conducting interstate transportation. The most common complaint is that collection of urine samples represents an unwarranted search and seizure of evidence without reasonable suspicion of drug use; that is, employees were presumed guilty and forced to provide incriminating evidence against themselves. In two landmark cases, the U.S. Supreme Court held that such searches are reasonable, citing compelling public safety concerns for the positions involved (armed customs inspectors and railroad employees).

Critics have also argued that drug testing is a violation of privacy rights. Although a general right to privacy is not explicitly stated in the U.S. Constitution, some states, such as California, do incorporate such a right in their state constitutions. However, employers may still be able to prevail in these states if they can show that the information obtained by the drug test is relevant. Courts generally seem inclined to accept such an argument for drug testing, particularly when it is based on public safety considerations.

Drug use and testing are also addressed by the Americans with Disabilities Act and the Civil Rights Act of 1991, although both provide more protection for addicted employees than for applicants. These laws specifically allow employers to conduct preemployment drug tests at any point in the hiring process, unlike other medical tests that can be required only after an offer of employment has been extended. Moreover, while employees with a drug addiction must be treated as having a disability, this requirement is waived for employees who are *currently* using drugs.

Is Drug Testing Fair?

Although drug testing is generally legal, some employees and applicants feel that it is unfair and unreasonable, particularly for jobs where the safety of coworkers or the public is not an issue. One reason for negative reactions is that "suspicionless" drug testing makes employees feel as if they have to prove that they're not drug users even when there is no specific reason to suspect that they are. The problem is even worse for nonusers who erroneously test positive. Since many drug-testing programs don't use confirmatory testing or MROs, this kind of mistake is fairly common and nearly impossible for an applicant to correct.

Another reason that many people object to drug testing is that providing a urine sample represents a significant invasion of privacy. And, as if being required to provide a urine sample weren't bad enough, the proper technique involves collecting the sample under the watchful eye of a nurse or laboratory technician who can ensure that the sample belongs to the person being tested and that a "clean" sample has not been substituted. Nor does the threat of invasion of privacy end when you've finished at the lab and come home, because you don't know what other uses are being made of your urine sample. In addition to detecting drug metabolites, urinalysis can also determine whether an applicant is pregnant or using birth-control medication, has diabetes or other chronic illnesses, or even is genetically predisposed to future illness.

These concerns about privacy are of more than passing interest. Studies have shown that applicants who object to a potential employer's hiring practices are less likely to seek or accept a job from that employer, thus increasing the cost and difficulty of recruitment. Although some studies suggest that job applicants are becoming more used to drug testing, many qualified applicants will still resent the process.[28] Some of these applicants may feel compelled to accept a job despite their concerns about what they see as unfair hiring practices; research shows that they may begin work with a chip on their shoulder that can affect their commitment and performance.[29] You need to weigh the benefits of drug testing against the potential costs of alienating applicants and employees who perceive such testing as unfair and invasive of privacy. You also want to use testing procedures that minimize negative reactions. Particularly for preemployment screening purposes, integrity tests may represent a less offensive and equally effective alternative to urinalysis.[30]

Is That a Red Flag You're Waving at Me? Being Alert for Signs of Counterproductive Behavior During Hiring

When people are applying for a job, they are usually trying to be on their best behavior and present the best record possible; this makes it harder to detect counterproductive behavior. Remember, though, that your goal is to identify and screen out the small number of applicants who have a strong tendency toward, and recent history of, such behavior. Signs and actual examples of counterproductive behavior can even occur during the application process, and you need to be alert to them. Since most applicants are putting their best foot forward, problem behavior should stick out like a red flag.

By reminding you to be alert to counterproductive behavior, we emphatically do not mean that you should treat every applicant as a potential miscreant. But when signs show up, you need to pay attention to them and not ignore or minimize them. These signs only show up in a small number of applicants, but when they do they deserve your attention. One good rule is to be as certain as possible before you offer employment to any candidate that you have ruled out an active history of counterproductive behavior. Focusing on active histories of behavior will also help you to keep within the guidelines of the Americans with Disabilities Act when dealing with behaviors related to alcohol and drug abuse.

It's important to be fair and conscientious in your assessments of potential counterproductive behavior, but fairness does not mean ignoring information, your senses, or your good judgment. When an applicant waves a red flag, you should proceed with great caution before hiring. Let's look at how these red flags can show up during the hiring process.

Applicants Show You or Tell You About Counterproductive Behavior Themselves

It seems almost impossible that someone would tell you about such behavior, doesn't it? But some applicants do "show and tell" and it's important to take these signs seriously when they occur and make your decisions accordingly. Here are a few such red flags, each taken from real-life examples:

- Applicants who tell you about settling a score with an old employer when they explain why they're changing jobs or why they think you would be a great potential employer
- Applicants who make sexually charged remarks or innuendos about people they encounter during the hiring process
- Applicants who show up for an interview visibly intoxicated or drug-impaired, or reeking of alcohol or marijuana
- Applicants who disclose a past serious instance of sexual harassment in an attempt to minimize the problem or preempt your own analysis

These blatant behaviors may not happen frequently, but they do happen, and they are too often ignored when they do. We remember helping the CEO of an entrepreneurial company interview a job candidate. The candidate showed up well dressed, carrying a well-prepared résumé, and, as it turned out, well tanked. Her speech was slurred and her eyes somewhat glazed. During the first portion of the interview, as she spoke to the CEO, we grew increasingly uncomfortable with her incoherence. And when she finally turned across the table to speak to us, the overpowering smell of alcohol was unmistakable—not perfume or mouthwash but good old-fashioned booze. We cut our questions short, but the CEO continued on. When the interview finally ended, he began a discussion of her qualifications, remarking partway through that she must be a bit nervous by disposition and may have had "a drink" at lunch to steady her nerves.

Why would an applicant do this? People who habitually engage in deviant behavior may come to think of it as normal, which also explains why applicants who are completing integrity tests willingly admit having stolen in the past. They may even be habituated enough to believe that you won't notice anything out of the ordinary, like the smell of booze or the offhand racial slur.

Applicants may also make a partial disclosure of problem behavior in the belief that you will accept their presentation of facts, ignore the situation, or be too squeamish to learn more on your own. A red flag is being waved, for example, when an applicant tells you of being unfairly persecuted by an unreasonable person for sexual harassment. That is certainly a valid possibility, but you would be prudent to gather more information and proceed cautiously, rather than to accept the applicant's presentation of the situation at face value.

A similar faulty logic may underlie the behavior of applicants who make crude remarks about members of the opposite sex during the application process, get drunk during a social function that's part of the application process, disclose a disregard for their current employer's rules and procedures, or list in detail all the reasons they will need to be absent during their first few months on the job. (No, we are not making any of these up.) These candidates are asking that you ignore and tolerate this behavior before you even employ them. After hiring such a candidate, as with those who make partial and preemptive disclosures of serious issues, you are likely to hear, "You knew about all this when you hired me."

Applicants Indicate Counterproductive Behavior in Their Application or Résumé

Several red flags can be raised by applicants' applications or résumés. Here are a few:

- Gaps in a résumé, or time filled with vague or unverifiable activities. Obviously, many people have quite legitimate reasons for gaps in employment, chief among them taking time to raise a family. It's the assertion of work that you can't pin down or that seems incongruous that should give you pause. In some instances, this has turned out to mean time spent hiding out in a forest, serving an undisclosed prison sentence, or fleeing overseas. A recurring pattern to many red flags is information that can't be verified as either true or false, and this is no exception.

- An unusual number or status of references. Why should people feel that they need ten people to vouch for them, and why is Mother Teresa listed as a reference for a candidate for management trainee?
- An overabundance of generic letters of reference, written at some time in the past. There may be quite legitimate reasons for having such letters, but they should never stop you from following all of your standard procedures for checking both references and past supervisors.
- Work experience or locations that can't be verified, particularly if they are in the United States. You may not be able to find out what the applicant doesn't want you to know about his or her activities, but the lack of verification should raise a red flag.
- Incongruities or unnecessary misrepresentations. We remember an applicant for an office management position who described her graduate degree as being in science, ethics, and economics. We questioned her about her thesis and her topic seemed incongruous for such a program (the first small red flag). A call to her university revealed that her graduate degree was real, but it was actually in religion (the second red flag). Careful checks of her work history then showed that a key job-related part of her history—implementing an extensive computerization effort for an office operations center— was a convincing fabrication.
- Written applications or cover letters that are inconsistent with making a diligent effort to get a job. Many great employees have poor handwriting, get nervous when applying for jobs, or have poor written English skills, particularly in jobs where these skills are not job-related. But an application that indicates that a candidate is neglectful even when applying for a job, or may have been impaired while doing so, raises another red flag.

Applicants' References Tell You About Counterproductive Behavior

The disadvantage you have in finding out about counterproductive behavior in an applicant is that you haven't actually worked with him or her. People who have may provide a more complete picture. Be wary when an applicant asks you not to check references with a past employer (as compared with a current employer), or to discount the information you receive. Almost everyone has had at least one negative employment experience, and these, by themselves, are not red flags. But in most situations, people are willing to let the chips of their past work fall where they may.

When an applicant asks you not to obtain information from past employers or to disregard information, you should become *more* alert. Ask the applicant specifically why he or she is making that request, and ask for the specifics about any problem situation or supervisor. When there is no hidden problem, you will get a complete explanation and will likely get a very similar one when you talk to the former employer, even if there were difficulties or hard feelings. But at other times, you will find out that the problem was related to counterproductive behavior, such as alcohol or drug abuse, theft, or sexual harassment. In such instances, you will want to proceed with extreme caution and with care about the information you are getting from both the applicant and his or her former employers.

Should you not contact a past employer at a candidate's request? We feel that you owe your duty to your own organization, not to the candidate, and you should make contact. Again, you will want to be cautious about accepting what you hear. On the other hand, it is quite legitimate for an applicant to ask you not to contact a *current* employer, and it is just as legitimate for you to make sure that you can contact the current employer to verify employment information after any job offer you may make has been accepted.

Past employers will often let you know about counterproductive behavior if you ask while checking references in a job-related way. (Supplied references are less likely to do this.) How do you ask? Politely, respectfully, after you have established rapport, very straightforwardly, and in a way that doesn't put the past employer in the position of slandering the candidate. You might ask (in your own words):

"Is there anything related to this person's conduct on the job that I haven't asked you about that might affect performance on the job for which he or she is applying?"

"Did you have concerns that the employee worked with his or her performance impaired [or impaired by alcohol or drug use on the job]?"

"Did you have any concerns about this person's professional conduct with coworkers or subordinates, and specifically in regard to sexual harassment?"

Some past employers will react with surprise to these questions, and not everyone will answer them. But often, once a question has been put straightforwardly, the person you are speaking with will feel a duty to be straightforward with you in return and will do so. That is why you are asking the questions.

When you are confronted with counterproductive behavior—or red flags suggesting the possibility of such behavior—you must make use of that information. It can indicate serious problems and almost always warrants further investigation. You don't want to leap to faulty conclusions, but you have a duty to act as a reasonable and prudent person when presented with this type of information. You don't need to have overwhelming evidence that the applicant would become a problem employee. You are not in a courtroom, trying to convict the applicant of a criminal offense; you are trying to make a critical business decision about whether to devote your organization's resources to hiring this person. Do so prudently.

Summary

High-impact hiring involves an assessment of the whole range of job-relevant factors an applicant will bring to the job. While most of this book has focused on determining whether applicants have the knowledge, skills, and abilities to perform the job, it is also important to determine whether they are likely to behave in a counterproductive fashion on a job. If an applicant has all the necessary knowledge, skills, and abilities to be a wonderful pilot but is inclined to have three martinis before flying, none of us wants to have that person in the cockpit. If we hire an accountant who embezzles, a manager who harasses female subordinates, or a shipping department worker who threatens coworkers, we similarly demonstrate bad hiring decisions.

In this chapter we have described the use of integrity tests and drug tests as ways of screening out applicants who are predisposed to engaging in these and other forms of counterproductive behavior. We have also described other signs of counterproductive behavior that can emerge during the hiring process. Although none of the procedures are perfect, they can provide useful complements to background checks and can improve your odds. However, it is important to remember that not all integrity and drug tests are equal, and to use particular care in evaluating vendors according to the standards described in Chapters Six and Nine. It is also crucial to remember that these tests will not magically solve all your workplace problems. Effective management practices are still needed to create a positive work environment that will make counterproductive behavior less likely.

Chapter Twelve

Making High-Impact Hiring Decisions

When we were developing a selection system for a unit of a Fortune 500 company, we worked with a manager who had experience at a previous job using a nationally known system of structured, behaviorally based interviewing, similar to the interviewing we recommend in Chapter Eight. We were delighted to work with someone who already understood the importance of performance orientation and validity. But when it came time for us to work out the decision process for the large number of hires in the unit each year, our friend was wary and skeptical of what she was sure we were going to recommend. She told us that she and her colleagues simply wouldn't have the time for the decision process recommended by the national system. "Tell us about that," we said. "Well," she said, "we were trained that all the managers in an operating unit have to come to consensus on hiring decisions, based on scores from the behavioral interviews. So whenever we were hiring, we'd have these long meetings with all the other managers, who didn't have to live with the results, and it took forever to reach consensus. We just don't have that kind of time here." "You're right," we said, "but you didn't have a lot of time there, either. So what did you do?" "Easy," came her reply. "All the managers got together and cut a deal: everyone voted for the candidate the hiring manager voted for. That way, we got 'consensus,' the managers got to hire the candidate they wanted, and we got done with those meetings fast."

By now you'll recognize that this performance-oriented hiring system got turned into a non-performance-based ritual. It wasn't the information-gathering process that became a ritual: it was the *decision-making* process. The purpose of this chapter is to help you think about high-impact decision making as a systematic, performance-oriented process that's an essential component of high-impact hiring. You'll learn how to gather and use information in ways that contribute to high-impact hiring decisions instead of to decision-making disasters. In this way, you'll be able to put every concept of every chapter in this book to use in the framework of making an effective hiring decision.

Humility: The Critical Ingredient in Hiring Decisions

The single most important ingredient you can bring to making a hiring decision effectively is *humility*. Humility may seem like an unusual word to be using in this context. We're not referring to a moral virtue, but instead to understanding accurately what you know, what you *can* know, what you *don't* know, and what you *won't* know, and then making the best possible decisions on the basis of that understanding. Socrates was referring to this kind of humility when he said that true wisdom is knowing what you know and knowing what you do not know.

To help us gain that humility, we're going to start by describing four fundamental limits that affect hiring decisions and how you can respond to them:

1. Limits on knowledge and accuracy
2. Limits on reasoning
3. Limits on predicting a changing future
4. A limitation we call "the tyranny of the best"

Limits on Knowledge and Accuracy

To make a fully informed hiring decision, you would have to know everything that was relevant to performance about every one of your candidates. But it's not possible to do this. You can't have all candidates come to work for six months and evaluate their performances, nor can you know everything you need to know about them. So there are practical limits to the amount of knowledge you can have when you decide to hire.

You make a hiring decision based on a subset of knowledge about each candidate. To make an effective decision, you want to be conscious that you know something, but not everything, about each candidate. You also want to design your selection system so that you are obtaining reliable information. Without careful attention to collecting data systematically and in a performance-oriented way, as outlined in Chapter Six, you will have different subsets of knowledge about each candidate, and your decision-making process will be flawed from the start. Applicants want to provide you with information that makes them seem more qualified, and they may withhold information that makes them seem less qualified. Our own research has shown that this process of distorting responses can have a substantial impact on which people you hire.[1,2]

Limits on Reasoning

It may seem insulting to suggest that you and the rest of us humans have limits on our capacity to reason, but we do. Our brains, with their inherent limits on size, and therefore on the number of neurons they contain, have some limit on their capacity to compute.[3] Complex problems that involve evaluation of different combinations, such as hiring decisions, exceed even a supercomputer's ability to solve them through brute-force crunching of all possible combinations. For example, think about the problem of how to assign people to jobs after they are hired. There is only one possible solution when you assign one person to a single position, two possible combinations of assignments to be evaluated when you assign two people to two positions, six possible combinations for three people and three positions, and twenty-four for four people and four positions. Assigning seventy people to seventy tasks, as you might do in a large company, for a start-up, or for seasonal hiring, requires evaluating almost 10^{100} combinations, a task that would exceed the capacity of supercomputers filling every planet in our solar system and running for millions of years.[4,5]

Even if you had perfect knowledge about every candidate—and it's critical to remember that you don't and can't—it's not possible to just reason your way through the wide range of relevant information about candidates and positions and come to an effective decision. Instead, we all adopt simplifications that allow us to make the decision workable. Experts in decision making have shown that when these simplifications are done intuitively, the resulting decisions are often of poor quality.[6, 7] The high-impact decision-making approach instead emphasizes the development of simplification strategies that lead to more effective decisions.[8, 9]

Limits on Predicting the Future

Expecting your hiring system to perfectly predict performance is a demand that it predict and control the future. As much as we'd all like to be error-free when hiring, this goal is excessively optimistic to achieve and unreasonable to operate on. Decision-making expert Kenneth Hammond points out the inherent limitations imposed on every decision simply because a decision, by definition, is about a future event that hasn't yet come to pass and therefore can't be fully understood.[10] And as we've noted elsewhere, human beings exercise choice, including choice about their work performance. Past performance is a good predictor of future performance, but human beings can and do choose to do things that are different from what they've done before. Learning, training, motivation, and persistence, for example, all improve performance as time goes on, and dissatisfaction, changes in the job, and counterproductive behavior can all decrease performance.

The Tyranny of the Best

All of these limitations result in a final limit, "the tyranny of the best." How many times have you heard someone say, "Go out and hire the best person for the job"? This single instruction may lead to more hiring errors than everything we've discussed until now. We'll demonstrate this brash statement with an example from an organization that has the skills and resources to do outstanding hiring.

AT&T, the world's leading telecommunications company, was searching for a successor to its current CEO. The instructions the CEO gave were to go out and "find the best and the brightest." Best at what? Brightest for what? To complicate matters, the search firms were told to recruit for the CEO of a marketing unit. The best and the brightest thus got defined as the best and brightest for marketing. The stock market's reaction to the resulting hire—a CEO who had had some marketing successes but far less experience with telecommunications technologies—was so intense that the value of AT&T stock dropped almost 5 percent on a day when other telecommunications stocks rose.[11, 12] One of the key issues for our purposes is the starting premise that the search should be for an elusive "best."

It's far easier and more useful to find excellent workable solutions to problems than it is to try to determine whether there is a single "best" solution to a problem, or what that best solution is. In fact, research suggests that focusing on workable solutions often produces better results than trying to find an optimal solution.[13] The lesson to be learned is that one of the most important ways to simplify and improve your hiring decisions is to stop looking for a "best" performer. Instead, start your hiring process by identifying performers whose qualifications predict that they can do the job effectively or, even better, excellently. The uncertainty inherent in even the best selection measures makes it difficult, if not impossible, to differentiate accurately between the predicted future performance of two closely ranked candidates. However, the measures are usually accurate enough to differentiate successful from unsuccessful employees.

We do not want our approach to be misread. We don't believe that different kinds of job performance are all acceptable, nor we do believe that it's impossible to know anything useful about the world around us, or about work performance. On the contrary, in the next section, we will show you how to use information you can gather to make good decisions about desirable, workable, and unworkable options in hiring. So join us in leaving the fantasy world of searching endlessly for "the best" and learn the extraordinary power of doing a consistently good job of hiring the good. As Herbert Simon sums it up in this twist on an old saying, sometimes "the best is the enemy of the good."[14]

A High-Impact Approach to Hiring Decision Making

Typical approaches to making a hiring decision fall into one of two camps, both of which are ill suited to most hiring situations. The first is the seat-of-the-pants, gut-instinct, trial-and-error methods we've described as warm-body and ritual hiring. The opposite approach is an idealized, highly quantitative decision-making process. While this approach is sophisticated and "scientific," it actually has a number of practical limitations, beginning with the assumption that you have the luxury of hiring from a large pool of qualified applicants. It also assumes that you have extensive, nearly perfect knowledge about these applicants; that you hire large numbers of these applicants on a regular basis; and that you, or your staff, have considerable statistical acumen.

We developed high-impact decision making for more typical hiring situations, in which these assumptions are not valid. High-impact decision making assumes that you are more likely to make your final choices from a small pool of applicants that may or may not meet your hiring needs. Our approach also recognizes that limitations on time and other resources generally cause your knowledge about applicants to be limited and imperfect. High-impact decision making compensates for these realities by helping you to:

- Develop solutions that overcome the fundamental limitations of decision making well enough to meet your hiring needs, even if the resulting decisions are not theoretically "optimal."[15]
- Use numerical-solution techniques that work well with small samples and that do not require you to be a statistician. If you can add, subtract, multiply, and divide, you can use these solutions to improve your hiring. In fact, we have developed one way of working through your hiring decision that requires no math at all!
- Adapt the complexity of your decision-making process to the difficulty of choosing among the group of people actually available to you to hire.

High-impact decision making, then, provides you with a practical way to make decisions that take advantage of what we know about effective decision making. It is designed to simplify hiring decisions by establishing three prioritized criteria:

1. Screen out applicants who will create serious performance problems. Eliminating the clearly incompetent—as well as the troublemakers—from your applicant pool can have a huge effect on the bottom line and should be your first priority.
2. Identify people who will at least satisfy your minimum requirements for work performance. Identifying these individuals is

generally easier than identifying the "best" applicants, and in some cases they may prove to be more cost-effective than hiring the cream of the crop.

3. Hire as many applicants as possible who *exceed* these minimum requirements, wherever that is practical.

A Hiring Decision Guide

When we develop a selection system for our clients, we prepare a customized decision-making guide that helps them to work through the hiring decisions. In this section we will help you to prepare your own guide: a method for assembling the critical information for making hiring decisions and working through your decisions. You will use the information contained in your Performance Attributes Matrix in a new way: to create a profile of successful performance and of desirable and acceptable levels of performance for each attribute in the matrix. Then, you will make your hiring decisions using the profiles.

High-impact decision making is designed to use minimal mathematics while still providing you with a systematic approach to evaluating and scoring the attributes of different candidates. We recommend using scores to represent your judgments, because having good information about applicants is not sufficient to make a good hiring decision. The information has to be evaluated, combined, and compared before you can make a high-impact hiring decision. And a structured process is the best way to accomplish this.

Some people have told us that they feel that using a score or rating takes their judgment out of the process and "reduces decisions about people to a number." In fact, we think that the opposite is true. We encourage you to use your judgment, focused in a high-impact way, on evaluating how well candidates' attributes fit with performance-based requirements. One of the purposes of the Performance Attributes Matrix is to guide you in using your judgment to evaluate the broad range and complexity of candidates' attributes in a systematic way, rather than to confound all this complexity and reduce it to a single nonperformance-based attribute called "gut feeling." As you make your evaluation of each attribute and each candidate, a score allows you to summarize and record your judgment so that you can make comparisons later. Without recording scores, you are likely to make decision-making errors that result from forgetting your evaluation, biasing your evaluation of one candidate against that of another, or aggregating your ratings into a single judgment to make it easier to remember. Imagine trying to remember your judgments of ten candidates on seven criteria without using some sort of scoring system!

For the decision-making process, the important information in the Performance Attributes Matrix is the performance attributes and the actual set of hiring tools you used to gather information on the attributes. At this point in the decision process, it's critical to use the matrix to keep your evaluation systematic. Doing so will help you to avoid the common mistake of combining all the information from a hiring tool into one overall score, rather than treating the score from each attribute measured by the hiring tool as a separate piece of information. An example would be to say that an applicant "did poorly" in an interview, rather than describing the person's performance on the particular attributes the interview was intended to assess. It's all too common for managers to try to come up with an overall score for the interview, reference check, résumé, and any tests. This has the effect of confounding and lumping together all of the attributes you worked hard to develop and is likely to add non-performance-related factors to your decision making.

The Performance Attributes Matrix is designed to help you to keep attributes distinct as you evaluate a candidate's qualifications and as you compare candidates to each other or with a standard. For example, your hiring decision might be based on scores for Conscientiousness, Work-Specific Knowledge, Attention to Detail, Numerical Reasoning, and Computer-Operating Skill. Some of these attributes may have been assessed by more than one hiring tool; for instance, Work-Specific Knowledge may have been measured in both the interview and a work sample. The matrix provides you with a way to combine scores from different measures, both for a given attribute and for different attributes.

Evaluating Qualifications: A Three-Tiered Approach

Another key consideration in high-impact decision making is how to evaluate the attributes measured by each of your hiring tools. One potential problem with measuring an attribute with different hiring tools is that the tools may have different ranges of scores.

For example, Dependability scores might range from 1 to 5 on your structured interview, from 1 to 4 on your scored reference-checking form, and from 0 to 50 on a personality inventory. How can you combine such disparate scoring systems to come up with an overall evaluation of an applicant's Dependability?

We recommend that you use three levels in evaluating most scores: unacceptable, minimally acceptable, and desirable. These categories fit with the ways most people think about work performance, and, more importantly, they define three categories of qualifications that are critical to high-impact hiring.

Unacceptable

You don't want to hire workers with unacceptable levels of qualifications. This defines your first level of qualifications. Not hiring workers with unacceptable levels of critical attributes is your first step in making your hiring decision a high-impact one. Rating each attribute separately instead of using a single overall rating will also keep you from hiring someone who has disqualifying characteristics in a few critical areas. One serious hiring error is to allow good ratings on some attributes to "average out" the effects of truly disqualifying ratings on other attributes. This kind of compensatory effect may be appropriate if a person has at least minimal qualifications, but it should never be allowed to operate when a person is truly unqualified on a particular attribute. A colleague of ours, for example, spent two years helping an organization out of a mess that was caused by hiring a candidate who was otherwise well qualified, but who had an established history of sexual harassment. Unqualified means disqualified in high-impact hiring, and it's important to have a rating scale and a decision-making process that says so. Being thorough about eliminating unacceptably qualified applicants from your pool allows you to hire with more confidence from the applicants who remain.

Acceptable

Next, you want to clearly identify a set of qualifications that define a minimum level of competency that will truly result in acceptable work. Acceptable work is work that will accomplish the most critical work outcomes as defined in your work analysis. Acceptable most emphatically does not imply hiring someone whose marginal performance impairs the ability of the organization to perform its work. Keeping this distinction in mind as you define what is minimally acceptable also helps to keep you focused on what's critical and what isn't. For example, if you are hiring for a call center in which all customer contact is by telephone, minimally acceptable levels of customer service orientation and verbal reasoning would be quite high, while minimally acceptable levels of personal grooming could be far lower.

The importance of deciding which attributes to base minimum competency on was brought home to us many years ago, when one of us was developing a selection system for a restaurant company. As part of the process, the management team had spent considerable time debating the relative importance of customer service orientation, food service skills, and professional appearance. A few weeks later, one of the district managers said, "I don't care what we talked about, I hire 'em if they're good-looking." That finally explained why his restaurants were consistently staffed by incompetent, unqualified, yet personally attractive wait staff. Defining minimal levels of competency is also required by the EEOC, and this example may go a long way to explaining why. No law requires that your organization hire anyone who isn't qualified to do the job. But you are required to define that minimal level in fair, job-related (and therefore performance-related) terms.

Desirable

Finally, we think it's critical to include the criteria that make for an outstanding performer, what we refer to as desirable levels of qualifications. As management expert Peter Drucker has pointed out, in order to hire excellent performers, you need to first be clear in your mind what excellent performance will look like.[16] By excellent performance, we mean performance that has a disproportionate impact on the work of your organization. Using the word "desirable" helps guide your hiring decision in two ways. First, when you find candidates who truly have desirable levels of qualifications of key attributes and no disqualifying scores, you want to hire them whenever possible. Second, "desirable" also implies "not essential," and that's important, too. If you've done a good job of defining "minimally acceptable" and are clear that unqualified candidates are never minimally acceptable, you should be able to do a good job of hiring, regardless of whether desirable candidates are in your pool for any given hire.

More quantitatively oriented readers may worry that our "unqualified, qualified, desirable" rating system is too simplistic to really capture differences between applicants. In reality, it's about as precise an evaluation as you can make in most hiring decisions, and it fits well with the way many people think when using numbers. Anything more fine-tuned is likely to make your ratings seem more precise than they really are, which can lead to decision-making errors. If you've done a good job of choosing valid hiring tools, it's very probable that a candidate with acceptable scores in all attributes will perform better than a candidate with unacceptable ratings. At the same time, if you have two candidates who rate acceptably on most attributes and who both rate desirably on the same attribute, chances are that there won't be significant differences in job performance between the two candidates. Although small differences between scores on an attribute are less critical than larger differences, if your measures are valid, then a candidate receiving a higher score has a higher probability of performing better on that attribute. If the desirable ratings were on different attributes, these differences would often tell you more about how the two candidates would do their jobs than they would about how good a job they'd do.

One reason you can be less concerned with these smaller differences in ratings among qualified candidates is that you have eliminated unqualified applicants from your pool. You can be more confident that small differences are differences between applicants who are at least "good enough."

Guidelines for Rating Applicants' Qualifications

For each attribute, you will need to determine what your basis will be for rating a candidate's qualifications as desirable, acceptable, or unacceptable. On a performance test that assesses actual or simulated work performance, doing this will be straightforward. Desirable candidates would have uniformly excellent performance, acceptable candidates would have performance that is satisfactory in all respects, and unacceptable candidates would have performance that would not meet minimum standards in your workplace.

The task is somewhat more difficult for attributes evaluated in interviews and reference checks, but still doable. Since these tools reflect judgments, applicants can be scored directly in terms of their acceptability on the attributes being assessed. "Desirable" ratings would indicate strong indications for an attribute, "acceptable" would indicate satisfactory levels without serious concerns, and "unacceptable" would indicate an absence of the attribute or serious warnings about deficiencies or problems.

The task is hardest on tests with raw scores, such as ability tests, personality tests, and cognitive ability tests. What is an acceptable level of Conscientiousness, for example? In developing standards for such scores, it's important to remember that we use such tests on the premise that, in general, people with more of a given attribute, and higher scores, tend to do better.

We recommend the following method for estimating scoring guidelines the first time you use such tests. As you continue to use your selection system and validate it, you can develop scoring guidelines from the relationship between hiring scores and later performance. First, using your experience in your job and in your industry, estimate what proportion of candidates have at least minimally acceptable levels of an attribute, or, alternatively, what proportion tend to be unacceptable. Use that percentage as a starting guideline for your ratings. For example, your experience may tell you that most of the people who seek employment are customer service–oriented, but fewer than a third have sufficient attention to detail. About half are conscientious enough. So you would estimate that anyone whose scores are in the top 80 percent on customer service (the twentieth percentile and up), the top third on attention to detail (sixty-sixth percentile and up), and the top half on Conscientiousness (fiftieth percentile and up) is at least acceptable. If you feel that you can reliably differentiate between acceptable and desirable levels of such traits, you can repeat the process to develop guidelines differentiating acceptable and desirable levels. As well, if you use tests that have national norms *for jobs and populations similar to yours* and that report percentile scores of applicants based on these norms, you can use these norms in place of your estimates. However, you want to know that the reported norms are based on samples of people similar to your applicants (see Chapter Nine for more discussion of norms).

Some additional key points should be made about using norms effectively in decision making. First, rating a lower-percentile score as acceptable does not mean that you are being less selective on an absolute basis. It means that you are estimating that a greater proportion of applicants tend to have acceptable levels. The example above, for instance, is common to work in resort communities: many people seeking employment in resorts are customer service–oriented, so a large proportion of candidates will have acceptable levels of customer service orientation. But while many "people people" are in resort communities to seek a resort career, others are there to escape from traditional workplaces, or from society, and you may find sharp differences in Conscientiousness scores.

Second, we prefer to think of our procedure for dealing with decision making on test measures as scoring guidelines rather than as cut scores. They clearly are based on estimates and need to be handled as approximations. Our method for combining scores in the decision table (presented later in this chapter) means that your approximations for desirable and acceptable levels will not include or exclude someone from employment on any single score. As you hire more and validate your system, your estimates should improve.

Making Hiring Decisions: The Categorical Approach

Once you've come up with a score for each applicant on each attribute, the next step is to combine this information in a way that will allow you to make a hiring decision. Candidates who score in the desirable range on every important attribute should be immediately and strongly considered for employment. Candidates who score desirably on some attributes and at least acceptably on all attributes should be put in a second group, to be reviewed carefully and compared with each other. Within this second group, candidates with desirable scores on important attributes should be considered first. Candidates with acceptable scores on all attributes but no desirable scores are considered next. Candidates who score unacceptably on any important attribute should be removed from further consideration, regardless of whether other attributes are rated as acceptable or desirable. Pretty simple. This method is not only intuitive and straightforward to use, but it is well established as providing good results under a variety of conditions.[17, 18] In many cases, this three-category approach is all you will need to know to make your final selection decision.

Yet every hiring decision is based on its own unique scenario, in which the most critical parts of the scenario are how many people you need to hire, how many candidates are available at a given level of predicted performance, and how much different levels of qualifications affect performance. So we want to build off this basic categorical decision method to provide you with additional options designed to help you deal with more complex hiring situations.

In many cases, you will need to make a choice about which people to hire within a group of applicants. That is, you may need to hire ten people, and you have five people who have all desirable scores and another twenty who have some acceptable scores. It's important to choose effectively within groups of applicants. For choosing within groups, we recommend that you pool attributes together for this purpose. For example, acceptable communication skills do not make up for substandard technical knowledge in a patent attorney. Once minimally acceptable competency is presented on all attributes, job performance is really based on combinations of different attributes and trade-offs among them. You want to find the combinations that provide a good fit with desired performance.

Evaluating different candidates' combinations of qualifications, then, requires combining scores of different attributes. We've developed a way to do this by creating a decision-making table of applicants and their attribute ratings, shown in Table 12.1. This can be prepared as follows:

1. List the attributes across the top of the chart, creating one column for every attribute you have rated in the selection system. If there are significant differences in importance between critical attributes, the most important attribute should be listed in the first column, the second most important in the second column, and so on. Don't worry too much about this; if all the attributes are about equal in importance, they can go in any order on the chart.
2. List the names of the applicants to the left of the first column of the chart, so that there is a row for each applicant.

Table 12.1. Decision Table for High-Impact Decision Making.

			Attribute		
Name	Work-Specific Knowledge	Conscientiousness	Attention to Detail	Numerical Reasoning	Computer Operating Skill
Lee	Acceptable	Desirable	Desirable	Acceptable	Acceptable
Tanya	Desirable	Desirable	Acceptable	Acceptable	Desirable
Alan	Desirable	Acceptable	Unacceptable	Acceptable	Acceptable
Karen	Acceptable	Acceptable	Acceptable	Acceptable	Acceptable
Frank	Desirable	Desirable	Desirable	Unacceptable	Acceptable
Sheri	Acceptable	Desirable	Acceptable	Desirable	Acceptable

3. Fill in the ratings for each applicant on each attribute. For most purposes, the desirable and acceptable ratings should work fine. Applicants with any unacceptable ratings who have not already been removed from the pool should be eliminated when these ratings show up on the table.
4. If all of the critical attributes are about equal in importance, you can rank-order your candidates by simply counting the number of attributes on which they have "desirable" scores.

For example, if you are measuring five attributes, applicants who have five attributes with desirable-level scores would be rated highest; those with four, three, two, and one desirable-level attributes would be ranked successively lower. Next would come those whose scores on all attributes were rated no higher than acceptable. Remember, candidates with unacceptable ratings on *any* important attribute need to be removed from consideration, regardless of whether other attributes were rated as desirable or acceptable.

As you can see, this is a simple method that helps you to differentiate between candidates and that often provides you with enough detail to make your final decisions. If not, a simple addition to this method provides finer distinctions, assuming that you have rated some attributes as significantly more important than others and want to give them more weight. This method allows you to add progressively more detail to your decision process, so be sure that you stop when you have enough detail to make a decision. Again, the simple method above is frequently sufficient.

Refer back to your decision table of applicants and attribute ratings and modify it as follows:

1. At the top of the table, note the most important attribute with a Roman numeral I, the second most important with a Roman numeral II, and so on. Or, if you prefer, prepare a new table in which the most important attribute is listed in the first column, the second most important in the second column, and so on. You can use the importance ratings that you developed in Chapter Two and used in Chapter Six.
2. Count up the number of attributes rated as desirable for each candidate. You may want to tally them at the right side of the table.

3. Circle or highlight the desirable-level ratings for the most important attribute.
4. Consider first those candidates who have high numbers of desirable ratings and who have attained desirable ratings on the most important attributes.
5. If you want finer detail within this group, start with the candidate who has a desirable rating for the most critical attribute and the highest number of desirable-level ratings. If you want even finer detail, out of those who attained desirable ratings on the most important attribute and high overall numbers of desirable ratings, consider first those who had the highest ratings on the *second* most important attribute.
6. Once you've considered the first candidate, you can continue down through the rest of the candidates who had desirable ratings on the most important attribute. Then you can proceed to those with desirable ratings on the second, third, fourth, and successively most important attributes. You can make finer ratings as needed using the same method.

Remember that in practice you are most concerned with deciding between two candidates only when you get to the point in the system where you are deciding which of the two you are going to hire. For example, assume that you are going to hire ten people for a position, and seven applicants have desirable ratings on your most important attributes and similar overall numbers of desirable ratings. It isn't useful for you to differentiate between these candidates. Plan to offer all of them employment. Once you know how many have accepted, you can get to the harder part of choosing who to hire further down in your pool. Assume that six of these seven applicants accept employment, leaving you with four slots to fill. Six applicants have been rated desirably on the second most important attribute. Of these, three were also rated desirably on four other attributes, including the third most important attribute. You offer employment to these three, leaving one slot to fill. Of the remaining three, applicant A isn't rated desirably on any other attributes, applicant B is rated desirably on the third most important attribute and two other attributes, and applicant C is rated desirably on a total of two attributes, including the fifth most important attribute. You choose to fill your last slot with candidate B.

You also need to remember that this more complex approach may not be necessary or useful. The finer the distinctions you draw between applicants, the less reliable the distinctions are likely to be. A performance-oriented selection system can help you to hire excellent candidates, but it cannot tell you as effectively which of two excellent candidates is better than the other.

Making Hiring Decisions: The Numerical Approach

You'll notice that we've just provided you with a way to make a hiring decision that doesn't involve making mathematical calculations. The decision-table method provides a way of making decisions based on several attributes, treating each attribute separately. The different elaborations of the method allow you to make fine distinctions while still dealing with nonnumerical ratings. As an alternative method, though, you may find it useful to rate candidates on numerical scores for each attribute and then combine these attributes into an overall score. You hire based on the level of the overall score. We want to provide an explanation of how to do this, and the math is simple and straightforward. But if you are still grateful to us for providing you with a nonmathematical approach in the decision table and want to skip over this section, you can do so.

Why would you want to use numerical scores? You may find combining numbers to be simpler than using a decision table, particularly if you are dealing with large numbers of qualified candidates. Or a large proportion of attributes may be numerically based to begin with. A third reason is that you may simply be more comfortable working with numbers.

Two cautions must be observed in order to maintain the integrity of selection decisions based on combined numerical scores. First and most important, as in the decision-table method, candidates with unacceptable rating levels on any attribute must be removed from the candidate pool. Otherwise, you can make the serious error of numerically creating an acceptable candidate by averaging an unacceptable and a desirable score. This result will be less visible than it is on a decision table. Unacceptable ratings are never compensatory!

Second, you must take care not to be fooled by your own numbers into believing that the combined or average scores are more precise than they are. As stated earlier, the larger the difference between two ratings (in this case, two scores), the more likely it is that the difference will be meaningful, all else being equal. Small differences in ratings probably won't make any consistent difference in work performance.

To make decisions numerically, you first need a way to combine different kinds of scores from different measures. For example, ratings of attributes made from the structured interview might range from 1 to 3, scores on a work sample might vary between 1 and 5, and raw scores from a personality measure might range from 1 to 100. How do you combine these scores into a number that makes sense? For high-impact hiring, we've developed a simple method for combining scores. This combined score is calculated only on the candidate's score in relation to the highest score possible for each attribute and measure. A more rigorous method, developing a type of combined scores called z-scores, involves first determining the standard deviation of the entire group of candidates for each attribute. We have a feeling that this calculation is something most hiring managers would just as soon skip. Our computer simulations show that the high-impact hiring method is generally as reliable as the rigorous method on which it is based.

You can do the calculations that follow with a calculator or on a spreadsheet. When we develop selection systems for clients, we develop customized software that makes these calculations automatically. If your eyes glaze over at math, we suggest again that you use the decision-table method and skip the following section. If you proceed, we promise that it's simpler than doing your income taxes!

The first step in creating a combined score is to convert all scores to a common scale. A simple way to do this is to divide each applicant's raw score on a measure by the maximum possible score on that measure as follows:

$$\text{CONVERTED SCORE} = \text{SCORE}/\text{MAXIMUM POSSIBLE SCORE}$$

For example, a candidate correctly answering 12 of 25 ability test questions and receiving a 3.5 on a five-point interview rating on Dependability would therefore have converted scores of .48 (12/25) for the ability test and .70 (3.5/5) for Dependability. If you prefer to work with percentages rather than decimals, you can multiply each result by 100. If these two attributes were equally important, and if there were no other important attributes, you could then add the scores together to get a combined score for this applicant.

In most cases, though, some attributes are more important than others. This means that different attributes make up different percentages of the overall combined score. In addition, if you use more than one measure for an attribute, each measure will make up a percentage of the score for that attribute. You can account for these different percentages by weighting the converted scores. You can calculate the weighted converted score for each attribute as follows:

WEIGHTED CONVERTED SCORE =
CONVERTED SCORE × IMPORTANCE OF ATTRIBUTE
× IMPORTANCE OF MEASURE

For example, suppose that you decided that the personality trait of Conscientiousness should be weighted as 20 percent of the basis for hiring accountants. You decide to measure Conscientiousness both in your interview and with a personality test, and you decide that each of them is an equally useful way to measure the trait. In other words, each measure will make up 50 percent of the Conscientiousness score. If you rated Juan 3 out of a possible 5 on Conscientiousness based on his interview, and he scored 36 out of 48 on the Conscientiousness portion of a personality test, Juan's combined weighted Conscientiousness rating would be calculated as follows:

1. From the interview, $(3/5) \times .20 \times .50 = .06$. The integer score (multiplied by 100) would be 6.
2. From the personality test, $36/48 \times .20 \times .50 = .075$ or $.08$. The integer score is 8.
3. The combined integer score for Conscientiousness would therefore be $6 + 8$, or 14. This score can then be added to combined weighted scores for other attributes to get a total combined score for Juan, which can be compared against a standard or against scores for other applicants.

Summary: Hiring Choices

Let's recap and summarize the process of making your choices about who to hire. If some candidates have scored at the desirable level across all attributes, and if the number of candidates in this group is less than the number you need to hire, you can immediately extend employment offers to each of these candidates. Depending on how many accept employment, you will know whether you will need to hire candidates who are more minimally qualified and how many additional candidates you will need to hire. In turn, this will help you to determine if you will be able to fill your hiring needs from your existing pool of candidates or if you will need to either recruit additional candidates or leave positions unfilled.

You may have more hiring needs than desirably qualified candidates. For example, you may need to hire ten people but have only five desirably qualified candidates, or you may have fifteen, of whom only seven accept your offer of employment. Now you are in the next phase: hiring minimally qualified candidates.

In some jobs, there is not a large difference in performance gained from increased qualifications. This is particularly likely for jobs in which performance is closely related to skills that are learned on the job and for jobs for which minimal qualifications, such as professional licensing, are so rigorous as to make the minimal qualification standards quite stringent. In such cases, you can proceed directly to hiring from the minimally qualified pool. Again, if your hiring needs are greater than or equal to the number of desirably and minimally qualified applicants, you can simply hire whoever is in that pool. Spending time and resources on detailed ranking is a waste.

If the difference in performance between minimal and desirable levels of qualifications is large, you need to consider the qualifications of your applicants in reference to your PATH for that position. (See Chapter Three for a discussion of PATHs.) If the PATH for the position indicates that you don't need to make an immediate hire, and if your past experience makes you confident of being able to recruit another group of desirably qualified candidates, do so instead of making minimally qualified hires. If your PATH indicates that you don't have the option of recruiting another pool or your experience shows that the pool isn't likely to improve, hire from the minimally qualified group.

The methods we have described will also work well when you are planning to hire only one candidate for a position. It's still critically important to eliminate unqualified applicants from your pool, and to hire an applicant with desirable qualifications whenever that is possible.[19] The decision-table and converted-score methods will help you to differentiate between desirable or acceptable candidates, if this becomes necessary in making a final selection.

Hiring Unqualified or Disqualified Candidates

Sometimes your pool will not result in any candidates who are minimally qualified. You may be tempted to hire candidates who are disqualified or unqualified. Don't do it. Find some more candidates. Change the way you operate. Pay more for temps. Close your business. But *don't do it*. Isn't there an exception? You can go back and review your criteria to make sure that you weren't overly selective or using minimal score guidelines that were too stringent. But the odds are that you weren't. Go out and find some more folks. Before you start to recruit this time, realize that you may have to change the job or the pay or the conditions or the people you are recruiting. Even though you may now be in a bind, make an effort to identify what you may need to do differently to recruit effectively.

Your Choices, Their Choices

These guidelines give you a method for deciding which candidates you will offer employment to first. The job market works both ways, and not everyone to whom you offer employment will come to work with your company. By using these decision-making guidelines, you can start with the candidates with the greatest likelihood of delivering outstanding performance and continue until you fill your hiring needs or run out of applicants who are at least minimally qualified. And you can feel confident in doing so.

A Final Word: About Personal Judgment and Performance

The purpose of high-impact hiring is not to remove your personal judgment from decision making. Rather it is to focus your judgment skills on effectively gathering relevant information to predict work performance, and on using this information to make good decisions. You have been making judgments about performance since you began your work analysis at the beginning of high-impact hiring.

People often ask us if there isn't room to include in a hiring decision whether you just *like* a given candidate. We have two answers. One is, sure, as long as you are talking about choosing between two equally skilled candidates and "liking" is not a code for illegal discrimination. But let us give you our preferred answer. We think that respect for skilled performance is of paramount importance in every workplace. We hope that you will hire people whose performance you will respect, and that mutual respect, even admiration, builds between you as you work together. We also hope that you have people in your life whom you just like: family, friends, and buddies. We hope that when you use high-impact hiring, hire systematically on the basis of performance, and come to develop a work group that's based on mutual respect for each other's performance, you will find yourself bragging to your friends about how great it is to work with people whose performance you really respect. We hope that your journey with us through high-impact hiring will begin your process of assembling that group of employees whose performance you respect. Your efforts to hire for performance will then continue to have a high impact on your life, and on the lives and work of the people you hire.

Afterword

Carrying Out Your Hiring Decisions

Toward the beginning of *High-Impact Hiring*, we told you that our preferred method for hiring when there is no time is to fight fires in the same way that the fire department does, by preparing in advance and rolling when time is critical. The following is a guideline to using high-impact hiring when you go to make a hire after you have set up your high-impact hiring system.

The key steps in high-impact hiring are:

1. Review your PATH for the position (our discussion in Chapter Three should be of help) and determine how much time you have to make the hire.
2. Review or conduct a work analysis of the job (refer to Chapter Two) so that you can develop or update a Performance Attributes Matrix for the job.
3. Determine how you will recruit for the position, internally or externally, and what methods you want to use, referring to Chapter Four as needed, and begin to implement your recruiting.
4. Use the Performance Attributes Matrix to help select the tools you want to use to gather information on critical performance attributes. An overview of the systematic approach to doing this is presented in Chapter Six. The following list of categories of selection tools may help you in developing your tool list for your hiring:
   - Application blanks, résumés, and biodata (Chapter Seven)
   - Structured interviewing (Chapter Eight)
   - Testing (Chapter Nine)

- Background and reference checking (Chapter Seven)
- Performance sampling (Chapter Ten)
- Honesty tests, drug tests, and other procedures to assess the likelihood of counterproductive behavior (Chapter Eleven)

5. Administer initial screening tools to applicants, using guidelines in Chapter Six, to eliminate unqualified applicants.

6. For applicants meeting the minimum qualifications on the initial instruments, proceed with interviewing. Use the high-impact hiring philosophy outlined in Chapter One and the techniques described in Chapter Eight to keep interviews focused on hiring for performance, and Chapter Five to make sure that your interviewing and testing process is fair and legal.

7. Administer performance tests and screening for counterproductive behavior if you have included them on the Performance Attributes Matrix, especially for applicants with desirable levels of qualifications.

8. Perform reference checks, at least on desirable candidates, using the guidelines provided in Chapter Seven.

9. As you are going through the selection process, record results from the different sources. Construct a high-impact hiring decision table, using the method described in Chapter Twelve.

10. Use your decision table to determine unacceptable, acceptable, and desirable candidates. Remember that you continue to make choices about candidates as you go through each stage of the hiring process, and you continue to bring information from each previous stage forward by including it in the Performance Attributes Matrix. Be particularly sure to:
    - Eliminate unqualified applicants from your pool whenever they do not meet minimum requirements.
    - Select desirable applicants when possible and minimally acceptable applicants when necessary for hiring. Chapter Twelve contains information on making these decisions effectively.

11. Before extending a job offer, make sure that apparently desirable applicants are actually desirable. Be particularly sure to:
    - Review all information about an applicant carefully.
    - Complete reference checks and background checks, using them as additional opportunities to verify job-related information from application forms, résumés, and interviews.

- Treat the decision to offer a job as carefully as you would a decision to extend any other contract in your business.

Carrying Out Your High-Impact Hiring Decision

The purpose of high-impact hiring is to help you make effective hiring decisions based on performance. How you carry out these decisions in your organization is beyond the scope of this book. But because we came to the topic of hiring from our broader interest in helping organizations to develop effective work performance, we have some perspectives to pass on to you about implementing your hiring decision in ways that are consistent with high-impact hiring. Obviously, these need to be implemented in the context of your organization's approaches and policies in these areas and other business and legal advice you might receive.

1. Use the decision-making categories to guide the way you make your offers. If you are hiring multiple candidates, you can begin to make offers to candidates with desirable qualifications and get their responses while continuing to make further selections among less qualified candidates.
2. Use your decision-making information and your PATHs to determine how you will go about making offers. For example, if you know from past experience that desirably qualified applicants perform much better than acceptable applicants, and there is a small number of these applicants, you will be more likely to do what it takes to get a desirable applicant to accept an offer. On the other hand, if there are plenty of both desirable and acceptable applicants, and you know there is little difference in performance between these groups, you can be less concerned about whether any given applicant accepts an offer.
3. Use your past experience, or build experience, to determine how long you need to wait for candidates to accept offers and how likely it is for candidates who accept offers to come to work. This varies between jobs and labor markets. Make sure that you keep sufficient candidates in the pool, at least until you are sure that you have enough firm acceptances to fill your hiring needs.
4. Make sure that you keep your high-impact hiring focus all the way through making an offer. You need to extend offers to candidates with better qualifications and not simply those who are

more like you. We know of one operating unit of a large corporation that implemented its own structured interviewing system at great expense and then never bothered scoring the interviews. The supervisors still hired the workers they thought would be most enjoyable to work with and most compliant to the supervisors' whims. They could never figure out why the same performance problems kept cropping up, even with their new hiring system. Reverting to gut feelings or likability at the time you make an offer can also cause adverse impact if it leads you to simply hire people who are more like you.

5. When making offers, remember that if the offer is accepted, you will be living with the atmosphere your offer creates for a long time. Fairness is a fundamental for workforce satisfaction, and you want to start out by dealing fairly and straightforwardly.

6. The same is true of candidates you offer jobs to who decline or applicants you reject. In dealing with applicants who get better offers, and also with those you must reject, remember that they had enough interest in and respect for your company to be interested in working there. Show them the same respect. You may want to hire them again, they may be customers or constituents of your business, and, one way or another, they are certainly members of your community.

Maintaining the Impact After the Hire

Make sure that you get new employees off on the right foot by welcoming them graciously to your organization. The same is true for welcoming someone selected from within your organization to a new position or to your team. Take the time to make sure that you and your organization are prepared for your new hire before the first day of work. Regardless of how much support you have from within your organization, it will still likely fall to you to ensure that new employees have a work area and an understanding of the work that will make them eager to get started.

Start new employees off with the kind of orientation and training that *you* would like to receive. Most people are both eager and apprehensive when they begin a new position. They want to succeed. Let them know right from the start that they can be successful and that you expect successful performance. A professional orientation, a good understanding of the work to be done, and effective training at their specific job are all essential to their successfully attaining performance. It's just as important to remember these factors when a new hire comes from within the organization.

Just as important as orientation and training are feedback and practice. People will appreciate receiving factual and constructive information early on about their performance. "Early on" means that feedback begins in the first week and the first month on the job, even the first day, and certainly well before the time of any initial formal performance appraisal. Opportunities for people to improve their performance through practice based on your feedback will be a great help.

Make your evaluations of new employees' performance on the same high-impact basis you used to hire them. You'll find the Performance Attributes Matrix to be invaluable in developing thorough performance evaluations and guiding the more frequent and informal feedback you provide.

Staying focused on high-impact techniques after the hire will help you to avoid two decision-making mistakes that managers frequently make. The first is to close prematurely on an assessment of the new employee as a great hire or a mistake. Remember that using high-impact hiring techniques makes it far more probable that an employee will perform effectively. Before reaching initial conclusions, give the new employee some time to settle in and settle down, make some initial progress and likely some mistakes, get constructive feedback, and practice doing better. You are looking for employees who will continue to improve and develop as they work with you, and you can't find that out all at once.

The second potential error is the opposite of the first. Your decision to hire someone is simply a prediction of his or her future performance. Your decision does not control the new hire's performance on the job. Certainly you want to help employees to succeed, in all the ways we've discussed and more. Ultimately, though, an employee is responsible for attaining effective performance. If all the evidence over a period of time points to problems with performance, don't turn away from these problems simply because you made the hire. If employment in your organization is not at will, then it's especially important to attend to performance problems constructively as soon as they arise, and especially to respond to them before the end of any probationary period your organization may have. When performance problems occur, focus on responding to them effectively and vigorously.

As you do more and more high-impact hiring, you may have fewer opportunities to hire as employees you hire perform better. Be sure to keep learning from the results of your hires, evaluating your system, and applying high-impact hiring techniques to the hires you make and to the performance of these new hires when they work with you.

Notes

Chapter One

1. J. G. March and H. A. Simon, *Organizations,* 2nd ed. (Cambridge, Mass.: Blackwell, 1993).
2. H. A. Simon, *Administrative Behavior: A Study of Decision-Making Processes in Administrative Organizations,* 3rd ed. (New York: Free Press, 1976).
3. D. F. Aberle, "Religio-Magical Phenomena and Power, Prediction, and Control," *Southwestern Journal of Anthropology* 22 (1966), 221–230.

Chapter Two

1. J. P. Campbell, R. A. McCloy, S. H. Oppler, and C. E. Sager, "A Theory of Performance," in N. Schmitt, W. C. Borman, and Associates, *Personnel Selection in Organizations* (San Francisco: Jossey-Bass, 1993).
2. J. P. Campbell, M. B. Gasser, and F. L. Oswald, "The Substantive Nature of Job Performance Variability," in K. R. Murphy, ed., *Individual Differences and Behavior in Organizations* (San Francisco: Jossey-Bass, 1996), pp. 258–299.
3. B. Schneider, "When Individual Differences Aren't," in K. R. Murphy, ed., *Individual Differences and Behavior in Organizations* (San Francisco: Jossey-Bass, 1996), pp. 548–571.
4. K. R. Murphy, ed., *Individual Differences and Behavior in Organizations* (San Francisco: Jossey-Bass, 1996), pp. 3–30.
5. Campbell, McCloy, Oppler, and Sager, "A Theory of Performance."
6. R. J. Harvey, personal communication, 1995.
7. D. Bowen, G. Ledford, and B. Nathan, "Hiring for the Organization, Not the Job," *Academy of Management Executive* 5 (1991), 35–51.
8. R. J. Harvey, "Job Analysis," in M. D. Dunnette and L. M. Hough, eds., *Handbook of Industrial and Organizational Psychology,* vol. 2, 2nd ed. (Palo Alto, Calif.: Consulting Psychologists Press, 1991), pp. 71–163.
9. K. P. Carson and G. L. Stewart, "Job Analysis and the Sociotechnical Approach to Quality: A Critical Examination," *Journal of Quality Management* 1 (1995), 49–64.

10. J. I. Sanchez, "From Documentation to Innovation: Reshaping Job Analysis to Meet Emerging Business Needs," *Human Resource Management Review* 4 (1994), 51–74.

11. L. M. Spencer and S. M. Spencer, *Competence at Work: Models for Superior Performance* (New York: Wiley, 1993).

12. S. R. Lawrence and E. C. Sewell, "Heuristic Versus Optimal Solution Schedules When Processing Times Are Uncertain," *Journal of Operations Management,* in press.

13. Harvey, "Job Analysis."

14. Harvey, "Job Analysis."

15. E. J. McCormick and P. R. Jeanneret, "Position Analysis Questionnaire," in S. Gael, ed., *The Job Analysis Handbook for Business, Industry and Government* (New York: Wiley, 1988).

16. Harvey, "Job Analysis."

17. Carson and Stewart, "Job Analysis."

Chapter Three

1. M. H. Bazerman and M. A. Neale, *Negotiating Rationally* (New York: Free Press, 1992).

2. J. L. Miller, "Organizational Commitment of Temporary Workers: A Combined Identity Theory and Psychological Contract Perspective." (Unpublished doctoral dissertation, University of Colorado at Boulder, Boulder, Colo., 1995).

Chapter Four

1. J. P. Wanous, *Organizational Entry: Recruitment, Selection, and Socialization of Newcomers* (Reading, Mass.: Addison-Wesley, 1980).

2. H. G. Heneman, R. L. Heneman, and T. A. Judge, *Staffing Organizations,* 2nd ed. (Middleton, Wis.: Mendota House, 1997).

3. R. B. Morgan and J. E. Smith, *Staffing the New Workplace* (Milwaukee, Wis.: ASQC Quality Press, 1996), pp. 217–218.

Chapter Five

1. P. D. Blanck, "Transcending Title I of the Americans with Disabilities Act: A Case Report on Sears, Roebuck and Co." *Mental and Physical Disability Law Reporter* 20 (1996), 278–285.

2. R. G. Rose, *Practical Issues in Employment Testing* (Odessa, Fla.: Psychological Assessment Resources, 1993).

3. *McDonnell Douglas Corporation* v. *Green,* 411 U.S. 792 (1973).

4. *United States* v. *Hayes International Corporation,* 4 FEP 411 (1972).

5. J. Ledvinka and V. Scarpello, *Federal Regulation of Personnel and Human Resource Management,* 2nd ed. (Boston: PWS-Kent, 1991).

6. K. L. Sovereign, *Personnel Law,* 3rd ed. (Englewood Cliffs, N.J.: Prentice Hall, 1994).

7. *Fernandes* v. *Wynn Oil Company* 653 F.2d 1275 (9th Cir. 1982).

8. Ledvinka and Scarpello, *Federal Regulation.*

9. *Kaiser Aluminum and Chemical Corporation* v. *Weber* 443 U.S. 193 (1979).

10. R. Risser, *Stay Out of Court: The Manager's Guide to Preventing Employee Lawsuits* (Englewood Cliffs, N.J.: Prentice Hall, 1993).

11. Sovereign, *Personnel Law.*

12. To obtain a copy of *Just Management,* contact Rita Risser, J.D., Stay Out of Court, P.O. Box 2146, Santa Cruz, CA 95063. To obtain copies of the state-specific employment law letters, contact M. Lee Smith Publishers, P.O. Box 198867, Nashville, Tennessee 37219–8867, (800) 274–6774.

Chapter Six

1. *Federal Register,* vol. 43, no. 166 (August 25, 1978), 38290–38315.

2. L. J. Cronbach, "Five Perspectives on Validity," in H. Wainer and H. I. Braun, eds., *Test Validity.* (Hillsdale, N.J.: Erlbaum, 1988).

3. R. M. Guion, "Personnel Assessment, Selection, and Placement," in M. D. Dunnette and L. M. Hough, eds., *Handbook of Industrial and Organizational Psychology,* vol. 2, 2nd ed. (Palo Alto, Calif.: Consulting Psychologists Press, 1991), p. 388.

4. R. D. Gatewood and H. S. Feild, *Human Resource Selection,* 3rd ed. (Fort Worth, Tex.: Dryden Press/Harcourt Brace College Publishers, 1994).

5. Society for Industrial-Organizational Psychology, *Principles for the Validation and Use of Personnel Selection Procedures* (College Park, Md.: Society for Industrial-Organizational Psychology, 1987).

6. R. Seymour, "Why Plaintiff's Counsel Challenge Tests, and How They Can Successfully Challenge the Theory of 'Validity Generalization,'" *Journal of Vocational Behavior* 33 (1988), 331–366.

7. J. G. Rosse, J. L. Miller, and M. D. Stecher, "A Field Study of Job Applicants' Reactions to Personality and Cognitive Ability Testing," *Journal of Applied Psychology* 79 (1994), 987–992.

Chapter Seven

1. J. M. Perry, "Résumé-Sorting Computer Helps Clinton Team Screen Thousands Seeking Administration Jobs," *Wall Street Journal,* Jan. 11, 1993, p. A18.

2. S. J. Herman, *Hiring Right: A Practical Guide* (Thousand Oaks, Calif.: Sage, 1994).

3. H. G. Heneman, R. L. Heneman, and T. A. Judge, *Staffing Organizations,* 2nd ed. (Middleton, Wis.: Mendota House, 1997).

4. E. C. Miller, "An EEO Examination of Employment Applications," *Personnel Administrator* 25 (1981), 63–70.

5. J. Frierson and J. Jolly, "Problems in Employment Application Forms," *Employee Relations Journal* 15 (1989), 53–61.

6. Bureau of National Affairs, "EEOC Guide to Pre-Employment Inquiries," *Fair Employment Practices* (Washington, DC: Author). (Periodically updated.)

7. B. N. Barge, "Using Biographical Data in Personnel Decisions," in J. Jones, B. Steffy, and D. Bray, eds., *Applying Psychology in Business: The Handbook for Managers and Human Resource Professionals* (San Francisco: New Lexington Press, 1991), pp. 260–274.

8. Heneman, Heneman, and Judge, *Staffing Organizations.*

9. T. W. Mitchell, "Practical Issues for Biodata Development" (Paper presented at the 11th annual meeting of the Society for Industrial and Organizational Psychology, San Diego, Calif., April 1996).

10. J. R. Glennon, L. E. Albright, and W. A. Owens, *A Catalog of Life History Items* (Greensboro, N.C.: The Richardson Foundation, 1966).

11. The two "generic" BIBs can be obtained by contacting London House, 9701 West Higgins Road, Rosemont, Ill. 60018–4720, (800) 237–7685.

12. The predeveloped BIB forms can be obtained by contacting Richardson, Bellows, Henry and Company, 1140 Connecticut Avenue, Washington, D.C. 20036, (202) 659–3755.

13. R. LoPresto, D. E. Micham, and D. E. Ripley, *Reference Checking Handbook* (Alexandria, Va.: American Society for Personnel Administration, 1986).

14. Heneman, Heneman, and Judge, *Staffing Organizations.*

15. R. D. Gatewood and H. S. Feild, *Human Resource Selection,* 3rd ed. (Fort Worth, Tex.: Dryden Press/Harcourt Brace College Publishers, 1994).

16. I. L. Goldstein, "The Application Blank: How Honest Are the Responses?" *Journal of Applied Psychology* 65 (1974), 491–494.

17. J. D. Bell, J. Castagnera, and J. P. Young, "Employment References: Do You Know the Law?" *Personnel Journal,* Feb. 1984, pp. 32–36.

18. Bell, Castagnera, and Young, "Employment References."

19. J. A. Branch, *Negligent Hiring Practice Manual* (New York: Wiley, 1988).

20. B. Leonard, "Reference-Checking Laws: Now What?" *HRMagazine,* Dec. 1995, pp. 57–62.

21. P. Falcone, "Getting Employers to Open Up on a Reference Check," *HRMagazine,* July 1995, pp. 58–63.

22. Herman, *Hiring Right.*

23. Herman, *Hiring Right.*

Chapter Eight

1. R. D. Gatewood and H. S. Feild, *Human Resource Selection,* 3rd ed. (Fort Worth, Tex.: Dryden Press/Harcourt Brace College Publishers, 1994).
2. Gatewood and Feild, *Human Resource Selection.*
3. B. Schneider and N. Schmitt, *Staffing Organizations* (Prospect Heights, Ill.: Waveland Press, 1992).
4. Gatewood and Feild, *Human Resource Selection.*
5. H. G. Heneman, R. L. Heneman, and T. A. Judge, *Staffing Organizations,* 2nd ed. (Middleton, Wis.: Mendota House, 1997).
6. Heneman, Heneman, and Judge, *Staffing Organizations.*
7. R. A. Levin, "Self-Presentation, Lies and Bullshit: The Impact of Impression Management on Employee Selection" (Paper presented at the annual meeting of the Society for Industrial and Organizational Psychology, Orlando, Fla., May 1995).
8. M. Yate, *Knock 'em Dead* (Holbrook, Mass.: Bob Adams, 1994).
9. R. L. Dipboye, *Selection Interviews: Process Perspectives* (Cincinnati: South-Western, 1992).
10. Schneider and Schmitt, *Staffing Organizations.*
11. L. R. Gollub and J. E. Campion, "The Employment Interview on Trial" (Paper presented at the annual meeting of the Society for Industrial and Organizational Psychology, St. Louis, Mo., April 1991).
12. M. A. McDaniel, D. L. Whetzel, F. L. Schmidt, and S. D. Maurer, "The Validity of Employment Interviews: A Comprehensive Review and Meta-Analysis," *Journal of Applied Psychology* 79 (1994), 599–616.
13. C. Searcy, P. N. Woods, R. D. Gatewood, and C. F. Lance, "The Structured Interview: A Meta-Analytic Search for Moderators" (Paper presented at the annual meeting of the Society for Industrial and Organizational Psychology, San Francisco, Calif., April 1993).
14. W. H. Weisner and S. F. Cronshaw, "A Meta-Analytic Investigation of the Impact of Interview Format and Degree of Structure on the Validity of the Employment Interview," *Journal of Occupational Psychology* 61 (1988), 275–290.
15. Gatewood and Feild, *Human Resource Selection.*
16. McDaniel, Whetzel, Schmidt, and Maurer, "The Validity of Employment Interviews."

Chapter Nine

1. M. Zeidner and R. Most, "An Introduction to Psychological Testing," in M. Zeidner and R. Most, eds., *Psychological Testing: An Inside View* (Palo Alto, Calif.: Consulting Psychologists Press, 1992), p. 2.
2. R. Hoffer, "Get Smart," *Sports Illustrated* (Sept. 5, 1994), p. 73.

3. J. E. Hunter, "Cognitive Ability, Cognitive Attitudes, Job Knowledge, and Job Performance," *Journal of Vocational Behavior* 29 (1986), 340–362.

4. Hunter, "Cognitive Ability."

5. R. G. Rose, *Practical Issues in Employment Testing* (Odessa, Fla.: Psychological Assessment Resources, 1993).

6. Hunter, "Cognitive Ability."

7. R. L. Thorndike, "The Role of General Ability in Prediction," *Journal of Vocational Behavior* 29 (1986), 332–339.

8. E. E. Ghiselli, *The Validity of Occupational Aptitude Tests* (New York: Wiley, 1966).

9. L. M. Hough and R. J. Schneider, "Personality Traits, Taxonomies, and Applications in Organizations," in K. R. Murphy, ed., *Individual Differences and Behavior in Organizations* (San Francisco: Jossey-Bass, 1996), pp. 31–88.

10. R. P. Tett, D. N. Jackson, and M. Rothstein, "Personality Measures as Predictors of Job Performance: A Meta-Analytic Review," *Personnel Psychology* 44 (1991), 703–742.

11. D. S. Ones, C. Viswesvaran, and F. Schmidt, "Do Broader Personality Variables Predict Job Performance with Higher Validity?" (Paper presented at the annual meeting of the Society for Industrial and Organizational Psychology, Nashville, Tenn., April 1994).

12. M. Barrick and M. Mount, "The Big Five Personality Dimensions and Job Performance: A Meta-Analysis," *Personnel Psychology* 44 (1991), 1–26.

13. P. T. Costa and R. R. McCrae, "Domains and Facets: Hierarchical Personality Assessment Using the Revised NEO Personality Inventory," *Journal of Personality Assessment* 64 (1995), 21–50.

14. L. M. Hough, "The 'Big Five' Personality Variables—Construct Confusion: Description Versus Prediction," *Human Performance* 5 (1992) 139–155.

15. Hough and Schneider, "Personality Traits."

16. Hough and Schneider, "Personality Traits."

17. Hough and Schneider, "Personality Traits."

18. R. Hogan and R. J. Blake, "Vocational Interests: Matching Self-Concept with the Work Environment," in K. R. Murphy, ed., *Individual Differences and Behavior in Organizations* (San Francisco: Jossey-Bass, 1996), pp. 89–144.

19. Rose, *Practical Issues in Employment Testing.*

20. R. D. Arvey and J. E. Campion, "The Employment Interview: A Summary and Review of Recent Literature," *Personnel Psychology* 35 (1982), 281–322.

21. Hogan and Blake, "Vocational Interests."

22. "How to Cheat on Personality Tests," in W. H. Whyte, Jr., *The Organization Man* (New York: Simon & Schuster/Touchstone, 1956), pp. 405–410.

23. M. Yate, *Knock'em Dead* (Holbrook, Mass.: Bob Adams, 1994).

24. J. Rosse, M. D. Stecher, J. L. Miller, and R. Levin, "The Impact of Response Distortion on Pre-Employment Personality Testing and Hiring Decisions," *Journal of Applied Psychology,* in press.

25. M. Zickar, J. Rosse, and R. Levin, "Modeling the Effects of Faking on Personality Instruments" (Paper presented at the 11th annual meeting of the Society for Industrial and Organizational Psychology, San Diego, Calif., April 1996).

26. L. M. Hough, "Can Integrity Tests Be Trusted?" *Employment Testing Law and Policy Reporter* 5 (1996) 97–103.

27. Hough, "Can Integrity Tests Be Trusted?"

28. R. C. Sweetland and D. J. Keyser, *Tests: A Comprehensive Reference for Assessments in Psychology, Education and Business,* 3rd ed. (Austin: Pro-Ed Publishing, 1991).

29. D. J. Keyser and R. C. Sweetland, *Test Critiques,* Vols. 1–6, 2nd ed. (Kansas City, Mo.: Test Corporation of America, 1988).

30. *Mental Measurements Yearbook,* 12th ed. (Highland Park, N.J.: Mental Measurement Yearbooks, 1996).

31. Rose, *Practical Issues in Employment Testing.*

32. R. D. Gatewood and H. S. Feild, *Human Resource Selection,* 3rd ed. (Fort Worth, Tex.: Dryden Press/Harcourt Brace College Publishers, 1994).

Chapter Ten

1. W. Cascio and N. Phillips, "Performance Testing: A Rose Among Thorns?" *Personnel Psychology* 32 (1979), 751–766.

2. P. Wernimont and J. Campbell, "Sign, Samples, and Criteria," *Journal of Applied Psychology* 52 (1968), 372–376.

3. H. L. Taylor, G. Lintern, C. L. Hulin, D. Talleur, T. Emanuel, and S. Phillips, *Transfer of Training Effectiveness of Personal Computer–Based Aviation Training Devices* (Technical Report ARL-96-3/FAA-96-2, University of Illinois at Urbana-Champaign Institute of Aviation, Urbana, Ill., 1996).

4. D. Robinson, "Content-Oriented Personnel Selection in a Small Business Setting," *Personnel Psychology* 34 (1981), 77–87.

5. R. D. Gatewood and H. S. Feild, *Human Resource Selection,* 3rd ed. (Fort Worth, Tex.: Dryden Press/Harcourt Brace College Publishers, 1994).

6. B. B. Gaugler, D. B. Rosenthal, G. C. Thornton III, and C. Bentson, "Meta-Analysis of Assessment Center Validity," *Journal of Applied Psychology* 72 (1987), 493–511.

Chapter Eleven

1. J. Rosse and H. Miller, "Absence and Other Employee Behaviors," in P. S. Goodman, R. S. Atkin, and Associates, *Absenteeism: New Approaches to Understanding, Measuring, and Managing Employee Absence* (San Francisco: Jossey-Bass, 1984).

2. J. Rosse and T. Noel, "Leaving the Organization: Individual Differences in Employee Withdrawal and Adaptation," in K. R. Murphy, ed., *Individual Differences and Behavior in Organizations* (San Francisco: Jossey-Bass, 1996).

3. S. L. Robinson and R. J. Bennett, "A Typology of Deviant Workplace Behaviors: A Multi-Dimensional Scaling Study," *Academy of Management Journal* 38 (1995), 555–572.

4. J. Greenberg and K. S. Scott, "Why Do Workers Bite the Hand That Feeds Them? Employee Theft as a Social Exchange Process," *Research in Organizational Behavior* 18 (1996), 111–156.

5. Greenberg and Scott, "Why Do Workers Bite the Hand That Feeds Them?"

6. K. R. Murphy, *Honesty in the Workplace* (Pacific Grove, Calif.: Brooks/Cole, 1993).

7. R. M. O'Bannon, L. A. Goldinger, and G. S. Appleby, *Honesty and Integrity Testing* (Atlanta, Ga.: Applied Information Services, 1989).

8. S. T. Hunt, T. L. Hansen, and G. E. Paajanen, "What Do Integrity Tests Measure? An In-Depth Look at One Widely Used, Predictively Valid, Personality Based Integrity Test" (Unpublished manuscript, Ohio State University, Columbus, Ohio, 1996). The PDI-Employment Inventory is available from Personnel Decisions International, 2000 Plaza VII Tower, 45 South Seventeenth Street, Minneapolis, Minn., 55402–1608, (800) 633–4410.

9. Greenberg and Scott, "Why Do Workers Bite the Hand That Feeds Them?"

10. P. R. Sackett, "Employment Testing and Public Policy: The Case of Integrity Tests," *New Approaches to Employee Management: Fairness in Employee Selection* 1 (1992), 47–59.

11. Sackett, "Employment Testing and Public Policy."

12. D. Z. Ones, C. Viswesvaran, and F. L. Schmidt, "Comprehensive Meta-Analysis of Integrity Test Validities: Findings and Implications for Personnel Selection and Theories of Job Performance [Monograph]," *Journal of Applied Psychology* 78 (1993), 679–903.

13. Ones, Viswesvaran, and Schmidt, "Comprehensive Meta-Analysis of Integrity Test Validities."

14. Sackett, "Employment Testing and Public Policy."

15. Ones, Viswesvaran, and Schmidt, "Comprehensive Meta-Analysis of Integrity Test Validities."

16. Sackett, "Employment Testing and Public Policy."
17. L. M. Hough, "Can Integrity Tests Be Trusted?" *Employment Testing Law and Policy Reporter* 5 (1996), 97–103.
18. G. M. Alliger, S. O. Lilienfeld, and K. E. Mitchell, "The Susceptibility of Overt and Covert Integrity Tests to Coaching and Faking," *Psychological Science*, in press.
19. M. Budman, "The Honesty Business: Written Integrity Tests for Hiring Purposes," *Across the Board* 30 (1993), 34.
20. M. M. Harris and M. L. Trusty, "Drug and Alcohol Programs in the Workplace: A Review of Recent Literature," in I. Robertson and C. Cooper, eds., *International Review of Industrial and Organizational Psychology* (New York: Wiley, 1997).
21. R. Cropanzano and M. A. Konovsky, "Drug Use and Its Implications for Employee Drug Testing," *Research in Personnel and Human Resources Management* 11 (1993), 207–257.
22. J. Normand, S. D. Salyards, and J. J. Mahoney, "An Evaluation of Pre-employment Drug Testing," *Journal of Applied Psychology* 75 (1990), 629–639.
23. L. Hunt and H. Winkler, "A Cost-Benefit Analysis of Georgia Power Company's Cause-Related Drug Testing Program" (Paper presented at NIDA Drugs in the Workplace Conference, Bethesda, Md., Sept. 1989).
24. J. Rosse, J. Miller, and R. Ringer, "The Deterrent Effect of Drug and Integrity Testing," *Journal of Business and Psychology* 10 (1996), 477–486.
25. Harris and Trusty, "Drug and Alcohol Programs in the Workplace."
26. H. Hansen, S. Caudill, and J. Boone, "Crisis in Drug Testing," *Journal of the American Medical Association* 252 (1985), 2382.
27. J. Bloch, "So What? Everybody's Doing It," *Forbes*, Aug. 1986, p. 102.
28. Harris and Trusty, "Drug and Alcohol Programs in the Workplace."
29. Cropanzano and Konovsky, "Drug Use and Its Implications for Employee Drug Testing."
30. J. Rosse, R. C. Ringer, and J. L. Miller, "Personality and Drug Testing: An Exploration of the Perceived Fairness of Alternatives to Urinalysis," *Journal of Business and Psychology* 10 (1996), 459–476.

Chapter Twelve

1. J. G. Rosse, M. D. Stecher, J. L. Miller, and R. A. Levin, "The Effect of Response Distortion on Personality Testing of Job Applicants," *Journal of Applied Psychology*, in press.
2. R. A. Levin, "Self-Presentation, Lies, and Bullshit: The Effect of Impression Management on Personality Testing" (Paper presented at the annual meeting of the Society for Industrial and Organizational Psychology, Orlando, Fla., April 1995).

3. C. Cherniak, *Minimal Rationality* (Cambridge, Mass.: MIT Press, 1986).

4. G. Dantzig, *Linear Programming and Extensions* (Princeton, N.J.: Princeton University Press, 1963).

5. F. Glover, D. Klingman, and N. V. Phillips, *Network Models in Optimization and Their Applications in Practice* (New York: Wiley, 1992).

6. M. H. Bazerman and M. A. Neale, *Negotiating Rationally* (New York: Free Press, 1992).

7. A. Tversky and D. Kahneman, "The Framing of Decisions and the Psychology of Choice," *Science* 211 (1981), 453–458.

8. G. Polya, *How to Solve It,* 2nd ed. (Princeton, N.J.: Princeton University Press, 1957).

9. H. A. Simon, *Administrative Behavior: A Study of Decision-Making Processes in Administrative Organizations,* 3rd ed. (New York: Free Press, 1976).

10. K. R. Hammond, *Human Judgment and Social Policy: Irreducible Uncertainty, Inevitable Error, Unavoidable Injustice* (New York: Oxford University Press, 1996).

11. J. J. Keller, J. S. Lublin, J. P. Miller, and S. Carey, "Why Did AT&T Choose John Walter?" *Wall Street Journal,* Oct. 24, 1996, pp. B1, B10.

12. M. Landler, "AT&T Reaches Out of Its World to Find Leader," *New York Times,* Oct. 24, 1996.

13. S. R. Lawrence and E. C. Sewell, "Heuristic Versus Optimal Solution Schedules When Processing Times Are Uncertain," *Journal of Operations Management,* in press.

14. H. A. Simon, *Models of My Life* (Cambridge, Mass.: MIT Press, 1996), p. 361.

15. Polya, *How to Solve It.*

16. P. F. Drucker, *The Effective Executive* (New York: HarperCollins, 1967), pp. 71–99.

17. L. J. Cronbach and G. C. Goldine, *Psychological Tests and Personnel Decisions,* 2nd ed. (Urbana: University of Illinois Press, 1965).

18. R. D. Gatewood and H. S. Feild, *Human Resource Selection,* 3rd ed. (Fort Worth, Tex.: Dryden Press/Harcourt Brace College Publishers, 1994).

19. S. Highhouse and M. A. Johnson, "Gain/Loss Asymmetry and Riskless Choice: Loss Aversion in Choices Among Job Finalists," *Organizational Behavior and Human Decision Processes* 68 (1996), 225–233.

Acknowledgments

A book like this really comes to fruition over a period of many years and countless interactions with many people. The hundreds and thousands of managers and workers we have worked with lead our list of people we wish to acknowledge. You are the reason we wrote this book, and a valued source of both questions and solutions. Equally important have been our numerous colleagues and our students who have imparted their wisdom, listened to our queries, and questioned our assumptions and conclusions.

The following people who were of particularly close assistance in shaping the concepts in this book are representative of a far larger number of you, all of whom we acknowledge with gratitude for making our work on this book possible: David Aberle, Murray Barrick, Jude Biggs, Rick Borkovec, Justin Bratnober, Bob Gatewood, John Gordon, Thomas Harris, Fred Holt, Chuck Hulin, Bob Keeley, and Jayson Webb.

There are three other groups of people who both of us would like to acknowledge for what they did to bring this book to fruition. The first are the entire Business & Management Series team at Jossey-Bass Publishers, including Larry Alexander, Bill Hicks, and Susan Williams, and Carrie Castillon and Julianna Gustafson. The second are our colleagues and associates at the University of Colorado and at the Center for Human Function and Work, particularly Missy Miller. The third are our families and our supportive friends who helped us to persist.

J.R
R.L

The Authors

JOSEPH ROSSE is associate professor of management at the Graduate School of Business and Administration at the University of Colorado at Boulder and senior associate at the Center for Human Function & Work in Boulder, Colorado. He received his B.S. degree (1976) from Loyola University in psychology and sociology and his Ph.D. degree (1983) from the University of Illinois in industrial and organizational psychology.

Rosse's teaching and research concern the development of high-performance hiring systems, as well as the effect of employee attitudes on performance and counterproductive behavior in the workplace. One of his passions is making high-quality workplace research useful to managers. He has consulted with numerous companies, large and small, in both the private and public sectors, on issues related to effective hiring, performance appraisal, and employee opinion surveys. He has been certified by the Human Resource Certification Institute as a Professional in Human Resources (PHR) and is a member of the Society for Human Resource Management, the American Psychological Society, and the Society for Industrial and Organizational Psychology. He has published over thirty articles and book chapters and presented nearly fifty papers at professional conferences. He is associate editor of the *Journal of Business and Psychology,* and along with Robert Levin, he writes a monthly newspaper column entitled "On Management" that explores controversial issues in managing work. Rosse has previously taught at the Industrial Relations Center at the University of Minnesota.

Along with his wife and two sons, Rosse enjoys living and playing in the Rocky Mountains. When he is not working with organizations or students, he enjoys skiing, scuba diving, tinkering with vintage Volvos, and surfing the Internet. He can be reached at Joseph.Rosse@colorado.edu.

ROBERT LEVIN is director of the Center for Human Function & Work, a private sector work performance research organization. The Center has been a University of Colorado at Boulder Research Park Organization since 1989. Levin also serves as an adjunct member of the management faculty of the College of Business and Administration at the University of Colorado at Boulder.

Levin founded the organization that is now the Center for Human Function & Work in 1986, with the twin aims of conducting research that would lead to a better understanding of work performance and of applying research in practical ways to help solve significant work performance problems. He has worked on hiring, selection, and performance issues for most of the Center's clients, including trucking companies, large resorts, government organizations, nonprofits, and health care organizations. Levin's research on performance has ranged from work physiology to industrial psychology, including research with Joseph Rosse and others on the effects that job applicants' efforts to distort responses have on hiring. He is a member of the International Society for Performance Improvement and the American Association for the Advancement of Science.

Levin has worked as the national director of the country's largest coaching education and training program; as the director of Nordic skiing for a ski training center, including serving on the national clinic faculty of the U.S. Ski Coaches Association; and as a U.S. Forest Service fire management foreman. He received his B.A. degree (1979) from Reed College in biology. He has written a wide range of materials on management, coaching, and hiring, including his monthly column "On Management" with Joseph Rosse. Levin can be reached at 303–444–8797.

Levin enjoys living in the Rocky Mountain West, and spending time near his home in Boulder, Colorado, exploring Rocky Mountain wilderness areas, cross-country and downhill skiing, and traveling through the canyons and deserts of the Colorado Plateau.

Index

atic information gathering of, 5–7; tests and, 187–201, 203–204, 207–213; warm-body hiring versus, 9–11. *See also* Decision making; Hiring; Hiring process; Hiring system; Performance; Tools of hiring

High-impact recruiting, 59–78; analysis for developing, 60–61, 78; analysis for evaluating, 77; approach of, 59–60; classified advertising for, 65–68; community training organizations for, 73; crisis hiring versus, 59; deep versus narrow, 77; electronic/on-line, 74–76; employee referrals for, 68–69; employer-of-choice competitive advantage in, 61; employment agencies for, 69–71; evaluating, 76–77; executive search firms for, 69–71; foundation-building for, 60–61, 78; job fairs for, 73–74; methods of, 64–76; mutuality in, 59–60, 62; networking for, 64–65; public employment agencies for, 71–72; realistic job previews in, 62–63; repertoire development for, 64–76; school recruiting for, 72–73; tracking, 76–77; versus traditional, low-impact recruiting, 65, 66. *See also* Advertising; Job applicants/candidates

High school recruiting, 72–73

Hiring: continuous, 51–53; crapshoot versus systematic approach to, 1–3, 11–14; crisis, 44–46, 49, 59; in dynamic situations, 31; employment law and, 86–104; high-impact framework of, 2, 4–9, 14; legal context of, 80–82; legal perspective on, 84–85; low-impact approaches to, 9–14; moral-ethical perspective on, 85; performance perspective on, 82–84; planned, 44–58; problems with, 2–3; as purchasing decision, 2–3; ritual, 11–14; social context of, 80–82; in stable situations, 31; time resources for, 2–3, 10; using PATHs

to improve, 48–50; warm-body, 9–11. *See also* High-impact hiring

Hiring decisions. *See* Decision making

Hiring events: analysis of, 54–56; anticipating, 44–46; causes of, and responses to, 54–58; continuous hiring for, 51–53; defined, 44; due to employee turnover, 56–58; due to growth, 54–55; due to promotions, 57–58; due to recurring trends, 55–56; job design for, 53; Planned Alternative to Hiring (PATH) approach to, 47–50; replacement planning and, 46–47; strategies for responding to, 46–54; succession planning for, 50–51; temporary staffing approach to, 54. *See also* Employee departure; Hiring system; Planning

Hiring process: screening for counterproductive behavior during, 248–253; screening stage of, 131–143; stages of, 109–110. *See also* High-impact hiring

Hiring system: applicants' reactions to, 123, 125–128, 161, 247–248; comprehensive development of, 105–130; incorporating performance attributes into, 42–43, 106–112; industrial psychologist consultation for, 130; perceived fairness of, 123, 125–128; principles of, 106; replacement planning system in, 44–58; tools of, criteria for choosing, 112–129. *See also* High-impact hiring; Hiring events; Systematic information gathering; Tools of hiring

Hogan, R., 196

Hogan Assessment Systems, Inc., 210

Honesty tests. *See* Integrity tests

Hulin, C., 217

Human behavior, and change, 8–9

Human differences, 105

Humility, in decision making, 256–259

Hunter, J., 189